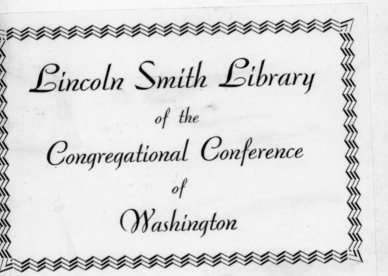

The University of Chicago Publications in Religious Education

EDITED BY

ERNEST D. BURTON   SHAILER MATHEWS
THEODORE G. SOARES

CONSTRUCTIVE STUDIES

STUDIES IN THE FIRST BOOK
OF SAMUEL

THE UNIVERSITY OF CHICAGO PRESS
CHICAGO, ILLINOIS

Agents

THE BAKER & TAYLOR COMPANY
NEW YORK

THE CUNNINGHAM, CURTISS & WELCH COMPANY
LOS ANGELES

THE CAMBRIDGE UNIVERSITY PRESS
LONDON AND EDINBURGH

THE MARUZEN-KABUSHIKI-KAISHA
TOKYO, OSAKA, KYOTO, FUKUOKA, SENDAI

THE MISSION BOOK COMPANY
SHANGHAI

SAMUEL AND HIS TWO SONS

STUDIES IN THE FIRST BOOK OF SAMUEL

FOR THE USE OF CLASSES IN SECOND-ARY SCHOOLS AND IN THE SECONDARY DIVISION OF THE SUNDAY SCHOOL

By

HERBERT LOCKWOOD WILLETT

THE UNIVERSITY OF CHICAGO PRESS
CHICAGO, ILLINOIS

Composed and Printed By
The University of Chicago Press
Chicago, Illinois, U.S.A.

TO
MY MOTHER
My First Teacher

TABLE OF CONTENTS

ILLUSTRATIONS AND MAP

EDITOR'S PREFACE

This book constitutes a companion volume to the previously published "Studies in the Gospel According to Mark." It aims to meet the same need in Old Testament study as that which the latter supplies in the case of the New Testament. Both are prepared for the same grade of pupils.

The editor of the series in which this volume appears holds the firm conviction that the Sunday school should have a curriculum of study, based on thorough knowledge of the Bible and intelligent understanding of the principles of teaching. Such a curriculum will, in the nature of the case, be graded both with respect to the Scripture material employed in its successive years and in respect to the method of using this material. The Epistle to the Ephesians cannot profitably be employed in teaching children six or seven years old, nor are children of that age ready for broad historical generalizations.

Though well aware that experience is likely to call for modification of any curriculum that, with the limited experiments that have yet been made in Sunday-school teaching under a graded curriculum, can now be framed, the plan which has most commended itself to the editors of this series, as a working scheme on which to undertake the preparation of the textbooks for such a curriculum, is the following:

I. THE ELEMENTARY DIVISION

The Kindergarten.—Elementary moral and religious truths, conveyed through the medium of the simple story, and made real to the child by his having immediate opportunity to express in play or picture-work his idea of the truths presented to him.

Grades 1–3.—Stories and verses from the Bible, with free use of pictures for purposes of illustration.

Grade 4.—The books of the Bible: an elementary course in Biblical Introduction intended to give the pupils a true conception of the Bible as a collection of religious books of varied literary form and specific purpose, including reading of appointed portions and the memorizing of selected passages. Such a course should, availing itself of the narrative character of much of the biblical literature, and of the historical setting of that which is not narrative in character, cast its instruction very largely in story-form, and so adapt it to the stage of intellectual development which the pupils for which it is intended have reached.

Grades 5–7.—Biblical biography, including the lives of Old Testament heroes, of Jesus, and of the apostles.

II. THE SECONDARY DIVISION

Grades 8–10.—Studies of separate books of the Bible; *e.g.*, the Gospel of Mark and the Epistle to the Philippians; the First Book of Samuel, and one or more of the Minor Prophets.

Grades 11–14.—Biblical history, including both events and teaching: a year and a half on Old Testament history, a year and a half on the life of Christ, and a year on the apostolic age.

III. THE ADULT DIVISION

Elective courses.

The present book falls under Division II. It is intended for classes of the eighth to tenth grades, and for pupils of a similar degree of advancement in academies and other schools in which instruction in the Bible is given, or in the home. In the preceding stages of the curriculum, as marked out above, the unit of instruction, so to speak, is at first the story, lodged in the child's quick and retentive memory, and made the vehicle of religious instruction. Thus far he knows the Bible only in detached fragments and his horizon is in each case limited to the single narrative. Next he is given (in the fourth grade) a bird's-eye view of the whole Bible, and gains some impression of the richness and variety of its contents. Then the life-story of an individual is made the unit of study, and for a period of three years, in a series of simple biographical studies, the pupil makes the acquaintance of the great men of the Bible. He is presently to pass to a constructive study of biblical history in its successive periods in which the books of the Bible are to be the sources for such constructive historical work. As the stepping-stone to his historical study in which the pupil shall build up the great history of divine revelation through prophets, Christ, and apostles, this book, with others of a similar kind which it is hoped will follow it, takes a single book of the

Bible as the unit and seeks to find out its meaning.

Two specific purposes have been kept constantly in mind in the preparation of this volume. From the intellectual point of view, the aim has been to train the pupils in the proper way of approaching and using a book of the Bible; in short, to teach them in a simple and practical way the art of interpretation as applied to such books as those of the Bible. By no means losing sight of the religious aim which must pervade all Bible study in the Sunday school, the effort has been to promote the achievement of that end by joining with it in this particular book the intellectual purpose to illustrate, and by illustrating to teach, the art of interpretation. The importance of this has been, in my judgment, too little recognized in Sunday-school work. Rightly emphasizing the importance of making moral and religious impressions, yet impatient to make such impressions at once, we have overlooked the fact that it is precisely the facts and truths of the Scripture by which these impressions are to be made, and that these facts and truths are reached only by interpretation. For interpretation is simply the process of discovering the meaning of things; as applied to a book, the discovery of the thought of the writer of that book. The conviction, that to help the pupils in our Sunday schools to acquire the interpretative attitude toward the books of the Bible would be to render to them a most valuable service, has controlled the work from beginning to end.

But the book has a specific religious purpose also, not divorced from its intellectual aim, but inseparably associated with it. For in the very process of learning to interpret the Book of Samuel the pupils will at the same time acquire a thorough knowledge of one of those books which tell the story of God's revelation of himself to man in terms of human life. Pupils of the age for which this book is intended are precisely at that stage of development in which biography—the life of the individual—makes its appeal to them. Among the characters which the Old Testament presents, none are more interesting or instructive morally and religiously than the three with which this book deals—Samuel, Saul, and David.

The Questions, though the last portion of the material under each section to be used in the study of that section, are, after the text of Samuel itself, the center of the book. Though no classification of them has been introduced, both because it is desirable to make the structure of the book as simple as possible, and because the classification would be of no special benefit to the pupil, they fall, in general, into three classes—questions of attention, questions of investigation, and questions of reflection and application.

Much of the *meaning* which it is the business of interpretation to find can be gained even by young pupils simply by giving attention to what stands written on the page. And the teacher who seeks to teach interpretatively must ask many questions which the pupil can answer by simply giving attention to the text before him.

But not all the meaning of a book will for every reader yield itself to mere attention. To attention must be added investigation. Many questions are asked in this book which a pupil twelve years of age cannot answer by looking at the text, however attentively. The Book of Samuel does not tell where all the cities which it mentions are located, nor give the meaning of all the words that it uses, such as "Ashtaroth," "diviners," "teraphim." How is the pupil to obtain the answers to these questions? In so far as they pertain to the meanings of words, a dictionary of the proper sort will furnish the answer. And just because, on the one hand, searching for these words in a dictionary slowly lodges in the pupil's mind the thought that he is looking for meanings, and, on the other, most pupils of the Sunday school do not possess the kind of a dictionary which is needed for the study of Samuel, this book contains a Dictionary, which undertakes briefly to define or explain those words of the text which it may be supposed the pupil may not understand without such help. To direct the pupil's attention to the Diction-

ary and to cultivate the habit of using it, the words
defined or explained are marked where they occur in
the notes or questions with a †. The teacher is
urged to insist upon the pupil looking up all such
words in the Dictionary and fixing in mind the
meaning of such words as are there defined, and the
main facts about the persons and places there
described. Indeed, the teacher should do what the
book cannot well do—teach the pupil to form the
habit of referring to the Dictionary to define or
explain all words of which, on his first attentive reading of the text, he finds that he does not know the
meaning or reference.

But not all the information which a young student
needs consists in definitions of words or facts concerning persons or places mentioned in Samuel.
The necessary further information has been supplied in the Explanatory Notes. The pupil should
be taught not to make these his first resource for
the discovering of the meaning of the passage, but
to turn to them only when neither his own powers
of attention nor the help of the Dictionary give him
the key to the meaning of the passage under study.
Used in this way they will also serve the purpose of
suggesting to him matters that he may have so
entirely overlooked as not even to have raised a
question concerning them. Above all, let not the
teacher fall into the mistake, or allow the pupil to
commit the error, of thinking that the study of the

Explanatory Notes is the study of the text of Samuel.
It is the meaning of the text, the thought of the
writer, that is to be sought.   The Notes are merely
a last resource to assist in the achievement of this
end.

But not even thus is our whole purpose in studying
Samuel attained.   Were it so, questions of attention
and investigation would be the only ones called
for.   But that the results of interpretation may
really be appropriated by the student, made a part
of his mental possession valuable for his moral development, he needs to reflect upon the facts and truths
which interpretation gives him, and to consider how
these truths concern him.   And so there have been
included, though without any special label, questions
intended to lead to such reflection and to suggest such
applications.

The Review Questions do not differ materially
in aim from those which pertain to the separate
sections; they simply deal with the text in larger
portions and finally with the whole book.   For true
interpretation does not leave the book as a series of
detached pieces, but, while breaking it into parts for
study, seeks to bind them all together again into the
unity which the book constituted in the mind of the
author.

The Foreword to the Pupil suggests how he
should prepare his lesson.   The teacher may
profitably follow substantially the same method in

the preparation of the weekly or daily lesson. He will do well, however, to prepare himself for the work as a whole by making himself familiar with the history of the Hebrew people from the time of the conquest of Palestine to the death of David, that he may study Samuel against the background of the times to which he belonged, and gain a larger knowledge of the Book of Samuel than can be had by preparing the lesson week by week or day by day. For this purpose he will find Wade, *Old Testament History*, or Kent, *History of the Hebrew People*, Vol. I, useful helps. One or both should, if possible, be read through before beginning to teach the present book. To gain the needful acquaintance with the First Book of Samuel it should be read through repeatedly before beginning to teach it. Further help in this direction may also be gained by using A. R. S. Kennedy's *Samuel, Introduction, Revised Version, with Notes, Index, and Maps.*

It scarcely needs to be said, but it is of the highest importance for the teacher to remember, that to his study of the Scripture he should add sympathetic study of his pupils and a thoughtful consideration of the question how he can so bring the thought of the narrative before his pupils that it shall help them to understand the life and teachings of Samuel, as one of the prophets who by faithful and courageous work in his own generation prepared the way for the teachings of Jesus, in whom alone as the

Final Prophet and Savior of the world the affection and hope of the student must be centered.

The class exercise may consist in the practical repetition of the process of study, with the exception of the writing of answers to the Questions, or may be devoted to reading the text, asking the questions, and discussing the pupil's answers. The teacher who has prepared himself to teach in the spirit described above will not lack for opportunities to make his teaching religiously impressive. Often perhaps he will let the deed or teaching of the biblical hero make its own impression, yet he should always be alert to respond to the pupil's question or suggestion, and when opportunity favors, to deepen by a sympathetic and judicious word the effect of the Scripture on the pupil's mind. If the pupils have difficulty at first in grasping the method of study, it would certainly be wise to devote the class hour for a few Sundays to the study of the lesson, pupil and teacher together, the teacher having first made sure that he himself has learned the method.

The pupil's written answers should be handed to the teacher, who will carefully correct them at home, corrections and suggestions being made in writing, and the papers returned to the pupil the following Sunday.

Of the points already spoken of, three seem to be of sufficient importance to call for an additional word of emphasis and suggestion to the teacher.

First, do not let the study of the Notes displace, in
the mind of the pupil or in practice, the study of
the Bible itself. Cultivate the habit of attentive
reading of the Scripture as the beginning and basis
of all the work done on the lesson, using the Questions to stimulate attention and start investigation,
the Dictionary and Notes to furnish answers to
the Questions which attention alone cannot answer.
Secondly, do not lose sight of the interpretative nature
of your work.   Your ultimate aim is the moral and
religious well-being of the pupil; but you are to
achieve this by bringing the truth before his mind,
and that truth is to be reached by interpretation of
the narrative and to become effective by reflection.
The teacher need not, probably ought not to, say
much to his pupil about interpretation, but he will
accomplish his best work for the pupil if he keeps his
own ideals clearly before his mind, and seeks also by
example more than by precept slowly to train the
pupil to take the interpretative attitude.   Thirdly,
do not neglect the pupil's written work.   The writing of answers to a few well-selected questions each
week furnishes the pupil a definite task and gives
definiteness to the results of his study.   The study
of the answers by the teacher will help in the important task of understanding his pupil, gaining his
point of view, gauging his mental progress; and
judicious written criticisms on his answers will
stimulate the pupil to make constant improvement.

It is well to encourage the pupil to hand in his work on sheets of uniform size, and to preserve the corrected papers with the book itself; or, perhaps better still, to write out the answers after correction in a book provided for the purpose, and preserved with the textbook as a record of a real piece of Bible study on his part. This will still further cultivate the feeling on the part of the pupil that he is doing work that is to be of permanent value to him, and tend to make it such.

The length of the lesson to be assigned is left to each teacher to decide. First Samuel is divided into such sections as seem to represent the divisions which the writer himself intended to make. The structure of the book is indicated more completely in the Table of Contents, and in the analysis printed on p. xxxiv. Each teacher must decide each week how many sections his pupils can successfully study.

With the consent and approval of the University Presses of Oxford and Cambridge, publishers of the Revised Version of 1885, and owners of the copyright in the British Dominions, the text of that version of the Book of First Samuel has been employed in this book. It is reprinted without change, save that, the better to adapt the book for the use of those for whom it is intended, some of the more technical of the marginal readings have been omitted, and a few, of a simpler kind, added, and that in one or two instances the division of the text into paragraphs has been modified.

It is fitting that public acknowledgment should here be made of my indebtedness to my colleague, Dr. John M. P. Smith, who has read the manuscript and proofs, offered many valuable suggestions, and relieved me of much of the editorial labor and responsibility which my absence in the Orient, while the book was going through the press, made it impossible for me to carry.

E. D. BURTON

A FOREWORD TO THE PUPIL

This little book has been prepared and published with a twofold purpose: first, to help you, through the study of the Book of Samuel, to acquire a knowledge of the lives of the prophet whose name it bears, Saul the first king of Israel, and David the most conspicuous figure of the early history of the kingdom; and secondly to help you to form the habit of coming to all the books of the Bible with the question, "What does it mean?" These two purposes will not at all conflict with one another, but each will help to fulfil the other. Every book is the expression of the thought of some person or persons. That thought is the meaning of the book. If that meaning is good and valuable, the book is good and valuable. If we are to get from the book that in it which is good and valuable, we must find out its meaning. Having found this meaning we must, if we would gain the largest good from the book, lodge it in our minds, make it our own, that when we find ourselves in those circumstances to which this truth is applicable, it may be at hand, a guiding influence to shape our conduct and mold our lives.

How to find the meaning of the First Book of Samuel, section by section, and finally as a whole, this book will try to show you. But one or two things may well be emphasized at the outset.

First, begin your study of each section—the teacher will indicate how many sections are to be studied for a given lesson—by reading the Scripture text of the section through attentively, making it your aim to discover as fully as possible the thought of the writer, or of the speaker whose words he records. Attentive reading will give you much of the thought of the passage.

Secondly, if there are in the section any words or phrases the meaning of which you do not know, or the reference of which you do not understand, look up these words or phrases in the Dictionary at the end of the volume. Then read the section again to see if, with the meaning and reference of these words in mind, the meaning of the passage is clear to you.

Thirdly, if the meaning is still not wholly clear to you, try to frame a definite question which will express what you need to know in order to grasp the whole meaning of the passage, and then look through the Explanatory Notes on the section, and see if these notes will furnish you the needed information. If you still lack something of a clear understanding of the passage, write down your question and refer it to your teacher, or some other person who is competent to answer it.

Fourthly, with these questions answered as fully as you can answer them before going to the class, read the passage attentively again, storing its words and meaning in your memory, and thinking them over, so that you may gain from them whatever of helpfulness and suggestiveness they may have for you.

Fifthly, turn to the Questions and answer them one by one, writing out the answers to those that are marked with *. Always use paper of the same size for these answers; write at the head of the sheet the number of the section and the Scripture reference as given in the book, the date of the Sunday when you are to hand in the paper, and your name. These papers are to be handed to the teacher, who will correct them and return them to you the following Sunday. When you receive them back, look carefully over the corrections, and then put the papers away in a safe place. A large envelope properly labeled will be useful for preserving them. Or you may copy them, incorporating the corrections, in a blank book, placing the section number and the Scripture reference at the top of each group of answers. Give special attention to the Review Questions, that you may bind together the results of your study of the separate sections, and so at the end of your work have a good understanding of the book as a whole.

It is my earnest hope, as I am sure it will be that of your teacher, that the pupils who use this book will grasp by diligent study the thought of this part of the Bible, and that, by keeping toward all they thus learn an open and sensitive mind, they will acquire a good knowledge of one period in the history of that faith which came to its highest and most impressive expression in the life and teachings of Jesus.

H. L. W.

THE FIRST BOOK OF SAMUEL
INTRODUCTORY REMARKS

1. *Name.*—The section of the Old Testament which now includes the books of First Samuel, Second Samuel, First Kings, and Second Kings was originally undivided. The separation into four books was made by the Greek translators for convenience. To the first two of these books the name Samuel is given. This does not denote authorship, for the events of Second Samuel occurred after the prophet's death. The name is only appropriate to the earlier portion of First Samuel, as after that Samuel ceases to be the important figure in the narrative.

2. *Contents.*—The Book of First Samuel is a part of the continuous prophetic narrative which begins with the occupation of Canaan and closes with the exile (*ca.* 1200–586 B.C.). This narrative opens with the Book of Judges and continues through Second Kings. First Samuel recounts the events from the birth of Samuel to the death of Saul. The three important figures in the book are Samuel, Saul, and David. But as Saul plays a much less conspicuous part, and is always overshadowed by Samuel, it is appropriate to divide the book into two sections, (1) the life of Samuel, I Sam., chaps. 1–15; (2) the life

of David, I Sam., chaps. 16–31, and continued in II
Sam., chaps. 1–24. The portion of the life of David
included in First Samuel is the period of his struggle
with Saul. The second period, his reign, is the
theme of Second Samuel.

3. *Divisions.*—The divisions of First Samuel are
as follows: A, The life of Samuel, I Sam., chaps.
1–15; (1) Samuel the Judge, I Sam., chaps. 1–7; (*a*)
early life, 1:1—4:1*a*; (*b*) the family of Eli, 4:1*b*–22;
(*c*) wanderings of the ark, 5:1—7:1; (*d*) deliverance
from the Philistines, 7:2–17; (2) Saul made king,
I Sam., chaps. 8–12; (*a*) demand of the people,
chap. 8; (*b*) Saul chosen, chaps. 9, 10; (*c*) relief of
Jabesh-gilead, chap. 11; (*d*) Samuel's farewell,
chap. 12; (3) First years of Saul's reign, I Sam.,
chaps. 13–15; (*a*) Defeat of the Philistines, chaps.
13, 14; (*b*) Saul's disobedience and rejection, chap.
15.

B, Saul and David, I Sam., chaps. 16– 1; (1)
David at Saul's court, I Sam. 16:1—21:1; (*a*) David
anointed, 16:1–13; (*b*) David a minstrel at the court,
16:14–23; (*c*) David and Goliath, 17:1—18:5; (*d*)
Jealousy of Saul, 18:6–30; (*e*) Saul's efforts to kill
David, chap. 19; (*f*) David's flight, chap. 20; (2)
David's career as an outlaw, I Sam., chaps. 21–26;
(*a*) David at Nob, 21:1–9; (*b*) David the fugitive,
21:10—22:5; (*c*) Saul's murder of the priests, 22:6–
23; (*d*) Saul's pursuit of David, chap. 23; (*e*) Saul
spared by David, chap. 24; (*f*) Nabal and David,

chap. 25; (g) Saul again spared by David, chap. 26;
(3) David in the Philistine service, I Sam., chaps.
27–31; (a) David as vassal of Achish, chap. 27; (b)
The despair of Saul, chap. 28; (c) David rejected by
the Philistines, chap. 29; (d) David's pursuit of the
Amalekites, chap. 30; (e) Death of Saul at Gilboa,
chap. 31.

4. *Sources.*—It is evident from even a casual
reading of First Samuel that the historian who wrote
the book made use of older documents. This is
shown in a variety of ways: (1) In several instances
there are duplicate accounts of the same event,
apparently taken from different sources; e.g., Saul's
election, chap. 9, 10:1–16; cf. chap. 8, 10:17–25;
Saul's rejection, 13:8–14; cf. 15:10–31; David's
arrival at the court, 16:14–23; cf. 17:12–31,
55–58; (2) Some portions of the narrative represent a point of view so different from others
that the only adequate explanation appears to
be the use of different documents; e.g., Samuel's
attitude toward the choice of a king in 8:4–6
as contrasted with chap. 9; the complacent mention of family teraphim in 9:13 as contrasted with
the stern denunciation of 15:23; and the view
of Jehovah's limited domain, 26:19 as contrasted
with the conception of his power beyond Israel,
5:1–5. A careful study of the book reveals two series
of narratives, one concerned particularly with the
life of Saul, the other with Samuel. Of these the

former is evidently much the older, its religious ideas being more primitive. The two sets of narratives have been combined by a later historian in the book as we now possess it, with occasional attempts to reconcile their variations (e.g., 11:12–14; 17:15, 31) and a few insertions of material from other sources (e.g., 2:1–10; 20:1—21:1). In the lessons that follow attention will be drawn to the source from which the particular narrative is taken.

5. *The purpose of the book.*—The book of First Samuel is not a complete history of the times with which it deals. In fact, it is not meant to be history at all in our sense of an orderly narrative of national events. Its purpose is religious rather. It gathers for recital such events as have value in illustrating and enforcing the preaching of the prophets. Its narratives must have been used constantly as preaching material by the religious teachers and reformers of Israel. They were not concerned with the history of the nation as such. But they selected from it those events and traditions which offered the best vehicles for religious instruction to the people. The book corresponds, therefore, less to a national history than a collection of prophetic teachings based upon that history, like sermons which make large use of past events, but whose purpose is present instruction and warning.

6. *The religious value of First Samuel.*—The book is a part of the collection of writings called the

Old Testament, and like all the other books of that
group its purpose is to develop the character of the
nation of Israel and the individual members of the
nation in harmony with the principles of conduct
proclaimed by their religious teachers, especially the
prophets.   At the same time it must be remembered
that religious education is a long process, and the
lessons and methods suited to a child or a child-race
are not those of a maturer period. The prophets
of Israel were men of God, but they were also men
of their own age. Their views of God were partial
and imperfect. Even so great a man as Samuel
exhibits something of the limitations, the prejudices,
and the fierce race hatreds of his time. Yet he is
the noblest figure of the age, and was the most
potent instrument for the elevation of Israel from
the rough life of mere tribesmen to the settled and
organized condition of a nation. The book must
therefore be understood not as a textbook on conduct, setting forth a final and satisfactory state of
society, but rather as a chapter in the history of
religion. The faults of that age were pointed out
by later prophets. Through successive generations
the religious teachers of Israel labored to bring in
better views of God and of social conduct. The
appeal, therefore, is to be made not to Samuel and
his age, but to the later and greater prophets, such
as Amos, Hosea, Isaiah, and their successors,
and most of all to Jesus, the final prophet, who

in contrast with Moses, Elijah, and all the holy men of the past, was pointed out as the Son of God, the final and authoritative teacher of the world.

SECTION I

SAMUEL'S PARENTS, I SAM. 1:1-9*a*

1 Now there was a certain man of Ramathaim-
zophim, of the hill country of Ephraim, and his name
was Elkanah, the son of Jeroham, the son of Elihu,
the son of Tohu, the son of Zuph, an Ephraimite: and
2 he had two wives; the name of the one was Hannah,

EXPLANATORY NOTES

This portion of I Sam. is taken from the late narrative of
Samuel's life which took form in the northern kingdom. It
emphasizes the prophetic work of Samuel as the most important
factor in the history of the period. See Introd., 4.

Vs. 1, "Ramathaim-zophim": a town whose site has not been
identified with certainty. It seems to mean "height (or heights)
of the Zuphites," with a possible reference to the family of Zuph,
who is mentioned in this verse as an ancestor of Samuel. Probably the town was situated at the site of the modern Ramallah,
three miles southwest of Bethel, about twelve miles southwest of
Shiloh and nine north of Jerusalem. "Hill country of Ephraim"†:
the central highland section of Palestine, of which the strong
tribe of Ephraim was the possessor. "Elkanah": The name
means "God has acquired;" his genealogy is traced back four
generations, after the manner of the Hebrew records. "An
Ephraimite": This designates not only residence within the tribal
limits of Ephraim, but membership in that tribe. In I Chron.
6:26-28, 33-38 Samuel is given a position in the tribe of Levi
This is probably due to the fact that he performed priestly functions, which in the later age in which Chronicles was written
were reserved to the Levites. Vs. 2, "two wives": Polygamy
was common in the Old Testament times, and was not regarded
as wrong. Education in morality is a slow process, and the

and the name of the other Peninnah: and Peninnah had children, but Hannah had no children. And ₃ this man went up out of his city from year to year to worship and to sacrifice unto the Lord of hosts in Shiloh. And the two sons of Eli, Hophni and Phinehas, priests unto the Lord, were there. And when

RUINS OF SHILOH

the day came that Elkanah sacrificed, he gave to Peninnah his wife, and to all her sons and her daughters, portions: but unto Hannah he gave a ₅ double portion: for he loved Hannah, but the Lord had shut up her womb. And her rival provoked ₆ her sore, for to make her fret, because the Lord had shut up her womb. And as he did so year by year, ₇

when she went up to the house of the Lord, so she
provoked her; therefore she wept, and did not eat.
8 And Elkanah her husband said unto her, Hannah,
why weepest thou? and why eatest thou not? and
why is thy heart grieved? am not I better to thee
9 than ten sons? So Hannah rose up after they had
eaten in Shiloh, and after they had drunk.

Hebrews, like other nations, could be taught only by degrees.
"Hannah" ("grace"): Every woman desired children. Like
Rachel (Gen. 30:1) she felt keenly the sorrow and disgrace of being
childless. "Peninnah" ("coral" or "pearl"): Her character is
disclosed in vs. 6. Vs. 3, "went up": The custom of making
journeys to sanctuaries is very old, and prevails among many nations. Three annual feasts† were held among the Hebrews
(Exod. 34:23), but probably few of the people felt the obligation
to make the pilgrimage more than once annually (vs. 21). "To
sacrifice": The animal, usually a bullock was taken to the sanctuary where it was killed; certain parts were burned on the altar,
a portion was given to the priest as his fee, and the remainder
was boiled and eaten by the worshiper and his family. "Lord
of hosts": "Jehovah of armies," i.e., the armies of Israel. "Shiloh"†: nineteen miles north of Jerusalem. The sanctuary was
here. "Sons of Eli"†: Eli was the priest, and his two sons
assisted in the services of the sanctuary. Vs. 4, "Gave portions":
It was his custom to give the different members of his family
portions of the sacrificial meat. Vs. 5, "double portion": The
translation of this verse is uncertain. It may be read: "He
gave a double portion, for he loved Hannah." This would indicate that the choice portion given to the favorite wife was a mark
of affection (such as Joseph showed toward Benjamin, Gen.
43:34). Or it may be read: "He gave to Hannah one portion,
though he loved her." This would mean that Hannah, having
no children, needed only a small allotment of food. Probably
this is the better reading. This constantly reminded Hannah of

her misfortune in being childless. Vs. 6, "her rival": the other wife, Peninnah, who was proud of her children and jealous of Elkanah's greater affection for Hannah. Vs. 7, "provoked her": The annual journey to the tabernacle gave more opportunity than any other event of the year for contrast between the conditions of the two women. It was at this time that Hannah most keenly felt the humiliation of having no child. Vs. 8, "better than ten sons": Her husband tried to comfort her with proofs of his affection. Yet nothing could give her consolation. Vs. 9, "rose up": She was very unhappy, and left the feast as soon as it was possible for her to withdraw. She wished to be alone, where she could find comfort in prayer.

QUESTIONS

(1) Whose career is recorded in I Samuel? (2)* Where was Ramathaim-zophim? (3) Who were Samuel's parents? (4) What were the names of Elkanah's wives? (5) Was it right for this man to have more than one wife? (6) What was the custom of that age? (7)* What was Elkanah's annual pilgrimage? (8) Where were the sacrifices held? (9) Who were the priests at this time? (10)* What were the duties of the priest†? (11) What did Elkanah give to Peninnah and her children? (12)* Why did he give a different amount to Hannah? (13) What was Hannah's great sorrow? (14) *Why were children, especially sons, greatly desired by Hebrew families? (15) What was Peninnah's treatment of Hannah? (16) What was her reason for this conduct? (17) What light does this hatred between the two wives throw on the evil of polygamy? (18) How did Hannah show her sorrow? (19) Did her husband sympathize with her? (20)* How did he attempt to comfort her? (21) Why did she leave the feast? (22)* How far, and in which direction, had Elkanah and his family traveled from their home to Shiloh? (23) Would you think Elkanah's family, where all were accustomed to attend religious service regularly, a model for today?

SECTION II

HANNAH'S VOW, I SAM. 1:9b–19a

Now Eli the priest sat upon his seat by the door-
10 post of the temple of the Lord. And she was in
bitterness of soul, and prayed unto the Lord, and
11 wept sore. And she vowed a vow, and said, O Lord
of hosts, if thou wilt indeed look on the affliction of
thine handmaid, and remember me, and not forget
thine handmaid, but wilt give unto thine handmaid
a man child, then I will give him unto the Lord all
the days of his life, and there shall no razor come
12 upon his head. And it came to pass, as she continued

EXPLANATORY NOTES

This section belongs to the northern narrative of Samuel's
prophetic ministry. See Introd., 4.

Vs. 9, "Eli† the priest": the aged priest and judge, who had
given over to his two sons the conduct of affairs at Shiloh. "The
temple"†: the sanctuary, or building in which worship was held
in Shiloh. At its door Eli sat to judge the people. Vs. 10, "in
bitterness": Hannah was distressed over her childless condition;
prayer and tears were her only resource. Vs. 11, "a vow": a
pledge made to God to devote to him some service or object in
return for the blessing asked. Such vows are recorded in the
cases of Jacob (Gen. 28:20–22), Jephthah (Judg. 11:30, 31),
and the parents of Samson (Judg. 13). "I will give him": Hannah promised to devote her son to the service of God, if she might
only enjoy the privilege and honor of motherhood. He was to be
dedicated to God as a Nazirite†. "No razor": He was to keep
his hair uncut as a sign of his consecration. The hair was a symbol
of life. All powers were to be dedicated to God. Vs. 12, "Eli

5

praying before the Lord, that Eli marked her mouth.
Now Hannah, she spake in her heart; only her lips 13
moved, but her voice was not heard: therefore Eli
thought she had been drunken. And Eli said unto 14
her. How long wilt thou be drunken? put away
thy wine from thee. And Hannah answered and 15
said, No, my Lord, I am a woman of a sorrowful
spirit: I have drunk neither wine nor strong drink,
but I poured out my soul before the Lord. Count 16
not thine handmaid for [1]a daughter of Belial: for
out of the abundance of my complaint and my provocation have I spoken hitherto. Then Eli answered 17
and said, Go in peace; and the God of Israel grant
thy petition that thou hast asked of him. And she 18
said, Let thy servant find grace in thy sight. So
the woman went her way, and did eat, and her countenance was no more sad. And they rose up in the 19
morning early, and worshipped before the Lord, and
returned, and came to their house to Ramah.

[1] Or, *a wicked woman*

---

marked": The old priest noticed Hannah, and saw that her lips
moved. Vs. 13, "in her heart": She was not speaking aloud.
"Drunken": At the sacrificial feasts wine was used. The sons
of Eli were immoral men, and their evil example may easily have
led to scenes of revelry and drunkenness, even near the sanctuary.
Vs. 14, "put away": Perhaps Eli had been compelled to rebuke
more than one woman for intoxication in those evil times. Such
is the implication of his command. Vs. 15, "No, my lord": Mark
the dignity and quietness of Hannah's reply. Though stung by
the severity of the needless rebuke, she does not resent it, but
corrects the aged priest. "Poured out": Prayer is such a pres-

entation of one's cause as puts one in communion with God and
brings relief of spirit. Vs. 16, "daughter of Belial"†: a vile or
wicked woman. "Provocation": The tauntings of her rival,
Peninnah, aggravated the bitterness of Hannah's misfortune.
Vs. 17, "Go in peace": Eli saw his mistake and felt compassion
toward the unhappy woman. "Grant thy petition": The priest
did not promise her the positive fulfilment of her request, but
encouraged her to believe that her prayer would be answered.
Vs. 18, "find grace": Hannah wished Eli's good will toward her.
Perhaps she felt that his prayers in her behalf would be a help in
obtaining her desire. "Did eat": She was no longer distressed,
but was full of hope. Vs. 19, "rose up early": in preparation for
the journey home. "Worshipped": Their final religious duties
were performed. These would naturally consist of prayer and
sacrifice. "To Ramah": This town, the home of Elkanah and
his family, is called Ramathaim-zophim in vs. 1. It was probably about twelve miles southwest of Shiloh.

QUESTIONS

(1) Where was Eli accustomed to sit? (2)* What is meant
by "the temple"†? (3) What did Hannah do in her trouble
(vs. 10)? (4) What is a vow? (5)* What vow did Hannah
make? (6) To what kind of life did she dedicate the child
she hoped for? (7) How did this plan of Hannah's shape
the life of Samuel? (8) Do you think a child will be helped
to live a useful life by such a plan of his mother's? (9) What
caused Eli to notice Hannah (vs. 12)? (10)* What did the
priest think about her (vs. 13)? (11) What reason had he
for so thinking? (12) Did drunkenness prevail at the sanctuary? (13) What did Eli say to Hannah (vs 14)? (14)
What was Hannah's answer (vs. 15)? (15) What were the
causes of Hannah's sorrow? (16) What did Eli do when he
understood her case (vs. 17)? (17) What effect did the kind
words of the priest have upon the sorrowful woman? (18)
Where was the home to which Elkanah and Hannah returned?
(19) Do you think that all good requests made to God will be
answered?

SECTION III

And Elkanah knew Hannah his wife; and the Lord remembered her. And it came to pass, when the 20 time was come about, that Hannah conceived, and bare a son; and she called his name Samuel, saying, Because I have asked him of the Lord. And the 21 man Elkanah, and all his house went up to offer unto the Lord the yearly sacrifice, and his vow. But Hannah went not up; for she said unto her 22 husband, I will not go up until the child be weaned, and then I will bring him, that he may appear before the Lord, and there abide for ever. And Elkanah 23

EXPLANATORY NOTES

In this section and throughout the first four chapters of the book the later Ephraimite or northern account of Samuel's life is followed. See Introd., 4.

Vs. 19, "remembered her": Her prayer had not been in vain. Similarly we read of God's remembrance of Rachel (Gen. 30:22), who had cried, "Give me children or I die" (Gen. 30:1). Vs. 20, "bare a son": Sons were the most prized possession of a Hebrew family. Vs. 21, "went up": to Shiloh, the city where the sanctuary stood (vs. 3). "The yearly sacrifice": probably the feast† of the Passover. "His vow": Nothing was said of Elkanah's vow on the previous visit. This assumes that he had made one. Vs. 22, "weaned": The child would then be two or three years old, and could remain, as his mother had promised. Vs. 23, "establish his word": He hopes that

8

her husband said unto her, Do what seemeth thee
good; tarry until thou have weaned him; only the
Lord establish his word. So the woman tarried and
24 gave her son suck, until she weaned him.   And when
she had weaned him she took him up with her, with
[1]three bullocks, and one ephah of meal, and a [2]bottle
of wine, and brought him unto the house of the Lord
25 in Shiloh; and the child was young.   And they slew
26 the bullock, and brought the child to Eli.   And she
said, Oh my lord, as thy soul liveth, my lord, I am
the woman that stood by thee here, praying unto
27 the Lord.   For this child I prayed; and the Lord
hath given me my petition which I asked of him:
28 therefore I also have [3]granted him to the Lord; as
long as he liveth he is granted to the Lord.   And
[4]he worshipped the Lord there.

[1] Or, *a bullock of three years*
[2] Or, *skin*
[3] Or, *lent*
[4] Or, *they*

---

their lives may be spared to realize the divine purpose. Vs. 24,
"Three bullocks": The marginal reading, "a bullock of three
years," is better. Even thus the offering was a costly one.
"Ephah"†: about one bushel. "Bottle"†: literally a "skin,"
holding several gallons. These provisions were for the sacrificial
feast, to which no doubt friends were invited. Vs. 25, "they
slew": This may refer to Elkanah and his servants, but more
probably to the priests. "Brought the child": Certain portions
of the slaughtered bullock were given to the priest as his portion.
At such a moment the child was presented. Vs. 26, "as thy soul
liveth": a common form of emphasis, meaning "truly" or "assuredly" (see 20:3). "Stood by thee": Hannah refers to the
time when she made the vow and received Eli's blessing (vss.
13–17). Vs. 27, "my petition": She recognized the birth of
Samuel as the direct answer to her prayers. Vs. 28, "granted

him": "lent him" would perhaps best express the thought. As she had asked for a child, so she gives over the child to God, in grateful fulfilment of her vow. "He worshipped": This may be read, "He (Samuel) bowed before Jehovah," or "He (Elkanah) worshipped," or perhaps "They worshipped": but probably the best reading is, "He (Eli) worshipped," in thankful recognition of the mercy of God in the gift of the child, first to Hannah, and now to the service of the sanctuary.

QUESTIONS

(1) Where did Elkanah go yearly? (2) Was this annual pilgrimage a good example of household religion? (3)* Why did Hannah remain at home? (4) Do you suppose she wished to keep Samuel with her as long as she could? (5) How did Elkanah feel when she told him of her wish to stay at home till the child was older? (6)* When did Hannah go to Shiloh? (7) What offering did she take? (8) What was done with Samuel? (9) Must it not have been hard for Hannah to leave her son? (10) Who probably took care of him in Shiloh? (11)* How does this section illustrate the faithfulness and devotion of Samuel's mother? (12) How would you describe Hannah's character?

SECTION IV

2 And Hannah prayed, and said:
  My heart exulteth in the Lord,
  Mine horn is exalted in the Lord:
  My mouth is enlarged over mine enemies;
  Because I rejoice in thy salvation.
2 There is none holy as the Lord;
  For there is none beside thee;
  Neither is there any rock like our God.
3 Talk no more so exceeding proudly;
  Let not arrogancy come out of your mouth:
  For the Lord is a God of knowledge,
  And by him actions are weighed.

EXPLANATORY NOTES

The song here inserted appears to be a national hymn of thankfulness for victory rather than an utterance of Hannah's. The reference to the birth of children in vs. 5 is probably the cause of its being assigned to its present position by the later editor.

Vs. 1, "prayed": In this song the power of God is celebrated, with warnings to those defiant of the divine will. There are no particular references to Hannah's circumstances, but the note of triumph may represent her sentiments. "Horn": The horn is the symbol of strength and honor. With it animals defend themselves (Ps. 92:10). But the strength and honor of the good come from God. "Mouth is enlarged": The singer is no longer silent in the presence of foes. "Salvation": deliverance from peril and reproach. Vs. 2, "none beside thee": no God other

The bows of the mighty men are broken,   4
And they that stumbled are girded with strength.
They that were full have hired out themselves for 5
  bread;
And they that were hungry ¹have ceased;
Yea, the barren hath borne seven;
And she that hath many children languisheth.
The Lord killeth, and maketh alive: 6
He bringeth down to ²the grave and bringeth up.
The Lord maketh poor, and maketh rich: 7
He bringeth low, he also lifteth up.
He raiseth up the poor out of the dust,   8
He lifteth up the needy from the dunghill,
To make them sit with princes,

---

than Jehovah. Most nations believed that there were many
gods. Even the Hebrews shared this view. It was the work of
the prophets to teach them that there is but one God. "Rock":
symbol of stability and protection (II Sam. 22:32). "Arrogancy":
pride, presumption. Is Peninnah addressed here, or are these
words a general rebuke to boastful people? "Weighed": Actions
are tested, even as goods are weighed. Vs. 4, "bows": One
important division of an army was the archers, or bowmen.
"Girded": Putting on a belt was a preparation for action. God
disarms the strong, and strengthens the weak. Vs. 5, "hired
out": Once rich, they have become so poor that they became
servants in order to obtain a living. "Have ceased": The opposite picture; they once were in want, but now they need toil no
longer. "Borne seven": This appears to be the most direct
reference to Hannah's condition, and yet it is general rather than
specific. Seven is the number indicating completeness. The
meaning is that the childless now has complete happiness in the
blessing of motherhood. "Languisheth": becomes weak and

And inherit the throne of glory:
For the pillars of the earth are the Lord's,
And he hath set the world upon them.

9 He will keep the feet of his ³holy ones,   ³ Or, godly
But the wicked shall be put to silence in darkness;
For by strength shall no man prevail.

10 They that strive with the Lord shall be broken to
    pieces;
Against them shall be thunder in heaven;
The Lord shall judge the ends of the earth;
And he shall give strength unto his king,
And exalt the horn of his anointed.

11 And Elkanah went to Ramah to his house.   And the
child did minister unto the Lord before Eli the priest.

---

of small importance through the death of her children.   This
does not seem to refer to Hannah's rival, but illustrates the con-
trasts seen in life.   Vs. 6, "Killeth": The Hebrew, who knew
nothing of secondary causes, or the laws of nature, attributed
the reward of good and the chastisement of evil directly to God.
In the largest sense it is true that the issues of life and death are
with God.   "To the grave:" Sheol†, the underworld of the dead,
according to Hebrew belief.   Vs. 8, "dust . . . . dunghill":
To "sit in dust" (Isa. 47:1) was to be in extreme poverty and
wretchedness.   The dunghill (Lam. 4:5) was the refuse-heap
outside an oriental town, where beggars and lepers resorted.   "Sit
with princes": These lines denote rapid advancement and
prosperity coming to those who had been very poor and obscure.
(See Ps. 113:7–9, which seems to be a copy of this passage.)
"Pillars of the earth": The figure of a house is used.   Pillars
denote strength.   Jehovah is the creator of the earth (Ps. 75:3).
Vs. 9, "keep the feet": safeguard the goings of his chosen ones.
"Put to silence": Evil men, no matter how successful, fail in the

end. Their lives count for nothing. Vs. 10, "broken in pieces": It is useless to defy the divine purpose. "Thunder": a dramatic description of God's majestic and eternal hatred of sin. "Ends of the earth": His government includes the most remote places. "His king": The king of Israel, as ruler of the chosen nation, is to be protected, strengthened, and raised to honor by God. The same use of "horn" as the symbol of power is seen here as in vs. 1. Vs. 11, "Ramah": already mentioned in 1:1, 19. Hannah's return to Ramah with her husband is not mentioned, but is to be understood. "Minister": The boy Samuel staid with Eli and was taught to perform such tasks as he could in the sanctuary.

QUESTIONS

(1)* What would be Hannah's feelings after the fulfilment of her wishes? (2) Was it natural that she should give expression to her joy in a hymn of praise? (3) Is there any direct reference to Hannah's personal experience in this song? (4) *Does the song seem the expression of one who thought of her own blessings, or of the national welfare? (5) Does the song in any manner resemble Mary's hymn of praise over the birth of Jesus, Luke 1:46-55? (6)* How does it show the beauty of gratitude for blessings received? (7) Do you think it possible for a noble and generous nature to receive benefits and remain unthankful?

SECTION V

THE SINS OF ELI'S SONS, I SAM. 2:12–17

12 Now the sons of Eli were ¹sons of Belial; they
13 knew not the Lord. And the custom of the priests
with the people was, that, when any man offered
sacrifice, the priest's servant came, while the flesh
was in seething, with a fleshhook of three teeth in his
14 hand; and he struck it into the pan, or kettle, or
caldron, or pot; all that the fleshhook brought up
the priest took therewith. So they did in Shiloh

¹ Or, *wicked men*

EXPLANATORY NOTES

The late narrative of Samuel's prophetic work, a northern
document, is here continued. The contrast of Eli's sons with
Samuel's character is disclosed.

Vs. 12, "sons of Belial"†: worthless, wicked men. (Recall
the term "daughter of Belial" in 1:16.) It is the purpose of this
section to show the urgent need for a change in the conduct of
religious affairs, such as Samuel introduced. Vs. 13, "seething":
boiling; after the Lord's portion, the fat, was taken to be burned
on the altar, the remainder of the usable meat was boiled and
eaten by the worshiper and his family. "A fleshhook": The
custom of giving the priest a part of the sacrifice as his reward was
no doubt very old. At first it was apparently optional with the
offerer whether or not he should give the priest a portion, and how
much it should be. Later on there arose the custom, here described, of permitting the priest to thrust in the three-pronged hook
among the boiling pieces and take whatever came out. Vs. 14,
"kettle": The cooking-vessels were kept at the sanctuary for
the convenience of the worshipers. "Priest took": The meat he

unto all the Israelites that came thither. Yea, before 15
they burnt the fat, the priest's servant came, and
said to the man that sacrificed, Give flesh to roast
for the priest; for he will not have sodden flesh of
thee, but raw. And if the man said unto him, They 16
will surely burn the fat ²presently, and then take as
much as thy soul desireth; then he would say, Nay,
but thou shalt give it me now: and if not, I will
take it by force. And the sin of the young men was 17
very great before the Lord; for ³men abhorred the
offering of the Lord.

* Or, *first*

³ Or, *the men despised*

---

brought out of the kettle with his fork was his fee, or reward, for
helping the worshiper in the preparation of his sacrifice. "All
the Israelites": Shiloh was a central sanctuary, and the most
important one, though there were other places where sacrifices
were made. The custom spoken of was practiced in the case of all
worshipers at Shiloh. Vs. 15, "before they burnt": A violation
of the usual custom is here noted. The fat was to be burned on
the altar as the first act of sacrifice. These priests did not wait
to perform their functions at the altar, but wanted their part of
the meat first. "Sodden": boiled; here was a second violation
of the custom. These unworthy sons of Eli not only wanted their
perquisite or "tip" first, but they would not take it from among
the boiling pieces, but wanted it raw, so that they might cook it at
home. Vs. 16, "burn the fat presently": The worshiper would
naturally be surprised and say, "Wait till the sacrifice of the fat
(God's part) has been made; then help yourself." The man
who made the offering was right in supposing that the gift made
to God was the important item. Not so these priests; they were
concerned only to secure their own rewards. "By force": This
disgraceful threat would fill any worshiper with astonishment and
indignation. Vs. 17, "Sin . . . . very great": The sin, of making
money out of religion, could have no place in the life of a true and

faithful priest. "Before the Lord": Not only was it disgraceful in men's estimation, but God looked on and marked their conduct. "Abhorred the offering": Such conduct by the priests made people think little of the importance of sacrifice, and dislike to visit a place where such things were practiced.

QUESTIONS

(1) What were the duties of the priests? (2) What kind of men were Eli's sons? (3)* In what way did they demand more for themselves than had been the custom? (4) What right had the priests to any part of the offering? (5)* To what acts did the selfishness of these men lead them? (6) Is there any worse vice than selfishness? (7)* How does this section show that the meanest faults may appear in connection with the most sacred work? (8) What do people think of religion when those who lead in the work of the church appear selfish? (9) Does it prevent others from doing right? (10)* What is its evil result? (11) Is it right to allow the evil conduct of others to prevent us from being good?

SECTION VI

SAMUEL'S GROWTH, I SAM. 2:18-26

But Samuel ministered before the Lord, being a 18
child, girded with a linen ephod. Moreover his 19
mother made him a little robe, and brought it to him
from year to year, when she came up with her
husband to offer the yearly sacrifice. And Eli 20
blessed Elkanah and his wife, and said, The Lord
give thee seed of this woman ¹for the loan which was
lent to the Lord. And they went unto their own
home. And the Lord visited Hannah, and she 21
conceived, and bare three sons and two daughters.
And the child Samuel grew before the Lord.

¹ Or, *for the petition which was asked for the Lord*

EXPLANATORY NOTES

Vs. 18, "Samuel ministered": There were many tasks about
the sanctuary which even a child could perform. The purpose
of this section is to show the simple piety and helpfulness of the
child who was not of the priestly family, in contrast with the
irreverence and baseness of the sons of Eli, the priests. "Linen
ephod": The ephod was a garment covering the shoulders and
girded around the waist. It was worn by priests (vs. 28; 22:18),
but also occasionally by others (II Sam. 6:14). Vs. 19, "little
robe": Samuel's mother supplied him with his necessary garments,
aside from the linen ephod. The one here mentioned was the
ordinary coat or robe worn as an outer garment. Vs. 20, "Give
thee seed": The blessing of Eli included the hope that Elkanah
and Hannah might have other children, since Samuel had been
devoted by them to God. Vs. 21, "visited Hannah": The expression "the Lord visited" is often used in the Old Testament to

22 Now Eli was very old; and he heard all that his
sons did unto all Israel, and how that they lay with
the women that did service at the door of the tent of
23 meeting.   And he said unto them, Why do ye such
things? for I hear of your evil dealings from all this
24 people.   Nay, my sons, for it is no good report that
I hear: ye make the Lord's people to transgress.
25 If one man sin against another, God shall judge him:
but if a man sin against the Lord, who shall entreat
for him?   Notwithstanding they hearkened not
unto the voice of their father, because the Lord would
26 slay them.   And the child Samuel grew on, and was
in favour both with the Lord, and also with men.

---

describe God's remembrance of one in need of help, deliverance,
or comfort. "Three sons and two daughters": Hannah's happiness was made complete in thus having not only her first request
for a child granted, but in becoming the mother of several others.
She had no further occasion for sorrow.   It is significant that no
further mention is made of Peninnah. "Before the Lord":
All that took place at the sanctuary might well be described as
"before the Lord," in his presence.   Vs. 22, "very old": Even
before Samuel's birth Eli had given over to his sons the conduct
of affairs. "All that his sons did": The conduct of Hophni and
Phinehas was notorious. Everyone knew of their greed in
demanding unlawful gifts, their cruelty in exacting their demands,
and their shameful behavior. "Did service": Women were
employed as servants to perform various duties at the sanctuary,
or tent of meeting (Exod. 38:8). Vs. 23, "Why do ye?": Eli
was not unconcerned, but was apparently helpless to correct the
behavior of his sons. He reproved them, but to no purpose.
Vs. 24, "transgress": It was bad enough that they were evil
men; but still worse was the fact that their influence caused

others to become indifferent or base. Vs. 25, "who shall entreat ?":
Where men only are concerned in a dispute, there is a higher
Power to act as umpire between them; but if a man sin against
God, there is no one who can act as judge. "Hearkened not":
Perhaps Eli had not corrected them in their youth; in that case
he was reaping the evil fruits of his own weakness. "Would
slay them": The evil consequences of sin are certain; and sometimes the Bible explains them in terms of God's will. God does
not wish the death of any (Ezek. 18:32), but in this world, whose
laws are his own, evil conduct persisted in brings destruction.
God is too loving to separate sin from its consequences. The
death of these bad priests was the only way in which the nature
of their lives could reveal itself, and others be warned against
imitating them. The same law holds good today. Yet it is not
true that sin always results in immediate misfortune to the sinner.
But the prophets wished to point out those instances in which this
consequence followed. Vs. 26, "grew on": In contrast with
these unworthy priests, the child increased not only in years and
strength, but grew in the affections of the people, and in a character pleasing to God.

QUESTIONS

(1)* In what place did Samuel live ? (2) How often did his
mother visit him ? (3) How did she show her love ? (4)
What was Eli's feeling for the family ? (5) How many other
children did Hannah have ? (6) Do you suppose that these
took the place of Samuel in her affection ? (7)* What did
Samuel do at Shiloh ? (8) Why is the character of Samuel
so attractive ? (9) What sort of men were the sons of Eli ?
(10) Was Eli at fault for their behavior ? (11)* In what manner is a father to blame when his children do wrong ? (12) Is
a father usually blamed when his children misbehave ? (13)
In what sense is a child responsible for the good name of his
father or mother ? (14) Does God wish to slay evil men ?
(15) Are such men always punished ? (16)* In what manner
is the prosperity of evil men one of the problems of life ? (17)
In what respect is Samuel's life a model ?

SECTION VII

A PROPHET'S WARNING, I SAM. 2:27–36

27   And there came a man of God unto Eli, and said
unto him, Thus saith the Lord, Did I reveal myself
unto the house of thy father, when they were in Egypt
28 in bondage to Pharaoh's house? And did I choose
him out of all the tribes of Israel to be my priest,
to ¹go up unto mine altar, to burn incense, to wear   ¹ Or, *offer upon*
an ephod before me? and did I give unto the house
of thy father all the offerings of the children of Israel

EXPLANATORY NOTES

Vs. 27, "a man of God": a prophet†, whose name is not
given. This would indicate that the work of religious instruction
was not confined to Eli and his unworthy sons. "Thus saith the
Lord": Such words were usually employed by the prophets to
introduce their messages. They imply a knowledge of God's
will, and the authority of his representatives. "Did I reveal?":
This question, of course, implies the answer "yes." God revealed
himself to Israel in Egypt, when the people were in bondage
(Exod. 4:14–17, 27; 12:1). "House of thy father": Eli was a
member of the tribe of Levi, and of the family of Aaron, the
brother of Moses, through whom God's revelation was made
to Israel in Egypt. "Pharaoh"†: the king of Egypt, who oppressed Israel (Exod. 1:8–14). Vs. 28, "did I choose?": another
question implying the answer "yes." The reference is to Aaron,
the ancestor of Eli, who was counted the first priest among the
Hebrews. "Mine altar": One of the duties of the priest was to
offer the sacrifices at the altar of God. "Burn incense:" This
was a special form of sacrifice, performed in the sanctuary at a
small altar, by sprinkling a powder made of spices upon the

made by fire? Wherefore ²kick ye at my sacrifice 29
and at my offering, which I have commanded in my
habitation; and honourest thy sons above me, to
make yourselves fat with the chiefest of all the offerings of Israel my people? Therefore the Lord, the 30
God of Israel, saith, I said indeed that thy house,
and the house of thy father, should walk before me
forever: but now the Lord saith, Be it far from me;
for them that honour me I will honour, and they that
despise me shall be lightly esteemed. Behold the 31
days come, that I will cut off thine arm, and the arm
of thy father's house, that there shall not be an old

---

coals, producing a fragrant smoke. "Wear an ephod": or, "carry
an ephod;" it is not clear here whether the reference is to the
priestly garment, which identified the wearer as a member of the
order of priests, or to the image used by the priests in securing
oracles. The user of the ephod was connected especially with
the giving of oracles. "All the offerings": The priests had
a share in all the materials brought for sacrifice upon the altar;
this was their living. Vs. 29, "Wherefore kick ye?": "trample
upon" is perhaps a better rendering. Another reading is, "why
do you look with envious eyes upon my sacrifices?" Eli's sons
had shown that they were unworthy of the high honor conferred
upon their tribe and family; their conduct took away all the
sacredness of the sacrifices made by the people. "Honourest thy
sons": By permitting his sons to act as they did, Eli became
partaker in their sin of dishonor to God. "Make yourselves
fat": The offerings demanded from the people by Hophni and
Phinehas were probably sold by them, and so became their
means, not merely of livelihood, but of gaining wealth. Vs. 30,
"I said indeed": This refers to the arrangement in Israel that
the family of Aaron should hold the priestly offices. This was,

32 man in thine house.   And thou shalt behold ³the
   affliction of my habitation, in all the wealth which
   God shall give Israel: and there shall not be an old
33 man in thine house for ever.   And the man of thine,
   whom I shall not cut off from mine altar, shall be to
   consume thine eyes, and to grieve thine heart; and all
   the increase of thine house shall die in the flower of
34 their age.   And this shall be the sign unto thee, that
   shall come upon thy two sons, on Hophni and
   Phinehas; in one day they shall die both of them.
35 And I will raise me up a faithful priest, that shall do
   according to that which is in mine heart and in my

³ Or, *an adversary in my habitation*

---

of course, regarded as the will of God. "Far be it": The conduct of these priests had made necessary a change. Their
particular branch of the Levites was to be deposed from priestly
offices. Vs. 31, "cut off thine arm": The arm is the sign of
power; the family of Eli was to be crippled, cut off, destroyed.
"Old man": They were to die prematurely. Vs. 32, "Behold the
affliction": If this is the correct translation, the meaning is that
Eli's descendants should see the sanctuary neglected, as the
result of the disfavor into which it had been brought, while the
rest of the nation enjoyed prosperity. Perhaps a better reading
is, "Thou shalt see a rival in my house," intimating that another
and worthier was to receive the priestly office. These words
probably referred to Samuel when uttered; but such also became
the case when Solomon removed Abiathar, a descendant of Eli,
from the priesthood, and put Zadok, of another clan of the tribe,
into the place (I Kings 2:26, 27, 35). Vs. 33, "not cut off":
Some of Eli's descendants would probably continue as priests,
but even they should either be a disgrace to their tribe, or have
cause to mourn over their loss of honor. "Shall die": Such a
fate overtook the entire group of priests at Nob in Saul's reign

mind: and I will build him a sure house; and he shall walk before mine anointed for ever. And it 36 shall come to pass, that every one that is left in thine house shall come and bow down to him for a piece of silver and a loaf of bread, and shall say, Put me, I pray thee, into one of the priests' offices, that I may eat a morsel of bread.

(I Sam. 22:9–19). Vs. 34, "sign": From the one event which was to happen in Eli's own lifetime he might know the certainty of the entire prophecy. "They shall die": Chap. 4 records the fulfilment of these words in the events of the battle of Aphek. Vs. 35, "a faithful priest": Reference is here made to Samuel, but the oracle was also fulfilled in the choice of Zadok, whom Solomon placed in office instead of Abiathar (I Kings 2:35), and in whose elevation the author sees the punishment of Eli's family. "Sure house": an abiding position as head of the priests. "Mine anointed": the king of Israel, whoever he might be at any particular time; the sons of Zadok were the priests throughout the later history. Vs. 36, "Bow down to him": Eli's descendants could secure a living only by begging a place of service from Zadok and his posterity.

QUESTIONS

(1) To whom did the unknown prophet come? (2)* What warning did he bring to the priest and his household? (3) What had they done that was wrong and needed rebuke? (4) What threat did he utter against them? (5) Did these predictions come true? (6) Do you think it is ever possible to escape the consequences of evil-doing? (7) Do those consequences always come in the same way? (8)* In what ways besides physical punishment do the results of bad conduct cause disaster to the guilty one? (9) Would it not be a great humiliation to a descendant of Eli to have to beg bread from

the priests? (10) *Is it always true that people are punished for wrong-doing? (11) Is it always evident, or are there inner and hidden ways in which the consequences of sin manifest themselves? (12) Has any prophet a higher duty than to warn men against evil, and threaten them with its results?

A YOUNG ARAB

SECTION VIII

SAMUEL'S NIGHT CALL, I SAM. 3:1-9

And the child Samuel ministered unto the Lord 3
before Eli. And the word of the Lord was ¹precious
in those days; there was no ²open vision. And it 2
came to pass at that time, when Eli was laid down
in his place (now his eyes had begun to wax dim,
that he could not see), and the lamp of God was not 3
yet gone out, and Samuel was laid down to sleep, in
the temple of the Lord, where the ark of God was;

¹ Or, *rare*
² Or, *frequent*

EXPLANATORY NOTES

This narrative is taken from the story of Samuel's prophetic
career as told in the Ephraimite document which extends from
1:1—5:1.

Vs. 1, "Samuel ministered": the same expression as that
in 2:11; but the child must have grown to boyhood by this
time. Probably he was twelve years old, or more. "Precious":
"rare;" there were few prophets, and little communication between God and the people. This was one of the sad results of
the decay of religion at Shiloh. Vs. 2, "In his place": Eli slept
not far from the ark, perhaps in the same apartment. "Wax
dim": Eli was already an old man before Samuel was born;
years had added to his infirmities. He was almost, if not totally,
blind. Vs. 3, "lamp of God": In the sanctuary there was a
candlestick, and the light was kept burning at night. "Not yet gone
out:" Samuel's call came late in the night, well toward morning.
"In the temple"†: The sanctuary at Shiloh is meant, of course.
Its arrangements were very simple. Samuel had his bed near
the ark, and Eli was not far away. "Ark† of God": the sacred

4 that the Lord called Samuel: and he said, Here am
5 I. And he ran unto Eli, and said, Here am I; for

AN ORIENTAL LAMP

thou calledst me. And he said, I called not; lie
6 down again. And he went and lay down. And
the Lord called yet again, Samuel. And Samuel
arose and went to Eli, and said, Here am I; for

---

chest, the visible symbol of the presence of God. Vs. 4, "the
Lord called:" The call of a prophet to his ministry was usually
associated with some striking event in his experience. In this case
the prophetic narrator represents Samuel as hearing the voice of
God. "Here am I": It was not a dream, for the child was awake.
Vs. 5, "ran unto Eli": Samuel slept near the ark and not far from
the infirm priest, so that he could guard the one and assist the
other in case of need. "I called not": Samuel supposed the
voice was that of Eli; but this the old man denied. Vs. 6,

thou calledst me. And he answered, I called 7
not, my son; lie down again. Now Samuel did
not yet know the Lord, neither was the word of
the Lord yet revealed unto him. And the Lord called 8
Samuel again the third time. And he arose and
went to Eli, and said, Here am I; for thou calledst
me. And Eli perceived that the Lord had called the
child. Therefore Eli said unto Samuel, Go, lie 9
down; and it shall be, if he call thee, that thou shalt
say, Speak, Lord; for thy servant heareth. So
Samuel went and lay down in his place.

"called yet again": The incident was repeated exactly. Vs.
7, "did not know the Lord": He had not begun to teach
as yet, though he was already "in favor with God" (2:26).
Vs. 8, "Eli perceived": At last the priest understood why
Samuel came so often to him; it could mean only that he
had received a divine message. The response which Eli told
him to make if the voice spoke again represents what ought to
be the listening, attentive, and obedient attitude of every child of
God.

QUESTIONS

(1) How old must Samuel have been at this time? (2)*
Why was the word of God rare in those days? (3) Did the
people have the Bible then? (4) On what did they depend
for religious instruction? (5)* Where did Eli and Samuel
sleep? (6) How was the sanctuary lighted? (7) What was
the ark? (8) Why was it kept in the tent? (9)* What did
Samuel hear? (10) Do you understand that Samuel actually
heard a voice, or that he became conscious at that time that
there was a religious work for him to perform? (11) To
whom did he go? Why? (12)* Why did not Samuel under-

stand the purpose of the call? (13) What did Eli perceive? (14) What were his instructions to Samuel? (15)* Was Eli likely to be sorry or glad that Samuel had now been called to a prophet's work? Would not Samuel be likely to become a rival to Eli and his sons? (16)* Does God call men to his service now? Does he call them in the same way? (17) What means are used in influencing people to undertake the work of God in our day? (18) What ought to be the response of those whom God calls? (19) Does he not call everyone to goodness and service as truly as he called Samuel?

SECTION IX

THE MESSAGE TO SAMUEL, I SAM. 3:10—4:1a

And the Lord came, and stood, and called as at 10
other times, Samuel, Samuel. Then Samuel said,
Speak; for thy servant heareth. And the Lord said 11
to Samuel, Behold, I will do a thing in Israel, at
which both the ears of every one that heareth it shall
tingle. In that day I will perform against Eli all 12
that I have spoken concerning his house, from the
beginning even unto the end. For I have told him 13
that I will judge his house for ever, for the iniquity
which he knew, because his sons did bring a curse
upon themselves, and he restrained them not. And 14

EXPLANATORY NOTES

Vs. 10, "Came and stood": God's actions are often in the
Bible represented in terms of human life; the third call to Samuel
was as if someone stood beside him. "At other times": just as
he had done twice before. Vs. 11, "ears . . . . shall tingle":
It was fitting that the first message to Samuel should concern the
house of Eli. What was to happen would be astonishing and
terrible. Vs. 12, "all that I have spoken": God had already
spoken through the unnamed prophet (2:27–36). "Beginning
. . . . end": first and last; the expression denotes the completeness of the punishment. Vs. 13, "I will judge": Sins such
as those of Eli's sons could not escape a just and enduring punishment. "Bring a curse": The margin reads, "speak evil of God."
They added impiety and blasphemy to avarice and lust. Vs. 14,
"not be purged": Sacrifice could be of no value where the

therefore I have sworn unto the house of Eli, that the
iniquity of Eli's house shall not be [1]purged with   [1] Or, *expiated*
15 sacrifice nor offering for ever. And Samuel lay
until the morning and opened the doors of the house
of the Lord. And Samuel feared to shew Eli the
16 vision. Then Eli called Samuel, and said, Samuel,
17 my son. And he said, Here am I. And he said,
What is the thing that the Lord hath spoken unto
thee? I pray thee hide it not from me: God do
so to thee, and more also, if thou hide any thing from
18 me of all the things that he spake unto thee. And
Samuel told him every whit, and hid nothing from
him. And he said, It is the Lord: let him do what
19 seemeth him good. And Samuel grew, and the
Lord was with him, and did let none of his words
20 fall to the ground. And all Israel from Dan even to

---

sinner continued impenitent and wicked. Vs. 15, "lay until the
morning": He was no longer in doubt as to the truth he had
heard. Terror and grief must have overwhelmed the boy.
"Opened the doors": This shows what was at least one of
his duties. "Feared": He might well dread the effects of such
a message upon the old man against whose family it was spoken.
"Eli called": He knew that Samuel had received a call from
God, and probably a message. That it concerned him and his
wicked sons he might well fear. Vs. 17, "God do so," etc: A
strong form of adjuration; a most urgent command. Eli wanted
to know all, even the worst. Vs. 18, "told him every whit":
every thing or word. "Let him do": Eli could not complain
that the sentence was too severe; he submitted with resignation.
Vs. 19, "fall to the ground": Samuel, although still young, now
began to discharge the duties of a prophet; he spoke with con-

Beer-sheba knew that Samuel was established to be
a prophet of the Lord. And the Lord appeared 21
again in Shiloh: for the Lord revealed himself to
Samuel in Shiloh by the word of the Lord. And the 4
word of Samuel came to all Israel.

---

viction and authority, and his words were heeded. Vs. 20,
"Dan† . . . . Beer-sheba"†: two border cities, one in the
extreme north, the other far to the south; the expression signifies
the entire land. The people came from all quarters to consult
him. Vs. 21, "the Lord appeared again in Shiloh": This is
one reading, and may well refer to the time when God did not
appear, because of the wicked priests. Another reading is
"Israel appeared," that is, the people began once more to visit
Shiloh to worship, which they had largely ceased to do. Vs. 1,
"came to all Israel": Samuel's fame went everywhere among the
people, and they gave attention to his utterances.

QUESTIONS

(1) How did God reveal himself to Samuel? Was there
any other way to represent Samuel's perception of the divine
will than in some such way as this? (2) Who had told
Samuel what to say? (3)* What did Samuel learn that God
was going to do? (4) What had been spoken against Eli's
house? (5) What had Eli's sons done to deserve chastisement? (6)* What was charged against Eli himself? (7)
Are fathers responsible for the evil conduct of their children?
(8)* Why could not sacrifice expiate the sins of Eli's house?
(9) What were Samuel's feelings, in all probability, when
he heard this message? (10) What was one of his duties in
the morning? (11)* Why did he hesitate to tell Eli his vision?
(12) How did Eli know that Samuel had received a message
from God? (13) How did he show his great anxiety to know
what it was? (14) Was it best for Samuel to tell Eli? (15)*

How did Eli receive the news? (16) What did he say? (17) Would it have been better if Eli had been more aggressive and less indulgent in his treatment of his sons? (18)* What were the marks of Samuel's increasing popularity? (19) Where were Dan and Beer-sheba? (20) What was Samuel's new work? (21) How wide was his influence? (22)* How does the story of Samuel and the sons of Eli illustrate the danger of ruin of successful but evil men? (23) How does it illustrate the opportunity for an obscure but faithful young man to succeed?

SECTION X

Now Israel went out against the Philistines to battle, and pitched beside Eben-ezer; and the Philistines pitched in Aphek. And the Philistines 2 put themselves in array against Israel; and when they joined battle, Israel was smitten before the Philistines; and they slew of the army in the field about four thousand men. And when the people 3

EXPLANATORY NOTES

The narrative combines the material of two different sources, the Ephraimite story of Samuel's life and the early Judean document which is the main prophetic account of all the early history of Israel. See Introd., 4.

Vs. 1, "against the Philistines"†: These people had oppressed Israel for some years. Their home was in the region lying along the Mediterranean seacoast, southwest of central Palestine. Probably this campaign was one of their raids into Hebrew territory for plunder, and the men of Israel were only defending their land. "Eben-ezer"†: "stone of help;" a place whose location is not certain, but it probably lay in the Plain of Sharon, west of Shiloh. "Aphek"†: The situation of this place is also uncertain; the two were not far apart. It may be located in the Plain of Sharon, somewhat north of Lydda (see map). Vs. 2, "Israel was smitten": The Philistines were probably making a raid into the Hebrew country, and the men of Israel attempted to stop them, but without success. "Four thousand": The Hebrews had no horses or chariots; foot soldiers were their only force. The loss of four thousand men would be a great disaster in a small country. Vs. 3, "the elders": the old men, who

were come into the camp, the elders of Israel said,
Wherefore hath the Lord smitten us to-day before
the Philistines ? Let us fetch the ark of the covenant
of the Lord out of Shiloh unto us, that it may come
among us, and save us out of the hand of our enemies.
4 So the people sent to Shiloh, and they brought from
thence the ark of the covenant of the Lord of hosts,
which[1] sitteth upon the cherubim; and the two sons
of Eli, Hophni and Phinehas, were there with the
5 ark of the covenant of God. And when the ark
of the covenant of the Lord came into the camp, all
Israel shouted with a great shout, so that the earth
6 rang again. And when the Philistines heard the
noise of the shout, they said, What meaneth the
noise of this great shout in the camp of the Hebrews ?
And they understood that the ark of the Lord was

[1] Or, *dwelleth between*

---

would naturally take counsel in a time of peril. "Let us fetch
the ark"†: They attributed their defeat, not to the valor of their
enemies, but to the disfavor of God. Their expedient was to
take the ark with them when the battle was renewed. They
thought God would give them the victory for the sake of the ark
alone, which was sacred to him. "Sitteth upon the cherubim"†:
The cherubim were the figures of angels upon the top of the ark
in the temple. There the glory of God rested. Vs. 4, "Hophni
and Phinehas were there": These two priests went along as
attendants of the ark. Vs. 5, "all Israel shouted": The people
believed they would now be victorious, and were wild with joy
when the ark was brought. "Earth rang": The very ground
trembled at the noise. Vs. 6, "this great shout": The Philistine
camp was not far off. They were terrified as much as the Hebrews
were delighted at the arrival of the ark, not doubting its power.

come into the camp. And the Philistines were afraid, 7
for they said, God is come into the camp. And they
said, Woe unto us! for there hath not been such a
thing heretofore. Woe unto us! who shall deliver 8
us out of the hand of these mighty gods? these are
the gods that smote the Egyptians with all manner of
plagues in the wilderness. Be strong, and quit 9
yourselves like men, O ye Philistines, that ye be not
servants unto the Hebrews as they have been to you.

Vs. 7, "not been such a thing": The Hebrews had never before
resorted to such means to win the victory. Vs. 8, "these mighty
gods": The Philistines had heard of the God of the Hebrews, and
probably thought they had several gods, as most of the nations
had. "Smote the Egyptians": The terrors of the exodus were
in their minds, when Egypt was smitten with dire plagues (Exod.
7 f.), and Pharaoh's host overthrown in the sea on the borders
of the wilderness (Exod. 14). Vs. 9, "quit yourselves like men":
The Philistines believed that their danger was great, but they
resolved to meet it bravely and not yield. These are almost the
precise words used by Paul in one of his exhortations to courage
(1 Cor. 16:13).

QUESTIONS

(1)* Who were the Philistines? Locate their country on
the map. (2) Why was Israel at war with them? (3) Where
were the two camps located? (4) What was the result of the
first battle? (5)* Why did the Israelites attribute their
defeat to God, rather than to the Philistines? (6) Why did
they wish to take the ark to the battle? Was it right so to do?
If not, why not? (7) How far did they have to bring the ark?
(8)* Is it probable that Eli was willing to have the ark go?
(9) How did the people manifest their joy at the arrival of the
ark? (10)* Why were they glad? (11) How did the Phil-

istines feel when they heard the shouting? (12) Why should they fear the presence of the ark? (13)* What did they know about the God of the Hebrews? Why did they speak as if there were more than one? (14) In what condition had the Philistines held the Hebrews? (15) Is it ever worth while to depend upon other aids than courage, aggressiveness, and the power of God?

SECTION XI

THE DISASTROUS BATTLE OF APHEK, I SAM
4:10–22

And the Philistines fought, and Israel was smitten, 10
and they fled every man to his tent; and there was
a very great slaughter; for there fell of Israel thirty
thousand footmen. And the ark of God was taken; 11
and the two sons of Eli, Hophni and Phinehas, were
slain. And there ran a man of Benjamin out of the 12
army and came to Shiloh the same day with his

EXPLANATORY NOTES

The sources used in this section are the early Judean and the
northern Samuel narratives interwoven.

Vs. 10, "Israel was smitten": Their false confidence in the
presence of the ark was rebuked. "Every man to his tent":
"Tent" is often used in the sense of house or home; there was a
panic of defeat, and the survivors made their escape home as best
they could. "Thirty thousand": This heavy loss meant the
practical destruction of the Hebrew army. Vs. 11, "ark of God
was taken": This was an unexpected triumph for the Philistines,
and the most signal feature of their success. To capture the flag,
standard, or most cherished possession of an enemy, adds glory to
a victory. "Hophni and Phinehas were slain": They may have
been killed while fighting to save the ark; more probably they
were cut down with the rest of the servants of the sanctuary who
were carrying it. Vs. 12, "a man of Benjamin": Benjamin was
the tribe whose territory lay just south of Ephraim. Jerusalem
was on its southern border. Running was a common practice,
and a man who could run a long distance and bear a message was
often widely known (II Sam. 18:19). The journey from Aphek

13 clothes rent, and with earth upon his head. And
   when he came, lo, Eli sat upon his seat by the wayside watching; for his heart trembled for the ark of
   God.   And when the man came into the city, and
14 told it, all the city cried out.   And when Eli heard
   the noise of the crying, he said, What meaneth the
   noise of this tumult?   And the man hasted, and
15 came and told Eli.   Now Eli was ninety and eight
   years old; and his eyes were set, that he could not
16 see.   And the man said unto Eli, I am he that came
   out of the army, and I fled today out of the army.
17 And he said, How went the matter, my son?   And

---

to Shiloh was twenty miles or more and would require most of a
day.   "Clothes rent": Tearing one's garments and throwing
dust upon one's head were signs of a great disaster or heavy
grief (Josh. 7:6; II Sam. 1:2).   Vs. 13, "Eli sat . . . . by the
wayside": Eli was sitting in his accustomed seat by the outer
door of the sanctuary (1:9), so that the messenger told his news
in the town before he reached the old priest.   "Trembled for the
ark": Even his anxiety about his sons was not so great as his fear
for the safety of the ark.   "All the city cried out": People in the
Orient are much more demonstrative than in the West.   The
whole population of Shiloh, mostly women and children, now
shrieked as they heard the terrible news.   It meant that most of
the men of Shiloh were dead.   Vs. 14, "What meaneth the
noise?": Eli could hear the cries and lamentations of the people
long before the messenger reached the sanctuary gate where he sat.
"Told Eli": The runner would naturally go on through the town
to the sanctuary, telling his news as he went, till he came to Eli.   Vs.
15, "eyes were set": He was already growing blind in 3:2; now he
was totally blind (cf. I Kings 14:4).   Vs. 16, "I am he": The
runner had to announce himself to the blind priest.   "How went

he that brought the tidings answered and said,
Israel is fled before the Philistines, and there hath
been also a great slaughter among the people, and
thy two sons also, Hophni and Phinehas, are dead,
and the ark of God is taken.   And it came to pass, 18
when he made mention of the ark of God, that he
fell from off his seat backward by the side of the gate,
and his neck brake, and he died; for he was an old
man, and heavy.   And he had judged Israel forty
years.   And his daughter-in-law, Phinehas' wife, 19
was with child, near to be delivered; and when she
heard the tidings that the ark of God was taken, and
that her father-in-law and her husband were dead,
she bowed herself and brought forth; for her pains
came upon her.   And about the time of her death 20

---

the matter?": If Eli could have seen the man's rent garments
and dust-covered head, he would have known at once that his
news was of the worst. Vs. 17, "ark of God is taken": The
messenger told his tidings in four statements, which reached
their climax in the last.   The capture of the ark was a calamity
far worse than all the rest.   Vs. 18, "he died": The news shocked
him so that he fainted, and so fell and was killed.   "Judged
Israel": He had held both religious and civil leadership in a
time when there was no king.   Vs. 19, "Phinehas' wife": The
incident of the death of the daughter-in-law of Eli further illustrates the consequences of the sins of his sons and the doom of
his family.   Vs. 20, "Fear not": Her women friends tried to
encourage her with the glad news that she was the mother of a
son.   But her grief was too great to be consoled.   Vs. 21, "Ichabod": The name was suggestive of the circumstances in which
the child was born (cf. 1:20; Gen. 35:18).   The name means

the women that stood by her said unto her, Fear not; for thou hast brought forth a son. But she answered 21 not, neither did she regard it. And she named the child[1] Ichabod, saying, The glory is departed from Israel; because the ark of God was taken, and be- 22 cause of her father-in-law and her husband. And she said, The glory is departed from Israel; for the ark of God is taken.

[1] That is, there is *no glory*

"no glory". Vs. 22, "ark of God is taken": Both Eli and his daughter-in-law put the loss of the ark above their personal sorrow over the death of Phinehas.

QUESTIONS

(1)* Where was this battle fought? (2) What was the occasion of the war? (3) What was the result of the contest? (4)* What did the survivors do? (5) How many men fell in the battle and the pursuit? (6) What befell the ark? (7)* In what respect could the death of Eli's sons be called a calamity? (8) How and by whom was the news brought to Shiloh? (9) Is it probable that messengers took the tidings to other towns? (10) Where was Eli waiting for news? (11)* How could the people of Shiloh judge the nature of the news from the messenger's appearance? (12) What was the effect of the tidings upon the people? (13) What was Eli's condition? (14)* What statements did the messenger make regarding the battle? (15) What were the results of the news to Eli? (16) Why was the loss of the ark so serious a matter? (17) How old was Eli, and how long had he been judge? (18) What caused the death of Phinehas' wife? (19) *What did she name her child, and why? (20) Is it probable that Shiloh was destroyed by the Philistines soon after this battle (cf. Jer. 7:12, 14; 26:9)? (21) *In what way does this story show that the consequences of evil conduct often fall on the innocent as well as the guilty? (22) How did the Israelites interpret the attitude of God toward them, as shown in the results of the battle? (23) How would the loss of the ark affect their belief that God always protected it?

AN ASSYRIAN

SECTION XII

THE ARK AMONG THE PHILISTINES, I SAM. 5:1–12

5 Now the Philistines had taken the ark of God, and they brought it from Eben-ezer unto Ashdod. 2 And the Philistines took the ark of God, and brought it into the house of Dagon, and set it by Dagon. 3 And when they of Ashdod arose early on the morrow behold Dagon was fallen upon his face to the ground before the ark of the Lord. And they took Dagon,

---

EXPLANATORY NOTES

The source from which this section is taken is the early Judean document, which, as would be expected, preserved the traditions regarding the sanctity and wonder-working power of the ark at Jerusalem. These stories of plagues wrought by the presence of the ark are to be taken as the reflection of the feelings of Israel against the Philistines, and the efforts of the prophets through popular traditions to discredit idolatry, rather than as literal history.

Vs. 1, "from Eben-ezer† unto Ashdod": Eben-ezer was the place near Aphek at which the men of Israel encamped before the battle. (cf. 4:1). Ashdod was one of the five cities of the Philistines, and was situated not far from the sea, and almost directly west of Jerusalem, about thirty-five miles distant. It was about twenty-five miles southwest from Aphek. Vs. 2, "House of Dagon": Dagon was the national god of the Philistines. There had been a temple of his at Gaza, but Samson is reported to have destroyed it (Judg. 16:21–31). The name Dagon probably signifies a fish-god, and it has been supposed that the idol had the head and hands of a man, but the body and tail of a fish. The idol was kept in a temple called "Dagon's house." "By Dagon": The ark was placed before the idol to show that the God of the Hebrews had been vanquished by Dagon. Vs. 3, "Dagon was

43

and set him in his place again. And when they arose 4
early on the morrow morning, behold Dagon was
fallen upon his face to the ground before the ark of
the Lord; and the head of Dagon and both the
palms of his hands lay cut off upon the threshold;
only the stump of Dagon was left to him. Therefore 5
neither the priests of Dagon, nor any that come into
Dagon's house, tread on the threshold of Dagon in
Ashdod, unto this day.

But the hand of the Lord was heavy upon them of 6
Ashdod, and he destroyed them, and smote them
with ¹tumours, even Ashdod and the borders thereof.
And when the men of Ashdod saw that it was so, 7
they said, The ark of the God of Israel shall not
abide with us: for his hand is sore upon us, and upon

¹ Or, *plague*
boils

---

fallen": One of the lessons the prophets tried to teach by such
narratives as this was that Jehovah would not endure association
with idols. Vs. 4, "head .... hands .... cut off": The
first fall of Dagon they may have attributed to accident. The
second could not be misunderstood. The idol was not only overthrown, but broken before the ark. Vs. 5, "tread on the threshold": A Philistine custom of leaping over the temple threshold
is traced to this incident by the writer. Perhaps this is referred
to in Zeph. 1:9. Vs. 6, "hand of the Lord was heavy": It was
not only the god of the Philistines that was brought low; the
entire population of Ashdod and vicinity was afflicted. The
people were attacked by boils or tumors, one of the features of
the oriental or bubonic plague, so much feared in the East. Vs.
7, "ark shall not abide": They attributed their affliction to the
presence of the ark, and wanted to have it removed as soon as
possible. Vs. 8, "lords of the Philistines": the rulers of the

8 Dagon our god. They sent therefore and gathered
all the lords of the Philistines unto them, and said,
What shall we do with the ark of the God of Israel?
And they answered, Let the ark of the God of Israel
be carried about unto Gath. And they carried the
9 ark of the God of Israel about thither. And it was
so, that, after they had carried it about, the hand of
the Lord was against the city with a very great discomfiture: and he smote the men of the city, both
small and great, and tumours brake out upon them.
10 So they sent the ark of God to Ekron. And it came
to pass, as the ark of God came to Ekron, that the
Ekronites cried out, saying, They have brought
about the ark of the God of Israel to us, to slay us
11 and our people. They sent therefore and gathered

---

five chief cities of their land. They were not independent kings
(though Achish is later called "king of Gath," 21:10; 27:2),
but were probably more like the judges in Israel. "Unto Gath"†:
The site of this town is unknown, though it has usually been
located southeast of Ashdod, on the border of Israel's territory.
The Philistines wished to determine whether or not the ark was
really the cause of their troubles, by taking it to a different city.
Vs. 9, "against the city": The same results were apparent here.
There was no Dagon temple, but the people were afflicted as at
Ashdod. Vs. 10, "came to Ekron"†: Ekron was on the way
toward Shiloh. Perhaps it was the writer's purpose to show that
the Philistines already realized that the ark must be sent back.
"Cried out": By this time all the people of the country had
learned what disasters followed the ark. Vs. 11, "Send away
the ark": In the sufferings which came upon them the Philistines
recognized the anger of Jehovah, the God of Israel, whose ark

together all the lords of the Philistines, and they said, Send away the ark of the God of Israel, and let it go again to its own place, that it slay us not, and our people: for there was a deadly discomfiture throughout all the city; the hand of God was very heavy there. And the men that died not were 12 smitten with the tumours: and the cry of the city went up to heaven.

---

they were detaining in their land. A fresh council of their rulers was therefore called, and they determined to restore the ark to Israel. Vs. 12, "cry of the city": This graphic picture of the distress in Ekron shows how urgent was the need for prompt action.[1]

QUESTIONS

(1) To what town was the ark taken by the Philistines? (2)* Where was Ashdod? (3) Where was the ark placed? (4)* Did they intend to honor the ark with worship like that accorded their idol, or to treat it as one of the spoils of war? (5) What happened to the image of Dagon in the night? (6) What happened the second night? (7)* With what custom of the priests of Dagon was this incident later connected? (8)* What plague broke out among the people of Ashdod? (9) To what did they attribute this affliction? (10) What did they decide to do? (11)* Why was not the ark sent di-

[1] In the account here given there is mention of only one form of plague. i. e., the boils or tumors. But in the Greek translation of the Old Testament (called the Septuagint† or LXX), vs. 6 has, in addition to our rendering, the words: "And mice sprang up in the midst of their land, and there was a very deadly destruction in the city." This would mean that there were two plagues: (1) the vast number of mice that overran the land, destroying the crops; and (2) the disease from which the people suffered. The offerings which were made by the Philistines (6:4) likewise imply a plague of mice. This may have been a later tradition.

rectly back to Israel from Ashdod? (12) What happened at
Gath? (13) Where was the ark sent from Gath? (14) Why
were the people of Ekron alarmed? (15) What council was
called? (16) *What did they decide to do? (17) Is it possible that any other plague than that of boils came upon the
Philistines? (18) What caused such traditions regarding the
wonder-working power of a sacred chest to take form? (19)
*What do you think was their value? (20) Might there be a
teaching value in a story even though it is not literal history?
(21) May it not be probable that the Philistines, who had
taken the ark in battle, actually did suffer from plagues which
as a superstitious people they attributed to the presence of the
Hebrew chest? (22) Is not God's power and providence far
more fully shown in the regular and constant care of his people
than in occasional wonders such as here described?

SECTION XIII

PREPARATIONS FOR THE RETURN OF THE ARK
I SAM. 6:1-9

And the ark of the Lord was in the country of 6
the Philistines seven months.[1] And the Philistines 2
called for the priests and the diviners, saying, What
shall we do with the ark of the Lord? shew us
wherewith we shall send it to its place. And they 3
said, If ye send away the ark of the God of Israel,
send it not empty; but in any wise return him a
[2]guilt offering: then ye shall be healed, and it shall
be known to you why his hand is not removed from

[1] The Sept. adds, *and their land swarmed with mice*

[2] Or, *trespass offering*

EXPLANATORY NOTES

The early Judean narrative, with its emphasis upon the sacredness of the ark, is the source from which this section is taken. It naturally magnifies the disasters wrought by the presence of the ark, and the recognition of Jehovah by the Philistines.

Vs. 1, "seven months": long enough to test the influence of the ark on the land of the Philistines. Notice the marginal reading from the Septuagint† and cf. note to the last section (p. 46). Vs. 2, "priests and diviners"†: The rulers had already decided that the ark should be returned to Israel. The men here named were consulted as to the gift or present that should be sent with it. Diviners were men who interpreted dreams and predicted the outcome of events. Vs. 3, "not empty": They were fearful of further trouble if they did not make an offering to Jehovah at the time his ark was returned. "A guilt offering": some compensation for the loss of the ark during the period of its absence. "It shall be known": If their trouble ceased as soon as the ark was restored, they would know that its detention was

48

4 you. Then said they, What shall be the guilt offering which we shall return to him? And they said,
Five golden tumours, and five golden mice according
to the number of the lords of the Philistines: for one
5 plague was on you all, and on your lords. Wherefore
ye shall make images of your tumours, and images of
your mice that mar the land; and ye shall give glory
unto the God of Israel: peradventure he will lighten
his hand from off you, and from off your gods, and
6 from off your land. Wherefore then do ye harden
your hearts, as the Egyptians and Pharaoh hardened
their hearts? when he had ³wrought wonderfully ³ Or, *made a*
among them, did they not let the people go, and *mock of*

---

the cause of their affliction. Vs. 4, "five golden tumours." It was
the custom among some ancient nations especially the Greeks
and Romans, to invoke the favor of deity in the cure of a disease
by offering a golden image of the limb or member of the body so
afflicted; and also to express thankfulness for recovery from such
an affliction, in a similar manner. It might have been either
such an image, or the likeness of the swelling or sore itself that
was offered by the Philistines. "Five golden mice": Here mice
are mentioned for the first time (but see marginal readings to
5:6 and 6:1, and also note to Section XII, p. 46). Such a
plague of mice was not uncommon, especially in Egypt, and
would be the cause of great damage. Five was the number of
the Philistine cities, all of which were involved in the common
disaster. "One plague": The entire territory of Philistia had
suffered. Vs. 5, "lighten his hand": They recognized their
trouble as probably due to a divine visitation. Vs. 6, "as the
Egyptians": The Philistines are supposed to have heard of the
wonderful deliverance of Israel from Egypt, and how Pharaoh,
the king of Egypt, had been humbled by the plagues that came

they departed? Now therefore take and prepare 7
you a new cart, and two milch kine, on which
there hath come no yoke, and tie the kine to the cart,
and bring their calves home from them: and take 8
the ark of the Lord, and lay it upon the cart; and
put the jewels of gold, which ye return him for a
guilt offering, in a coffer by the side thereof; and
send it away, that it may go. And see, if it goeth 9
up by the way of its own border to Beth-shemesh,
then he hath done us this great evil: but if not, then
we shall know that it is not his hand that smote us;
it was a chance that happened to us.

---

upon his land, but still hardened his heart (Exod. 8:15, 32). This
is the second reference the Philistines are represented as having
made to Israel's dealings with the Egyptians (cf. 4:8). Vs. 7,
"new cart": It was believed that whatever was used for God's
service should be new, so that he could have its first and best use;
so the cart was to be new, and the cattle such as had not been
yoked before. "Kine": an old word for cattle, cows. "Bring
their calves home": One would expect a cow to stay near her
calf; if then these cows, whose calves were left at home, should
of their own will take the ark away, it would appear that some
higher power controlled their actions. Vs. 8, "in a coffer": a
chest or box. Vs. 9, "to Beth-shemesh"†: This was a city of the
Israelites very near Philistia, the nearest point at which the ark
could reach the land of Israel from which it had been taken.

QUESTIONS

(1) Where was the country of the Philistines? What were
its chief cities? Locate them on the map. (2) How long did
the ark remain in Philistia? (3)* Why did the Philistines
wish to send a present back with the ark? (4) Whom did

they consult regarding it? (5)* How did they think they
would know whether their afflictions were sent by Jehovah
or not? (6) What did they decide to send as presents?
(7) Do you think God would really care for gold offerings
of the kind they sent? (8)* What was commendable in their
conduct in this instance? (9) In what respect were the
Egyptians a warning to the Philistines? (10) What preparations did they make to return the ark? (11) Why did they
use new things only? (12) Where were the golden images
placed? (13)* What means did they use to learn whether or
not their affliction was a divine rebuke? (14) Where was
Beth-shemesh? (15) If the cattle had gone in some other
direction, what would the Philistines have thought? (16) Do
you think the real explanation of this narrative is the wish of
its writer to show that Jehovah was as much to be feared in
Philistia as in Israel? (17)* Would such a tradition as is here
recorded be useful to teach the Hebrew people the reverence
due to God? (18) Do you think it is true that most great
reformations have come about by just such work as Samuel's
on the part of some great and consecrated man? (19) Compare the work of Samuel with that of Savonarola, Luther,
Knox, and Wesley, in so far as you are acquainted with their
lives.

SECTION XIV

THE ARK BROUGHT BACK, I SAM. 6:10—7:1

And the men did so; and took two milch kine, and 10
tied them to the cart, and shut up their calves at
home: and they put the ark of the Lord upon the 11
cart and the coffer with the mice of gold and the
images of their tumours. And the kine took the 12
straight way by the way to Beth-shemesh; they went
along the high way, lowing as they went, and turned
not aside to the right hand or to the left; and the
lords of the Philistines went after them unto
the border of Beth-shemesh. And they of Beth- 13

EXPLANATORY NOTES

For the source of the narrative in this section, see the opening
of the "Explanatory Notes" on the previous section (p. 48).

Vs. 10, "did so": Their plan to secure the proper return of the
ark, and the consequent favor of Jehovah, is told in vss. 7–9.
Vs. 12, " lowing as they went": The cattle took the nearest way
to reach the land of Israel. Their lowing, or calling for their
calves, indicated to the Philistines that they were driven on by a
higher power in spite of their motherly instincts. "Went after
them": The Philistine rulers wanted to see the outcome of the
experiment. "Border of Beth-shemesh"†: They went as far
as it was safe for them, into the fields near the town. Beth-
shemesh was in a valley opening out onto the plain. Vs. 13,
"wheat harvest": It was therefore in the spring or early summer.
The fields were cultivated by people who lived in the town for
protection, and most of the population went out to work in the
harvest. "Rejoiced": They saw the cattle bringing the ark up
the valley, and were happy that the symbol of Jehovah's presence

shemesh were reaping their wheat harvest in the valley: and they lifted up their eyes, and saw the ark,

14 and rejoiced to see it. And the cart came into the field of Joshua the Beth-shemite, and stood there, where there was a great stone: and they clave the wood of the cart, and offered up the kine for a burnt

15 offering unto the Lord. And the Levites took down the ark of the Lord, and the coffer that was with it, wherein the jewels of gold were, and put them on the great stone: and the men of Beth-shemesh offered burnt offerings and sacrificed sacri-

16 fices the same day unto the Lord. And when the five lords of the Philistines had seen it, they returned to Ekron the same day.

17 And these are the golden tumours which the Philistines returned for a guilt offering unto the Lord; for Ashdod one, for Gaza one, for Ashkelon

18 one, for Gath one, for Ekron one; and the golden

---

was once more in their possession. Vs. 14, "Joshua the Beth-shemite": One of the people of the town. "Great stone": The people believed that the occasion was worthy of a sacrifice, and they used the large and convenient stone which they found there as an altar. "Clave the wood": They felt that the cart and the cattle were sacred, and they used them for the sacrifice, splitting up the cart and killing the cows for the burnt offering. Vs. 15, "Levites": The Levites were members of the tribe of Levi, who performed priestly offices. Vs. 16, "they returned": The five rulers of the Philistine cities had followed behind the ark to see what would happen. Now they were satisfied, and returned home. Vs. 18, "golden mice": In the account in vs. 4 only five golden mice are mentioned. Here it appears that there were mice, according to the number of all the cities of the Philistines belonging to the five lords, both of fenced cities and of country villages: even unto the great stone, whereon they set down the ark of the Lord, which stone remaineth unto this day in the field of Joshua the Beth-shemite. ¹And he smote of the 19 men of Beth-shemesh, because they had looked into the ark of the Lord, even he smote of the people seventy men, and fifty thousand men: and the people mourned, because the Lord had smitten the 20 people with a great slaughter. And the men of

¹ The Sept. has, *And the sons of Jeconiah rejoiced not among the men of Beth-shemesh, because they saw the ark of the Lord; and he smote among them seventy men and fifty thousand men*

many more, representing even the smallest towns, as well as the five great cities. A "fenced" city was one defended by walls. "Unto this day": The clause should probably read, "And the stone . . . . is a witness unto this day," i.e., the day in which the writer lived. Vs. 19, "he smote": This verse is perplexing and probably wrong. As it stands, it would indicate that God was angry because the people looked at the ark. But this was just what they might be expected to do in their joy. The marginal reading seems better. One family or clan ("the sons of Jeconiah") showed no joy in the occasion, and their death was interpreted as a sign of God's anger. Among the Hebrews, as with most ancient people, plagues and calamities of every kind were believed to be the sign of divine anger. Later prophetic teaching and the New Testament show this view to be erroneous. "Fifty thousand": This is certainly a mistake. The entire population of Beth-shemesh could have been only a few hundred. Probably the reading should be "seventy men," and the "fifty thousand" was added by the mistake of some copyist. "Great slaughter": The death of seventy men was a terrible calamity in a small community; it was a mystery which they could not understand, but which they connected with the presence of the ark. Vs. 20, "to whom shall he go up": Like the people of Ashdod, they

Beth-shemesh said, Who is able to stand before the Lord, this holy God? and to whom shall he go up 21 from us? And they sent messengers to the inhabitants of Kiriath-jearim, saying, The Philistines have brought again the ark of the Lord; come ye down, 7 and fetch it up to you. And the men of Kiriath-jearim came, and fetched up the ark of the Lord, and brought it into the house of Abinadab in the hill, and sanctified Eleazar his son to keep the ark of the Lord.

---

wanted the ark taken away. As they were at the border of the hill country, the ark would have to go *up* in being taken toward Shiloh. Vs. 21, "Kiriath-jearim"†: a town about nine miles northwest from Jerusalem; it was on much higher ground than Beth-shemesh, and about nine or ten miles northeast from it: "Come ye down": They said nothing of the calamity that had befallen them; they seem to have felt sure that the people of Kiriath-jearim would be glad to receive the ark. Their words, "come down" and "fetch it up," again refer to the higher position of Kiriath-jearim. Vs. 1, "house of Abinadab": This was probably a suitable location; no special reason is given. "Sanctified Eleazar": There is no hint that he was a priest; they employed him to take charge of the ark.

QUESTIONS

(1) How was the vehicle prepared for the ark? (2) *What were the different things that were placed on the cart? (3) What road did the cattle take? What made it more remarkable that they should go away from home? How did they show their maternal instincts? (4) Why did the Philistine rulers follow them? How far did they go? (5)* Why were the people of Beth-shemesh out in the fields? At what time

of the year did the harvest come? (6) How did the people feel when they saw the ark? (7) What did they do to celebrate the return of the ark? For a similar use of cattle and farm implements read I Kings 19:19–21. (8)* What did the five Philistine rulers do? Is anything further said about the plagues among the Philistines? (9) Locate on the map the five cities of the Philistines named in vs. 17. (10)* What is represented as happening to the people of Beth-shemesh? How does the text differ from the marginal note in explaining this event? (11) How many are said to have died? (12) How did the people of Beth-shemesh feel after this misfortune? (13) To whom did they send? Where was Kiriath-jearim? Were the latter people glad to receive the ark? (14) What did they do with it? (15)* Why was it not sent to Shiloh again? (See Section IX, Question 23). (16) Is it probable that the priests and prophets of later days could make effective use of such narratives in deepening a feeling of awe regarding the ark and the sanctuary?

SECTION XV

SAMUEL'S WORK OF REFORM, I SAM. 7:2-4

2 And it came to pass, from the day that the ark abode in Kiriath-jearim, that the time was long; for it was twenty years: and all the house of Israel
3 ¹lamented after the Lord. And Samuel spake unto

¹ Or, *turned unto*

EXPLANATORY NOTES

With this section the account of Samuel's prophetic work, as given in the Ephraimite source is resumed. It continues as far as 8:22.

Vs. 2, "the time was long": One of the interesting characteristics of the Bible is illustrated in the short paragraph included in this section: some long narratives deal with events that occupied only a brief time, while in other very short accounts we have our only information regarding events that covered many years. The author does not mean to say that the entire time the ark remained in Kiriath-jearim was twenty years, but that from the time it was taken there twenty years were spent by Samuel in his efforts to bring Israel to a better condition. "The ark abode": The sacred chest, after being captured by the Philistines, was returned, and kept in the hill town mentioned. "Lamented after the Lord": The translation is not very satisfactory. Probably "turned unto" would be better. Samuel's work as a reformer resulted in getting the people interested in the religion of Jehovah, against which the conduct of the priests at Shiloh had turned them. Vs. 3, "Samuel spake": This is the first time he has been mentioned since 4:1. After the death of Eli and his sons, the young man was the recognized prophet and judge. He probably returned to his parents' home at Ramah (see 7:17), and made that his own headquarters. From it he went out on visits to different parts

all the house of Israel, saying, If ye do return unto
the Lord with all your heart, then put away the
strange gods and the Ashtaroth from among you,

Or, *direct*   and ²prepare your hearts unto the Lord, and serve
him only; and he will deliver you out of the hand
of the Philistines.   Then the children of Israel did 4
put away the Baalim and the Ashtaroth, and served
the Lord only.

---

of the country (see vs. 16) and preached the religion of Jehovah
and the necessity of repentance.   "Put away the strange gods"†:
In the days of Eli and his sons idolatry grew among the people,
because there was no one to hold their regard and affection to
Jehovah, and they easily fell into the idolatrous practices of their
neighbors.   "Ashtaroth"†: The images of the goddess Astarte,
which they were in the habit of worshiping.   "Serve him only":
The pure, imageless worship of Jehovah must never be mixed
with the unclean rites of the false gods.   "He will deliver you":
It must not be supposed that this was any one message of Samuel
to Israel.   It was what he was constantly preaching in all the
places he visited, all those years.   He told the people that victory
depended upon repentance and obedience.   Vs. 4, "put away the
Baalim"†: Baals, or images of the sun-god of the Canaanites,
whose worship was taken over by Israel.   "Served the Lord
only": This shows how wide must have been Samuel's work,
and how faithfully he pursued it.

QUESTIONS

(1) How had the ark come to Kiriath-jearim (see Section
XIV)?   (2) What does the twenty years include?   (3) During
this time what change took place on the part of the people?
(4)* How did Samuel reach "all the house of Israel"?   (5)
What did he command the people to do?   (6)* What were
the "strange gods"?   How were they worshiped?   (7) Why

was it necessary to worship Jehovah only? (8)* Did the people believe that there were other gods than Jehovah? How did they think of them? (9) By what people were Baal and Astarte worshiped? (10)* Why were the Philistines mentioned as the enemies Israel chiefly feared? (11) Was this message of Samuel's delivered on a single occasion only, or was it the burden of all his preaching? (12) What relation does the mention of twenty years bear to the statement of what Samuel was accustomed to preach? (13)* Where did Samuel live at this time? Why had he not remained at Shiloh? (14) What places did he visit in the course of his frequent journeys (vs. 16)? (15) What was the effect of his preaching? (16) In what ways could a preacher like Samuel secure the reformation of a nation?

SECTION XVI

THE BATTLE OF EBEN–EZER, I SAM. 7:5–17

And Samuel said, Gather all Israel to Mizpah, and 5
I will pray for you unto the Lord.   And they gathered 6
together to Mizpah, and drew water, and poured it
out before the Lord, and fasted on that day, and
said there, We have sinned against the Lord.   And
Samuel judged the children of Israel in Mizpah.

EXPLANATORY NOTES

The source in this section is the late Ephraimite account
of Samuel's life. The story of deliverance from Philistine oppression, with Samuel as the hero, is perhaps the parallel of the account in 13:2 f. of which Saul is the chief figure.

Vs. 5, "Gather all Israel": Messengers were despatched
to the different towns to summon the people. The fact that there
was sufficient unity of sentiment to make possible such a gathering
shows how successful had been Samuel's work of preaching the
need of union and obedience to God. "To Mizpah"†: A hill-
top five miles northwest of Jerusalem and about the same distance
southwest from Ramah, Samuel's home. "Will pray for you":
Only after years of teaching would the people have responded to
such an appeal. This shows somewhat the nature and effect of
the prophet's religious reforms. Vs. 6, "drew water": The
pouring out of water was not an ordinary form of sacrifice, but it
might well represent a feeling of contrition for sin a "pouring out
of the heart" to God. "Fasted": This was also unusual, but
in the later history it became a common religious practice (Zech.
8:19). "We have sinned": The gathering was for the confession
of sin and the completion of the people's covenant of faithfulness
to God. "Samuel judged": His leadership as a prophet easily
passed over into the authority of judge or king. People brought

7 And when the Philistines heard that the children of
   Israel were gathered together to Mizpah, the lords
   of the Philistines went up against Israel. And
   when the children of Israel heard it, they were afraid
8 of the Philistines. And the children of Israel said
   to Samuel, Cease not to cry unto the Lord our God
   for us, that he will save us out of the hand of the
9 Philistines. And Samuel took a sucking lamb, and
   offered it for a whole burnt offering unto the Lord:
   and Samuel cried unto the Lord for Israel; and the

---

to him their disputes for decision. The gathering at Mizpah
must have lasted some time. It was like one of the annual feasts.
Vs. 7, "Philistines† went up": They had been recognized as the
lords of the land since the battle of Aphek (chap. 4), and did not
wish to see the Israelites growing in strength and unity. They
may have regarded the meeting at Mizpah as a step toward
national federation and freedom on the part of the Hebrews.
They probably thought they could gain an easy victory over the
people at Mizpah, and thus fasten their rule on the land more
strongly than ever. Vs. 8, "Cease not to cry": The men of Israel
were terrified when they thought of their old and formidable
enemies. Probably few of them were armed, and they dreaded
the trained soldiers of the lowland. They could only trust Samuel
to invoke God's protection. Vs. 9, "whole burnt offering":
No part of the victim was used for food; all was consumed upon
the altar. This was a symbol of the entire consecration of the
nation to Jehovah and the deep fervor of their cry to him. "Cried
. . . . answered": Samuel prayed for the terrified people. God's
answer came in the deliverance that followed. Vs. 10, "the Lord
thundered": A storm broke upon the Philistines, such as dismayed
and disorganized them. The Hebrews recognized the event as
a providential interference in their behalf, and rushed forward to
complete the work which the storm had begun. Vs. 11, "under

Lord answered him. And as Samuel was offering 10
up the burnt offering, the Philistines drew near to
battle against Israel: but the Lord thundered with a
great thunder on that day upon the Philistines, and

BETHEL

discomfited them; and they were smitten down
before Israel. And the men of Israel went out of 11
Mizpah, and pursued the Philistines, and smote them,
until they came under Beth-car. Then Samuel took 12
a stone, and set it between Mizpah and Shen, and
called the name of it [1]Eben-ezer, saying, Hitherto
hath the Lord helped us. So the Philistines were 13

[1] That is, *The
stone of help*

subdued, and they came no more within the border
of Israel: and the hand of the Lord was against the
14 Philistines all the days of Samuel. And the cities
which the Philistines had taken from Israel were
restored to Israel, from Ekron even unto Gath; and
the border thereof did Israel deliver out of the hand
of the Philistines. And there was peace between
15 Israel and the Amorites. And Samuel judged Israel
16 all the days of his life. And he went from year to
year in circuit to Beth-el, and Gilgal, and Mizpah;

Beth-car": probably the modern Ain Karim, a short distance
west of Jerusalem. The storm and the onrush of the Hebrews
drove the Philistines in panic down the nearest valley past the
height of Beth-car toward their own country. Vs. 12, "took a
stone": It was a suitable memorial of such a victory. "Between
Mizpah and Shen": The latter name means "the tooth," and no
doubt refers to some rock not far from Mizpah. "Eben-ezer"†:
This "stone of help" is not the same place as the one mentioned in
4:1. It was somewhere in the highlands of Judah, and not far from
Mizpah. Vs. 13, "Philistines were subdued": This statement
is difficult to reconcile with the frequent narratives of conflict with
the Philistines later on, even during Samuel's life (cf. 13:5; 14:52;
17:1; 23:27, etc.). Materials from several writers went into the
book of First Samuel, and their information was not always the
same. The peace that followed the victory of Mizpah was
probably understood to have continued for many years. It is
possible also that this narrative of victory with Samuel as the hero
is a parallel to the Judean account in 13, 14, in which Saul is the
chief figure. Vs. 14, "cities . . . . were restored": another
fruit of the victory. Ekron† and Gath† were Philistine cities
near the border of Israel (see map). "The Amorites"†: a general
name for the older nations in Canaan, the neighbors of Israel.
Vs. 15, "Samuel judged Israel": His work as leader and prophet

and he judged Israel in all those places. And his 17
return was to Ramah, for there was his house; and
there he judged Israel: and he built there an altar
unto the Lord.

---

caused the people to submit to him all matters requiring judgment. "Went in circuit": Unlike a king, living in a capital,
Samuel visited different towns, holding sacrificial assemblies, or
public meetings. "Bethel"†: A town about half-way between
Shiloh and Jerusalem. "Gilgal†": not the place of that name
in the Jordan valley, but probably to be located about eighteen
miles north of Jerusalem, and seven miles north of Bethel. Vs.
17, "return to Ramah": This town, in which Samuel was born,
had now become his residence. At times when he was not absent
on his preaching tours he exercised the functions of prophet and
judge here. "Built there an altar": This was in the "high
place" (9:12, 13), where sacrificial feasts were held. In both
war and peace, Israel trusted the leadership of Samuel.

QUESTIONS

(1)* Why did Samuel want the people assembled? (2)
Why did he call them to Mizpah? Where was this place?
(3) Do you imagine the people from all the country came, or
only those of the vicinity? (4)* What three things did the
people do at Mizpah? What was the meaning of the pouring
out of water? (5) How did Samuel judge the people? (6)*
What was the difference between the condition of the nation
at this time and at the time when Samuel began his work?
In other words, what had he accomplished during those
years? (7) What report came to the Israelites at Mizpah?
What led the Philistines to attack them at that time? (8) How
did the people feel when they heard that their enemies were
coming? (9)* What did they beg Samuel to do? (10) What
did he do? (11)* What was it that caused the defeat of the
Philistines? (12) Do you not suppose there was a battle, in

which the Hebrews fought as well as they could? (13)* How did Samuel commemorate the victory? (14) What is the meaning of "Eben-ezer"? Why did they give it that name? Was it the only place of that name? (15) What does the writer say about the future relations of Israel and the Philistines? (16)* What part of the country was taken from the Philistines? (17) What were Israel's relations with its neighbors? (18) What were Samuel's duties? What places did he visit? Compare the work of Samuel with that of a modern circuit judge, or evangelist. (19) Where did he live? Did his parents probably reside there yet? (20) What did he build there? What other towns do you remember as having altars or sanctuaries? (21)* Make a list of all the places mentioned in this section, and locate them on the map as far as possible. (22) How does this story illustrate the value of a good ruler to a nation? Of what other rulers do you know as having proved a blessing to their people?

*REVIEW QUESTIONS

(All review questions should be answered in writing)

(1) Who were Samuel's parents, and what was his birthplace?

(2) What was the character of the worship at Shiloh, and of the priests who ministered there?

(3) What was the cause of Hannah's sorrow, how was it removed, and what was the expression of her gratitude?

(4) Describe the call of Samuel.

(5) What events led to the death of Eli the priest?

(6) What happened to the ark after the battle of Aphek?

(7) What were the causes and the method of its return?

(8) What was Samuel's method of doing the work of prophet and judge?

(9) On what occasion and in what manner were the Philistines defeated? What memorial of the event was erected?

SECTION XVII

THE DEMAND FOR A KING, I SAM. 8:1-9

And it came to pass, when Samuel was old, that **8**
he made his sons judges over Israel.   Now the name **2**
of his firstborn was Joel; and the name of his sec-

EXPLANATORY NOTES

With this section begins one of the two accounts of Saul's
elevation to the kingship.   The one is the early Judean narrative
of Saul's life (9:1—10:7, 9–16, 11:1—15) and the other is the late
account from the northern kingdom relating to Samuel (8:1–22,
10:17–27, 12:7–25).

Vs. 1, "made his sons judges": It will be noticed that many
years of Samuel's life are passed over without record.   Only a
very few incidents have been given, and he is already an old man.
Neither his marriage nor the birth of his sons has been mentioned.
It was natural that he should give his sons the work of assisting
him in hearing causes and settling disputes among the people.
Vs. 2, "judges in Beer-sheba": These sons of Samuel are not
known otherwise than by this notice of them.   Beer-sheba† was
far to the south, fully forty-five miles from Jerusalem, and on the
southern frontier of Judah.   Vs. 3, "turned aside after lucre":
The sins of Samuel's sons were similar to those of the sons of Eli,
save that they had not the opportunities which the priestly office
offered Hophni and Phinehas.   But they profited by their positions
as judges, taking presents of money as inducements to give dis-
honest decisions.   Vs. 4, "elders† of Israel": the men of age and
wisdom, the heads or sheiks of clans.   Vs. 5, "make us a king":
There had never been a king in Israel.   In the days of the judges,
a century or so earlier than Samuel's day, Gideon was offered the
honor of kingship, but refused it (Judg. 8:22, 23).   His son,
Abimelech, assumed the position of king or prince at Shechem, but
it was only a brief and local effort (Judg., chap. 9).   Now the
people feel that a king is needed.   Vs. 6, "displeased Samuel":

3 ond, Abijah: they were judges in Beer-sheba.   And
his sons walked not in his ways, but turned aside
after lucre, and took bribes, and perverted judgment.

4   Then all the elders of Israel gathered themselves
5 together, and came to Samuel unto Ramah: and they
said unto him, Behold, thou art old, and thy sons

A WELL AT BEERSHEBA

walk not in thy ways: now make us a king to judge
6 us like all the nations.   But the thing displeased
Samuel, when they said, Give us a king to judge us.
7 And Samuel prayed unto the Lord.   And the Lord
said unto Samuel, Hearken unto the voice of the
people in all that they say unto thee: for they have
not rejected thee, but they have rejected me, that I
8 should not be king over them.   According to all the
works which they have done since the day that I

brought them up out of Egypt even unto this day, in
that they have forsaken me, and served other gods,
so do they also unto thee. Now therefore hearken 9
unto their voice: howbeit thou shalt protest solemnly
unto them, and shalt shew them the manner of the
king that shall reign over them.

Our knowledge of Samuel's life comes from two different sources
which are woven together in the book we are studying. According to one account, Samuel thought it a mistake for the people to
wish a king. According to the other, he regarded it as the natural
result of his own work of teaching and unification, and in harmony
with God's purpose. Vs. 7, "they have rejected me": In this
account of the matter, the whole plan of choosing a king is considered as a mistake, displeasing alike to Samuel and God. Perhaps it took literary form in the later days when the evils of the
rule of bad kings were most keenly felt. Vs. 8, "served other
gods": Here the demand for a king is regarded as in line with the
many acts of disobedience and idolatry committed by the nation
ever since the exodus. Vs. 9, "thou shalt protest": Samuel is
to grant the popular request, but to take occasion to show how
much better it would be if the people would consent to be ruled by
God through his prophets.

QUESTIONS

(1) How is the fragmentary character of the record of
Samuel's life shown? (2) Why is it that so few of the acts of
Bible heroes are recorded? (3) What work did Samuel assign
to his sons? (4) What was the work of a judge? (5)* What
were the names of Samuel's sons? Where did they live? Was
not Beer-sheba too far from the center of the country to be
an appropriate place for them? (6) What kind of men were
Samuel's sons? How did they resemble Eli's sons? How
did they differ from them? (7) Do you think Samuel was

responsible for the character of these men? (8)* Who came to Samuel to complain about the situation? Where did Samuel live? (9) What were the two things which the people urged as causes of discontent? (10) What request did they make? Had there ever been a king in Israel? Did their conduct show that they still recognized Samuel as their rightful leader? (11)* What did they say was to be the work of the king? What nations did they know that were ruled by kings? (12) How did the request affect Samuel? Why should he feel troubled over it? (13) To whom did he take the matter? (14) What was the divine response? Who had really been rejected? (15)* How did this conduct of the people correspond to their previous record? (16) What instances of national sin do you recall in the earlier history of the people? (17)* What was Samuel commanded to do? If it had been wrong for the people to have a king, would it have been permitted at all? (18) How was Samuel to prepare the people for their new experiment? (19)* How does the demand for a king show the success of Samuel's work as judge? If he had not united them as a nation, would they have desired a king at all? (20) Compare the condition of the people at the time Samuel began his labors over them with their situation at the time they demanded a king. What elements of progress are evident? (21) Can you remember other instances in which the life of one man has been the means of organizing a nation? Would King Alfred and Washington be similar examples?

SECTION XVIII

SAMUEL'S WARNING, I SAM. 8:10-22

And Samuel told all the words of the Lord unto 10
the people that asked of him a king. And he said, 11
This will be the manner of the king that shall reign
over you: he will take your sons, and appoint them

EXPLANATORY NOTES

The northern source regarding Samuel's career as a prophet
is followed here. It emphasizes the disinclination of Samuel to
have a king chosen, and points out his warnings to the nation.

Vs. 10, "Samuel told . . . . the people": The previous verses
recount the popular demand for a king, Samuel's displeasure, and
his presentation of the matter to God in prayer. He was told to
consent to the people's wish while warning them of the danger
incurred. Vs. 11, "the manner of the king": the way in which
he would act. "For his chariots": In the early period the men
of Israel always fought on foot. It was not till the days of Solomon that chariots and cavalry were used. A king would need
standing armies, and the nation would have to furnish the soldiers
from its homes. "Run before his chariots": Kings were accustomed to have men run in front of their chariots to clear the way
(see II Sam. 15:1). This was a mark of royalty. Vs. 12, "captains of thousands:" The different grades of officers were designated according to the number of men they commanded. "Plow
his ground": Some were to be chosen as soldiers, some as officers,
and some as workers in the fields, and makers of tools. This
would point not only to enforced military service, but to a condi
tion of serfdom almost amounting to slavery. Vs. 13, "your
daughters": Women as well as men would have to serve the new
master whom the people were demanding. His court would
require perfumers, cooks, and other servants. Vs. 14, "take
your fields": Samuel suggested the most alarming possibilities

unto him, ¹for his chariots, and to be his horsemen;
12 and they shall run before his chariots: and he will
appoint them unto him for captains of thousands,
and captains of fifties; and he will set some to plow
his ground, and to reap his harvest, and to make his

¹ Or, over his chariots, and over his horses

FARMER AND PLOUGH

instruments of war, and the instruments of his
13 chariots. And he will take your daughters to be
²confectionaries, and to be cooks, and to be bakers.
14 And he will take your fields, and your vineyards,
and your oliveyards, even the best of them, and give
15 them to his servants. And he will take the tenth of
your seed, and of your vineyards, and give to his

² Or, perfumers

officers, and to his servants.   And he will take your 16
men-servants, and your maid-servants, and your
goodliest young men, and your asses, and put them
to his work.   He will take the tenth of your flocks: 17
and ye shall be his servants.   And ye shall cry out 18

---

in order to keep the people from wanting a king.   Nobody would
want to have his farm, or his grape vineyard, or his olive orchard
taken from him and given to some favorite friend of the king.
Indeed we know what happened on one occasion when King
Ahab tried forcibly to take possession of a field (I Kings, chap.
21).   Vs. 15, "tenth of your seed": The people would be taxed
10 per cent. of their incomes for the royal revenues, to support the
king and his court.   Vs. 16, "put them to his work": Nothing
would be exempt from his will.   Their servants and their beasts
he would demand from them.   Vs. 17, "his servants": his bond-
servants, or slaves.   This would be a disgraceful humiliation to the
free-born Israelites.   Vs. 18, "ye shall cry out": Samuel tries
to convince them that they will regret their demand for a king,
when they discover how expensive and humiliating is the condition
they wish to try.   "Will not answer you": It would be practically
impossible to get rid of their kings.   The choice, once made,
could not be revoked.   It is of course clear that the kind of king
here described came only in later years.   Neither Saul nor David
had any such court as is here pictured.   Solomon, and a few
of the later kings, may have approached it.   Not unlikely the
description, written down in the days of the kingdom, was filled
in with details taken from the actual conditions of the writer's
time.   Vs. 19, "we will have a king": Samuel's persuasions and
warnings were of no avail.   Vs. 20, "judge us . . . . and fight":
These were the two sides of the king's work, to govern his people,
hearing and settling disputes; and to fight at their head against
their enemies.   Vs. 21, "rehearsed them": repeated them.   Vs.
22, "hearken unto their voice": Again Samuel is told to grant
their request (cf. vs. 9).   "Go ye": Samuel dismissed them to

in that day because of your king which ye shall have chosen you; and the Lord will not answer you in
19 that day. But the people refused to hearken unto

AN OLIVE TREE

the voice of Samuel; and they said, Nay; but we
20 will have a king over us; that we also may be like all
the nations; and that our king may judge us, and go
21 out before us, and fight our battles. And Samuel

heard all the words of the people, and he rehearsed them in the ears of the Lord. And the Lord said to 22 Samuel, Hearken unto their voice, and make them a king. And Samuel said unto the men of Israel, Go ye every man unto his city.

---

their homes to wait for a favorable moment for the choice of a king. The story is continued in 10:17–27, which in its original form probably followed 8:22. The intervening verses (9:1—10:16), taken from the other source, tell a wholly different story of how Saul was chosen king.

QUESTIONS

(1) What had the people demanded of Samuel? How did their wish affect him? What did he do? What was he told to do in regard to the people's request? (2) What response did Samuel make to the people? (3)* For what purposes did he say the king would take their sons? (4) Was it not necessary to have a standing army? (5) What menial service would the king demand of the men of Israel? (6)* What would be the tasks of the women? (7) What property would the king seize? For what purpose? What were the chief crops raised? (8)* What kind of taxes would the king exact? (9) Why did Samuel make his description of the king so repulsive? If the writer lived in an age when the kings did such things, would that fact influence his report of Samuel's words? (10) Was Samuel able to check the popular demand for a king? (11)* What two things did they want the king to do? (12) When he had failed in his effort, what was Samuel told to do? (13) Why did he send the people home? (14)* Is it possible that this narrative is to be connected at once with the one in 10:17–27? If that is the case, and the assembly at Mizpah was called at once, how are we to account for the other story, 9:1—10:16? And how did the words of

8:22*b* get into the text? (15) Note Samuel's attitude of regret and reluctance in this story, as contrasted with his interest in making Saul king in 9:1—10:16. *What explanation can you give for it? (16) Is it possible that both stories of the choice of Saul were in circulation among the people? (17) Is not the fact that such different narratives regarding the same men were used by the prophets a proof that they considered the teaching value of a story of greater importance than the facts it contained? (18) May not this fact explain many discrepancies in Old Testament narratives?

SECTION XIX

SAUL'S SEARCH, I SAM. 9:1-14

Now there was a man of Benjamin, whose name **0**
was Kish, the son of Abiel, the son of Zeror, the son
of Becorath, the son of Aphiah, the son of a Benjamite, a mighty man of [1]valour.   And he had a son, **2**
whose name was Saul, a [2]young man and a goodly:
and there was not among the children of Israel a
goodlier person than he: from his shoulders and

[1] Or, *wealth*
[2] Or, *choice*

EXPLANATORY NOTES

It has been noted that there are two main lines of tradition
regarding the choice of Saul as king.   The older (Judean, 9:1—
10:16, chap. 11) represents the matter as providentially arranged by
the meeting of Saul and Samuel, and the public vindication of the
choice by Saul's victory over Nahash.   The second (Ephraimite,
chap. 8, 10:17-27, chap. 12) reveals Samuel as opposed to the
change but persuaded by God, and later holding the election at
Mizpah where Saul was chosen by the sacred lot.   It is the first
of these two accounts that is begun in this section.   Vs. 1, "man
of Benjamin": The tribe of Benjamin was one of the smallest,
after the events recorded in Judg. 20:12 f.   Its territory lay just
south of the tribe of Ephraim and included a portion of the city
of Jerusalem.   "Kish, the son of Abiel": In I Chron. 8:33 and
9:39 Ner is called the father of Kish, but such differences in
the reports of genealogies are not infrequent nor strange.   "Mighty
man of valour": The other rendering, "wealth," seems preferable.
Kish was a well-to-do farmer.   "Saul": The name means "asked."
It was also the home name of the apostle Paul, who was likewise
of this tribe of Benjamin.   Vs. 2, "choice man and goodly": Saul
was not necessarily young at this time, for soon after his son
Jonathan is introduced (13:2).   Saul was tall and of fine appear-

76

3 upward he was higher than any of the people. And
the asses of Kish Saul's father were lost. And
Kish said to Saul his son, Take now one of the
4 servants with thee, and arise, go seek the asses. And
he passed through the hill country of Ephraim, and
passed through the land of Shalishah, but they
found them not: then they passed through the
land of Shaalim, and there they were not: and he
passed through the land of the Benjamites, but they
5 found them not. When they were come to the land
of Zuph, Saul said to his servant that was with him,
Come and let us return; lest my father leave caring
6 for the asses, and take thought for us. And he said
unto him, Behold now, there is in this city a man of
God, and he is a man that is held in honour; all that

---

ance (9:2, 10:23). Vs. 3, "go seek the asses": The property
of Kish was in stock, and some of the asses strayed. There are
no fences in Palestine. Sheep, goats, cattle, and asses have to
be watched to prevent their wandering. A father had full control
of his children as long as he lived, and could send them on errands,
no matter how old they were. Vs. 4, "passed through the hill
country": The route of Saul and his servant is not very clear.
They probably started from Gibeah, Saul's home, and went
through the country to the northwest, descending to the plain of
Sharon to the west, and returning to the hills in the direction of
their home. Shalishah and Shaalim are not known, but they
probably lay somewhere in the plain. Vs. 5, "land of Zuph":
This appears to be the region of Ramah, Samuel's home, for
that town was called Ramathaim-zophim, or the "two Ramahs
of the Zuphites," and the father of Samuel was a descendant of
Zuph (1:1). Vs. 6, "in this city": probably Ramah, Samuel's

he saith cometh surely to pass: now let us go thither;
peradventure he can tell us concerning our journey
whereon we go.   Then said Saul to his servant, 7
But, behold, if we go, what shall we bring the man?
for the bread is spent in our vessels, and there is not
a present to bring to the man of God: what have we?
And the servant answered Saul again, and said, 8
Behold, I have in my hand the fourth part of a
shekel of silver: that will I give to the man of God,
to tell us our way.   (Beforetime in Israel, when a 9
man went to inquire of God, thus he said, Come
and let us go to the seer: for he that is now called a
Prophet was beforetime called a Seer.)   Then said 10
Saul to his servant, Well said; come, let us go.   So
they went unto the city where the man of God was.

---

home.   "Cometh surely to pass": The servant thought Samuel
was a fortune teller, whom it was worth while to consult.   The
servant's only partial knowledge of Samuel, and Saul's entire
ignorance of him, seem strange in view of the prophet's greatness
and authority in the nation.   We do not know all the facts.   We
have to accept the differences between the two accounts, and
attempt to ascertain what the narrators felt to be the teaching
value of each.   Vs. 7, "there is not a present": It was understood
by both Saul and his servant that they ought to take to the prophet
a gift of some kind.   Vs. 8, "fourth part of a shekel": a very
small coin worth about ten or twelve cents; but as it was all Saul
had, he was not ashamed to offer it.   Vs. 9, "called beforetime a
seer": i.e., a clairvoyant, one who sees hidden things, who tells
fortunes and predicts lucky days.   The writer describes the
custom in earlier days, before the prophets were well known.
Vs. 10, "went into the city": Ramah, where Samuel lived.   Vs.

WOMEN WITH WATER JARS

As they went up the ascent to the city, they found 11
young maidens going out to draw water, and said unto
them, Is the seer here? And they answered them, 12
and said, He is; behold, he is before thee: make
haste now, for he is come to-day into the city, for
the people have a sacrifice to-day in the high place:
as soon as ye be come into the city, ye shall straight- 13
way find him, before he go up to the high place to
eat: for the people will not eat until he come, because he doth bless the sacrifice and afterwards they
eat that be bidden. Now therefore get you up; for
at this time ye shall find him. And they went up to 14
the city; and as they came within the city, behold,
Samuel came out against them, for to go up to the
high place.

11, "went up the ascent": Ramah means "high place." It was
partly situated on a hill. "To draw water": In eastern lands
the women go to the public fountain or spring for water to carry to
their homes. Vs. 12, "he is come to-day": Samuel had probably
just returned from one of his preaching tours, and was going to
hold a sacrificial feast at the place of worship at the top of the hill.
Vs. 13, "find him": The two young men were advised to go to the
home of Samuel in the city, so that they might obtain the information they wished before he went up to open the services at the high
place. Vs. 14, "came out against them": They met the prophet
just coming out from his home to ascend to the high place.

QUESTIONS

(1) What is meant by "Benjamin"? (2)* Where was it
located, and how did it compare with other tribes in size?
(3) Who was Kish, and what was his position among his

neighbors? (4) How is Saul described? (5)* Why would such a man be desirable as a king? (6) What misfortune had happened to Kish? (7) What steps were taken to find the animals? (8) What regions did the young men visit? Estimate what distance they traveled. (9)* How is the "land of Zuph" connected with the earlier part of Samuel's life? (10) What was Saul's suggestion when they reached this point? (11) Who proposed the visit to the prophet? In what way did the servant describe him? (12) Does this description indicate that fortune tellers were common and were often consulted? (13)* Did the servant mistake the character and work of Samuel, or was he really a fortune teller? (14) What did Saul think they should take if they consulted the seer? Was it the custom to give a present for such services? (15) How much money did they have? Did they think so small a fee was sufficient? (16) In what city did Samuel live? (17) In what part of the country was it? (18) Of whom did they inquire concerning Samuel? What information did they receive? (19)* Where and in what manner were the sacrifices celebrated? (20) Does vs. 12 suggest that Samuel had just returned from one of his prophetic journeys? (21) Where did the young man meet the prophet? (22)* In what manner does this section emphasize the providential nature of Saul's acquaintance with Samuel? (23) Does it seem strange that Saul should not have known so famous a man as Samuel? (24) Does the fact that we have two quite different stories of Saul's choice as king help to explain this?

MEETING OF SAUL AND SAMUEL, I SAM. 9:15-25

Now the Lord had revealed unto Samuel a day 15
before Saul came, saying, To-morrow about this 16
time I will send thee a man out of the land of Benjamin, and thou shalt anoint him to be ¹prince over
my people Israel, and he shall save my people out
of the hand of the Philistines: for I have looked upon
my people, because their cry is come unto me. And 17
when Samuel saw Saul, the Lord said unto him,
Behold the man ²of whom I spake to thee! this

¹ Or, *leader*

² Or, *of whom I said unto thee, This same,* etc.

EXPLANATORY NOTES

The early Judean narrative of Saul's life is continued in this
section. Vs. 15, "had revealed": This statement prepares for
what follows by showing that Samuel already knew of Saul's
arrival, and of his fitness to be king. It is a part of the purpose
of the writer to show that the prophet was accustomed to receive
from God such intimations as were necessary for his work. Vs.
16, "shalt anoint": It is plain that the writer understood it to
be the will of God that Saul should be king. Kings, priests, and
sometimes prophets were set apart to their offices by pouring oil
on their heads (I Kings 19:15, 16; Lev. 8:12; Zech. 4:14).
"Shall save": As Israel's chief danger was from the inroads of
the Philistines, their greatest need was a war leader who could
organize their army and protect the land. Vs. 17, "behold the
man": Samuel saw at once the good qualities of Saul and was
convinced that he would be a king pleasing to God. Vs. 18,
"in the gate": Most ancient cities had walls and gates, but probably the principal entrance to the town is meant, whether walled

18 same shall have authority over my people.   Then
Saul drew near to Samuel in the gate, and said, Tell
19 me, I pray thee, where the seer's house is.   And
Samuel answered Saul, and said, I am the seer; go
up before me unto the high place, for ye shall eat
with me to-day: and in the morning I will let thee
20 go, and will tell thee all that is in thine heart.   And

A PALESTINIAN HOUSE

as for thine asses that were lost three days ago, set
not thy mind on them; for they are found.   And
[3] for whom is all that is desirable in Israel? Is it not
21 for thee, and for all thy father's house?   And Saul
answered and said, Am not I a Benjamite, of the
smallest of the tribes of Israel?   and my family the
least of all the families of the tribe of Benjamin?
wherefore then speakest thou to me after this man-

[3] Or, *on whom is all the desire of Israel? Is it not on thee, and on all*, etc.?

ner? And Samuel took Saul and his servant, and 22
brought them into the guest-chamber, and made
them sit in the chiefest place among them that were
bidden, which were about thirty persons. And 23
Samuel said unto the cook, Bring the portion which
I gave thee, of which I said unto thee, Set it by thee.

Or, shoulder And the cook took up the ⁴thigh, and that which was 24
upon it, and set it before Saul. And Samuel said,
Behold that which hath been reserved! set it before
thee and eat; because unto the appointed time hath
it been kept for thee, for I said, I have invited the
people. So Saul did eat with Samuel that day. And 25
when they were come down from the high place

⁵The Sept. has, *they spread a couch for Saul on the housetop, and he lay down* into the city, ⁵he communed with Saul upon the
housetop.

---

or not. Vs. 19, "go up before me": as a guest; the youth who
was looking for lost property is suddenly welcomed as the chief
guest of the town. "In thine heart": answer all questions;
perhaps Saul was already concerned about the unhappy condition
of the country. Vs. 20, "set not thy mind": do not concern
yourself about them; there are more important matters to receive
your attention. "All that is desirable": Compare the text with
the marginal translation; the one implies that all the riches of
Israel are at Saul's disposal as king, the other that he is desired
by the nation. Vs. 21, "smallest of the tribes": In the war
described in Judg., chap. 20, this tribe had barely escaped
extermination. Vs. 22, "guest-chamber": the building at the
high place in which the sacrificial feasts were held. "Thirty
persons": the few specially invited citizens who were honored
above the rest; probably the other people feasted outside. Vs.
23, "Bring the portion": Samuel had already informed the cook

that he should reserve a choice part of the meat for an expected guest. Vs. 24, "Samuel said": The text is uncertain; perhaps a better reading would be "(the cook) said, The meal is served! Eat! For to the appointed time we have waited for thee to eat with the guests." Vs. 25, "upon the housetop": The reading of the Greek version (see margin) is to be preferred, for the housetop was the usual sleeping place in the warm months.

QUESTIONS

(1) What preparation had Samuel received for the coming of Saul? (2)* What do you understand by the words, "the Lord revealed unto Samuel"? Would this imply a direct communication in words, or Samuel's perception of what would be most in harmony with the divine plan? (3) Why did Israel need a prince or leader? (4)* How do you reconcile vs. 16 with 7:13 which says the Philistines were completely subdued? Is it possible that the victory there described is the same one which Saul achieved later on (chap. 14)? (5) What was Samuel's feeling when he first saw Saul? (6) Where and how did the two men meet? (7) What was the prophet's treatment of Saul? (8)* What did Samuel mean by "all that is in thine heart"? What proves that it was not of the loss of the asses that he was speaking? (9) What are the two possible meanings of the last part of vs. 20? Which rendering yields the best meaning? (10) Was Saul's reply merely self-depreciation, or did he really think himself unworthy of the honor? (11) Why was his tribe smaller than the others? (12)* What light does the equality of treatment accorded to Saul and his servant throw on the customs of the time? (13) What was the guest-chamber? (14) What courtesies were shown the young men? (15)* What was the purpose of the gathering? (16) How many were invited? (17) What special preparations had been made by Samuel? (18) What part of the food was reserved for the chief guests? (19)* If Saul was entertained at a public feast, in what respect

was he Samuel's guest? (20) What occurred after the feast? (21) Where did Saul remain that night? (22) Is it clear that both God and Samuel are represented in this section as desiring a king for Israel? (23) Does not this fact as contrasted with Samuel's reluctance to have a king in Section XVII, show that we have two different accounts of the event?

MOUND OF BEISAN

SAUL ANOINTED, I SAM. 9:26—10:16

26 And they arose early: and it came to pass about
the spring of the day, that Samuel called to Saul on
the housetop, saying, Up, that I may send thee away.
And Saul arose, and they went out both of them, he
27 and Samuel, abroad. As they were going down at
the end of the city, Samuel said to Saul, Bid the servant pass on before us (and he passed on), but stand
thou still at this time, that I may cause thee to hear
10 the word of God. Then Samuel took the vial of
oil, and poured it upon his head, and kissed him, and
said, Is it not that the Lord hath anointed thee to be
2 prince over his inheritance? When thou art departed from me to-day, then thou shalt find two men
by Rachel's sepulchre, in the border of Benjamin at
Zelzah; and they will say unto thee, The asses

EXPLANATORY NOTES

In this section the early Judean story of Saul's career is the
source. Vs. 27, "end of the city": the border or outer part of
the town. Vs. 1, "vial of oil": used for consecrating men to
kingly office (II Kings 9:1, 3). From this custom of anointing
is derived the Hebrew word "Messiah" = "anointed," of which
the Greek word "Christ" is the equivalent. "Kissed him":
perhaps in token of reverence and submission, as a subject to a
king (cf. Ps. 2:12); but more probably as a mark of affection.
Vs. 2, "Rachel's sepulchre": Not the traditional tomb near
Bethlehem, but one on the northern border of Benjamin, on

which thou wentest to seek are found: and, lo, thy
father hath left the care of the asses, and taketh
thought for you, saying, What shall I do for my son?
Then shalt thou go on forward from thence, and 3
thou shalt come to the oak of Tabor, and there
shall meet thee there three men going up to God to

Saul's way home. "At Zelzah": No such place is known, and
the present form of the word may be due to a copyist's error.
"They will say": Samuel gives Saul several signs by which he
may be assured that his anointing is according to the will of God.
Vs. 3, "oak of Tabor:" Another unknown landmark on Saul's way
home; probably a well-known tree, revered as a sacred spot (cf.
Gen. 18:1, Judg. 4:5). "Up to God": Bethel had been regarded
as a holy place from early times. There was an altar there to
which these men were going. "Three kids . . . . three loaves,"
etc.: The offerings were for the shrine. Vs. 4, "give thee two
loaves": as an act of friendship, and perhaps also as expressing
their undefined recognition of his future greatness. Vs. 5, "hill
of God": Gibeah, Saul's home. "Band of prophets"†: It must
be remembered that the term prophet was of very wide application, being used not only of the nobler, saner men, like Samuel
and after him Elijah and Elisha, who were the religious leaders
and statesmen of their time, but even of men, who like those
mentioned here went about in groups or bands, stirring up religious excitement with shouting, and dancing, and musical instruments. Today even we use the term preacher with a scarcely
less wide range of meaning. Such groups of men went about
"prophesying," i.e., engaging in excited dances and shoutings,
accompanied with musical instruments. These bands represent
prophecy at its lowest level. It is notable that the greater prophets
like Samuel did not despise such men, but sought to influence
them for good, and to emphasize the saner and more effective side
of religion. "Psaltery," etc.: instruments corresponding to a lyre,
tambourine, flute, and harp respectively. Vs. 6, "spirit† of the

Beth-el, one carrying three kids, and another carrying three loaves of bread, and another carrying a
4 ¹bottle of wine: and they will salute thee, and give   ¹ Or, *skin*
thee two loaves of bread; which thou shalt receive
5 of their hand. After that thou shalt come to ²the   ² Or, *Gibeah*
hill of God, where is the garrison of the Philistines:

RACHEL'S SEPULCHRE

and it shall come to pass, when thou art come thither
to the city, that thou shalt meet a band of prophets
coming down from the high place with a psaltery,
and a timbrel, and a pipe, and a harp, before them;
6 and they shall be prophesying: and the spirit of the
Lord will come mightily upon thee, and thou shalt
prophesy with them, and shalt be turned into another

man.   And let it be, when these signs are come unto 7
thee, that thou do as occasion serve thee; for God
is with thee.   And thou shalt go down before me to 8
Gilgal; and, behold, I will come down unto thee, to
offer burnt offerings, and to sacrifice sacrifices of
peace offerings: seven days shalt thou tarry, till I
come unto thee, and shew thee what thou shalt do.
And it was so, that when he had turned his back to 9
go from Samuel, God gave him another heart: and
all those signs came to pass that day.

³ Or, *Gibeah*

And when they came thither to ³the hill, behold, 1c
a band of prophets met him; and the spirit of God
came mightily upon him, and he prophesied among
them.   And it came to pass, when all that knew him 11
beforetime saw that, behold, he prophesied with the

Lord": An expression often used in the Old Testament to denote
any strong influence or impulse (cf. Judg. 14:6; I Sam. 11:6, 7).
Seeming to be superhuman and to transport a man out of himself,
it was ascribed to God.   Saul would be irresistibly drawn into the
circle of these "prophets," so Samuel said, and would imitate their
wild conduct, thus acting very differently from his habit.   Vs.
7, "as occasion serve": i.e., "you will know what to do," an assurance that he will be equal to the emergency, and may rely upon the
divine help.   Vs. 8, "to Gilgal": This verse appears to interrupt
the order of the narrative, and to violate the very freedom to "do
as occasion" might suggest which Samuel has just granted Saul.
It is probably a later addition, preparing the reader for 13:7–15.
Vs. 9, "another heart": The entire current of his life was changed
by his interview with the prophet.   Vs. 10, "he prophesied":
imitated the men he met in their ecstatic actions.   Only one of
the "signs" referred to in the previous verses and in vs. 9 is

prophets, then the people said one to another, What is this that is come unto the son of Kish? Is Saul

12 also among the prophets? And one of the same place answered and said, And who is their father? Therefore it became a proverb, Is Saul also among

13 the prophets? And when he had made an end of prophesying, he came to the high place.

14 And Saul's uncle said unto him and to his servant, Whither went ye? And he said, To seek the asses: and when we saw that they were not found, we came

15 to Samuel. And Saul's uncle said, Tell me, I pray

16 thee, what Samuel said unto you. And Saul said unto his uncle, He told us plainly that the asses were found. But concerning the matter of the kingdom, whereof Samuel spake, he told him not.

---

mentioned. Vs. 11, "Saul also among the prophets?": The men of this class were usually considered of small importance (cf. II Kings 9:11), whereas Saul belonged to a well-to-do family. It astonished the people to see him among such men. Vs. 12, "who is their father?": A further comment on the obscure and indifferent estate of these roving "preachers" as compared with the well-born son of Kish. Vs. 13, "to the high place": to Gibeah, his home, near which he had met the strolling prophets. Vs. 14, "uncle": "Cousin" is probably a better reading.

QUESTIONS

(1) Where had Saul spent the night? (2)* What unusual courtesy did Samuel show his guest in bidding him farewell? (3) How did Samuel further secure privacy for his conversation with Saul? (4) What was the significance of the anointing? (5)* What was the purpose of the three "signs" that

Samuel gave Saul? (6) Where was he to meet the two men? Who was Rachel? (7) What was to happen at the oak of Tabor? Why were the men going to Bethel? (8)* What were they carrying? What was a "bottle" of wine? (9) Who were the Philistines? Why did they have a garrison at Gibeah? (10)* What kind of men were the "prophets" whom Saul was to meet? (11) How did they "prophesy"? What musical instruments did they have? (12) What do you think was the value of such practices? (13) What somewhat similar things happen today? Are they wholly good, or wholly bad, or partly good and partly evil? (14) What should be the attitude generally of people who count themselves both religious and intelligent to those who seem to them zealous but lacking in intelligence and discretion? (15) What was to happen to Saul when he met them? (16)* How was Saul changed by his interview with Samuel? (17) Do you understand this to imply some magical change that came over him, or the uplifting effect of his interview with Samuel? (18) How did Saul act when he met the band of prophets? (19) Do you understand that he "preached" or "predicted," or rather that he acted in the strange, excited manner of these men? (20) How did his conduct impress the people who knew him? (21)* What is the meaning of the proverb which arose from this event? (22) Where did he go when he recovered from the strange influence of the group of prophets? (23) What questions were asked him on his arrival at home? (24) Why did he not tell of Samuel's message to him? (25)* What was the leading purpose of the writer in recording this narrative?

SECTION XXII

SAUL CHOSEN KING, I SAM. 10:17–27

17 And Samuel called the people together unto the
18 Lord to Mizpah; and he said unto the children of
Israel, Thus saith the Lord the God of Israel, I
brought up Israel out of Egypt, and I delivered you
out of the hand of the Egyptians, and out of the hand

EXPLANATORY NOTES

In the regular progress of the narrative the present section
follows immediately after Section XVIII (8:10–22) which, like
this, is taken from the later Ephraimite story of Samuel's work.
Contrary to the spirit of 9:1—10:16, in which the choice of Saul
was divinely directed, and was highly pleasing to Samuel, this
account represents the popular demand for a king as a rejection
of both God and his prophet, and displeasing alike to both.
This difference in thought about the events of the history on the
part of the two writers whose writings are combined in this book,
illustrates a fact about the Old Testament historical books which
needs to be clearly recognized. The authors of these books were
"writing prophets": they were men who sought to do with the
history of their people what Jesus demanded that the scribes
should do with the events of their own time, viz., interpret them
(Luke 12:56), discover their meaning, and the instruction which
they yield for the guidance of life. In their endeavor thus to
interpret the history of the days of Samuel, the two writers were
led to take not fundamentally different views of God and his
relation to the world, but of the conduct of the people in demanding a king and of God's attitude and of the attitude of Samuel as
his prophet toward the appointment of Saul. Doubtless there
was truth in both views, but not quite the whole truth in either

of all the kingdoms that oppressed you: but ye have 19
this day rejected your God, who himself saveth you
out of all your calamities and your distresses; and
ye have said unto him, Nay, but set a king over us.
Now therefore present yourselves before the Lord
by your tribes, and by your thousands. So Samuel 20
brought all the tribes of Israel near, and the tribe of
Benjamin was taken. And he brought the tribe of 21
Benjamin near by their families, and the family of
the Matrites was taken: and Saul the son of Kish was
taken; but when they sought him, he could not be
found. Therefore they asked of the Lord further, 22
Is there yet a man to come hither? And the Lord
answered, Behold, he hath hid himself among the
stuff. And they ran and fetched him thence; and 23

---

one. Vs. 17, "to Mizpah"†: When the people would no longer
consent to any other rule than that of king (8:19–22) Samuel
called them together at the famous old sanctuary of Mizpah.
Here he addressed them in a tone of reproach because of their
ungrateful abandonment of his own simple method of government, approved of God. Vs. 19, "tribes . . . . thousands":
There were twelve tribes besides the Levites; "thousands"
signifies the clans of which a tribe was composed. Vs. 20, "Benjamin was taken": The choice was made by casting lots, the sup-
position being that the divine will was revealed in this manner.
Vs. 20, "could not be found": Saul was too modest to enjoy such
publicity, and had hidden when he became aware that his was the
name chosen. Vs. 22, "is there yet a man?": A better translation would be, "Did the man come hither?" The oracle assured
them that he was present, but in hiding among the baggage. Vs.
24, "none like him": Samuel wanted the people to see that if

when he stood among the people, he was higher than any of the people from his shoulders and upward.

24 And Samuel said to all the people, See ye him whom the Lord hath chosen, that there is none like him among all the people? And all the people shouted, and said, ¹God save the king.

25 Then Samuel told the people the manner of the kingdom, and wrote it in a book, and laid it up before the Lord. And Samuel sent all the people away,

26 every man to his house. And Saul also went to his house to Gibeah; and there went with him the ²host,

27 whose hearts God had touched. But certain ³sons of Belial said, How shall this man save us? And they despised him, and brought him no present. ⁴But he held his peace.

¹ Heb. *Let the king live*

² Or, *men of valour*

³ Or, *base fellows*

⁴ Or, *But he was as though he had been deaf*

---

they must have a king, the divine choice had been the best. "God save the king!": or, with the margin, "Let the king live!" (cf. II Sam. 16:16; I Kings, 1:25, 31; II Kings 11:12). Vs. 25, "wrote in a book": the rules and warnings for guidance of king and people. It may also have contained the warnings found in Samuel's rebuke (8:10-18). Vs. 26, "went with him": The assembly was entirely informal and popular, and at the completion of the business it broke up and the people departed for their homes. But as was natural, some brave men remained with Saul as a sort of bodyguard, being impressed with his appearance and spirit. Vs. 27, "brought him no present": There were some who thought Saul unequal to the task of being king. When the rest came to offer their allegiance and present their gifts in token of good-will, they declined to join. To such men he gave no heed, but bore himself with dignity as became a king.

QUESTIONS

(1) To what place did Samuel summon the nation?   (2) For what purpose?   (3)* When were the people delivered from Egypt?   (4) From what other kingdoms had God rescued them?   (5) In spite of these past mercies what was their present attitude toward God?   (6)* How does this feeling about the choice of a king compare with that in the narrative of 9:1—10:16?   (7)* How was the election held? (8) Who was finally selected?   (9) Where was he when the choice was made known?   (10)* Why did he hide?   (11) How did they discover him?   (12) What was his appearance? (13) How did the people receive their king?   (14)* What precautions for the future did Samuel take?   (15) Was the "manner of the kingdom" a book of rules to be followed, or of dangers to be avoided?   (16) Where was the book deposited?   What is meant by "before the Lord"?   (17) Where did the people go?   (18)* Where did Saul go?   Who went with him?   What was the purpose of these men in going with the new king?   (19) What is meant by the words "whose hearts God had touched"?   (20) What kind of men were "sons of Belial"†?   What did these men say? Why?   (21) How did they treat Saul?   Did he resent it?   (22)* How do you account for the two views presented in this and Sections XX, XXI regarding Samuel's attitude toward the kingship? (23) How do you account for the fact that both are given place in the book?   (24) Is it wrong to co-operate with those who have chosen what you regard as a wrong course, when once it is decided that this is the best course that they will consent to choose?   Would it be wrong for example, for a father to assist his son to succeed in business though he believed that the son ought to have chosen to get an education instead of going into business?   (25)* What answer to this general question do 8:19–22 and 10:19 suggest?   Is this answer right? Does such co-operation change the character of the previous choice or avert its possible evil consequence?

SECTION XXIII

RELIEF OF JABESH–GILEAD, I SAM. 11:1–15

11 Then Nahash the Ammonite came up, and encamped against Jabesh-gilead: and all the men of Jabesh said unto Nahash, Make a covenant with us,
2 and we will serve thee. And Nahash the Ammonite said unto them, On this condition will I make it with you, that all your right eyes be put out; and
3 I will lay it for a reproach upon all Israel. And the elders of Jabesh said unto him, Give us seven days' respite, that we may send messengers unto all the borders of Israel: and then, if there be none to save

---

EXPLANATORY NOTES

In the present section the narrative is taken from the early Judean story of Saul's life, the first portion of which is found in 9:1—10:16, and tells of the search for the asses, the interview of Saul and Samuel at Ramah, the private anointing, and the signs that were fulfilled on Saul's journey home. It will be borne in mind that the two stories present quite different views of Samuel's attitude toward the election of a king, that of favor being prominent in the document from which the present section is taken. Vs. 1, "Nahash the Ammonite": The Ammonites† were a people living east of the Jordan, and north of Moab (see map). "Jabesh-gilead†: .... all the men of Jabesh": They propose to surrender without attempt at resistance. Vs. 2, "right eyes be put out": not only a degrading sign of subjection, but a preventive of further fighting on their part, the custom of battle being to cover the body, all but the right side of the face, with the shield. Such maiming of captured enemies was not uncommon (see Judg. 1:6,7). Vs. 3, "seven days": So confident was Nahash,

97

us, we will come out to thee. Then came the mes- 4
sengers to Gibeah of Saul, and spake these words
in the ears of the people: and all the people lifted
up their voice, and wept. And, behold, Saul came 5
following the oxen out of the field; and Saul said,
What aileth the people that they weep? And they
told him the words of the men of Jabesh. And the 6
spirit of God came mightily upon Saul when he heard
those words, and his anger was kindled greatly.

---

that he contemptuously granted the request to wait a week. Vs.
4, "wept": Helpless to aid their countrymen in their distress, they
could only raise their cries of grief and rage. No one seems to
have thought of taking the news to Saul, who would have been
the first to learn of the facts had he been recognized as king. It
must be borne in mind that according to the source followed in
this section Saul's anointing was private, not even his own family
knowing the facts. To this writer the story of the public election
at Mizpah (Section XXII) was unknown. Vs. 5, "following the
oxen": Like the later Cincinnatus, Saul the farmer leaves his
plow to deliver his people. Like any other farmer of the place he
drove his cattle back to the town at night; but when he heard the
news he knew, as the rest did not, that the time to "do as occasion
might serve" had come. Vs. 6, "spirit of God"†: Saul rose to
the emergency, with courage stirred alike by his indignation at the
arrogance of Nahash (cf. Judg, 14:19) and his wish to save the
people, of whom he had the right to think as his own. Vs. 7,
"cut them in pieces": Such a startling summons would instantly
rouse the people. It resembles the Scottish "fiery cross" by
which the clans were assembled. In the call Saul linked Samuel's
name with his own. Vs. 8, "in Bezek"†: a town west of the
Jordan (see map), well situated as a point of departure for Jabesh-
gilead. "Children of Israel . . . . men of Judah": The narrative
was written after the separation of the land into two kingdoms,

7 And he took a yoke of oxen, and cut them in pieces, and sent them throughout all the borders of Israel by the hand of messengers, saying, Whosoever cometh not forth after Saul and after Samuel, so shall it be done unto his oxen. And the dread of the Lord fell on the people, and they came out as one

OXEN PLOUGHING

8 man. And he numbered them in Bezek: and the children of Israel were three hundred thousand, and 9 the men of Judah thirty thousand. And they said unto the messengers that came, Thus shall ye say unto the men of Jabesh-gilead, To-morrow, by the time the sun is hot, ye shall have deliverance. And the messengers came and told the men of Jabesh; 10 and they were glad. Therefore the men of Jabesh

said, To-morrow we will come out unto you, and ye
shall do with us all that seemeth good unto you.
And it was so on the morrow, that Saul put the people 11
in three companies; and they came into the midst
of the camp in the morning watch, and smote the
Ammonites until the heat of the day: and it came to
pass, that they which remained were scattered, so
that two of them were not left together. And the 12
people said unto Samuel, Who is he that said, Shall
Saul reign over us? bring the men, that we may
put them to death. And Saul said, There shall not 13
a man be put to death this day: for to-day the Lord
hath wrought deliverance in Israel.

Then said Samuel to the people, Come and let us 14
go to Gilgal, and renew the kingdom there. And 15
all the people went to Gilgal; and there they made
Saul king before the Lord in Gilgal; and there they
sacrificed sacrifices of peace offerings before the
Lord; and there Saul and all the men of Israel
rejoiced greatly.

Israel in the north and Judah in the south. The numbers of the
soldiers are of course much too great. The tendency to overstate
the size of armies is frequently met in ancient records, and the
Old Testament is no exception. Barak's army numbered 10,000
(Judg. 4:10). Vs. 11, "morning watch": between 2 A. M. and
daylight (cf. Exod. 14:24), the middle watch being from 10 P. M.
till 2 A. M. (cf. Judg. 7:19). Vs. 12, "said unto Samuel": No
mention is made of the prophet's going with the army to the relief
of the city, and the reference here to the refusal of certain men to
acknowledge Saul, an incident of the other document, makes it

probable that vss. 12, 14 were added by the compiler who fitted the two narratives together. "To Gilgal"†: the sanctuary which seems to have shared honors with Mizpah, Bethel, and Shiloh. "Renew the kingdom": This shows again the purpose of the compiler to harmonize the two accounts. Vs. 15, "made Saul king": Here the narrative of this source is completed. Saul, secretly anointed before, has showed that he possessed kingly qualities, and the people take him to Gilgal and make him their king.

QUESTIONS

(1) Having read the Scripture story carefully once or twice, look up on the map and in your dictionary the places mentioned; next, having read the Explanatory Notes with the Scripture passage before you, tell the story in your own words. Then answer the following questions:

(2)* Who were the Ammonites? (3) Of what nation were the people of Jabesh-gilead? (4) Had these peoples previously been friendly or unfriendly? (5) Does it appear that the Ammonites had any distinct cause of war against Jabesh-gilead? (6)* What was the meaning of Saul's symbolic message to the people of Israel? (7) What do you think of the conduct of the Ammonites in this matter? (8) What do you think of the conduct of the men of Jabesh-gilead as stated in vs. 1? (9)* What qualities does Saul show on this occasion? Try to state these distinctly. How far do they seem to you admirable qualities? Was he fighting for himself or for others? (10) What was the result to Saul of his conduct in this matter?

(11) Is it ever right to defend one who is attacked by another? Would you think it right or wrong to defend a sister or younger brother against attack? (12) Is it ever right to defend one's self from an attack? (13)* Is war between nations ever right? If so, when? (14) Read the words of Jesus in Matt. 5:38–41: If we should follow this teaching of Jesus and the spirit of his life what would always

be our attitude toward those who have wronged or who threaten to wrong us or others? (15) Read Matt. 5:43-45, and Luke 10:27, 28, and consider whether if we follow this teaching of Jesus we should be able to live at peace with all men. Would obedience to this teaching sometimes call for resistance to wrong? (16)* If you have to choose between doing wrong or suffering wrong, which is better?

RUINS OF A GATE

SECTION XXIV

12 And Samuel said unto all Israel, Behold, I have hearkened unto your voice in all that ye said unto me, 2 and have made a king over you. And now, behold, the king walketh before you: and I am old and gray-headed; and behold, my sons are with you: and I have walked before you from my youth unto this 3 day. Here I am: witness against me before the Lord and before his anointed: whose ox have I taken? or whose ass have I taken? or whom have I defrauded? whom have I oppressed? or of whose hand have I taken a ¹ransom to blind mine eyes

¹ Or, *bribe*

EXPLANATORY NOTES

This section follows immediately Section XXII in the original arrangement of the material, the intervening section coming from a different source. See on Section XXIII. Section XXII, following the record of chap. 8, states that in the assembly at Mizpah, which Samuel reluctantly called to choose a king, the will of the nation was accomplished in the selection of Saul by lot. Throughout this document (chaps. 8, 10: 17–27, and 12) the attitude of Samuel is one of opposition to the change of government from his rule as prophet of God to a kingship, and of regret at the necessity of selecting a king. His tone in the present section is one of reproval and anxiety. Notice that in vss. 3–5 Samuel speaks to the people of his own conduct toward them. Vs. 3, "his anointed": the anointed king, who had been selected by the sacred lot. "Ox . . . . ass": the most common property

therewith? and I will restore it to you. And they 4
said, Thou hast not defrauded us, nor oppressed us,
neither hast thou taken aught of any man's hand.
And he said unto them, The Lord is witness against 5
you, and his anointed is witness this day, that ye
have not found aught in my hand. And they said,
He is witness.

And Samuel said unto the people, It is the Lord 6
that appointed Moses and Aaron, and that brought
your fathers up out of the land of Egypt. Now 7
therefore stand still, that I may plead with you before the Lord concerning all the righteous acts of
the Lord, which he did to you and to your fathers.
When Jacob was come into Egypt, and your fathers 8
cried unto the Lord, then the Lord sent Moses and
Aaron, who brought forth your fathers out of Egypt,

---

of an agricultural people. "Blind mine eyes": The sin most
frequently denounced in the judges of Israel was the acceptance
of bribes to secure favorable judgment.

Vs. 6, With this verse Samuel begins a sketch of the history of
Israel from the days of Moses down to his own time, which he
reaches in vss. 11, 12. "Moses† and Aaron"†: the two brothers
who became the leaders of the nation in the period of the Exodus
from Egypt. Vs. 7, "may plead with you": present my case
against you. Vs. 8, "Jacob† . . . . into Egypt": The migration
of Jacob and his clan to Egypt led to the events of the Exodus,
after the people had endured the hardships of subjection for two
centuries or more. "This place": the land of Canaan, or Palestine as it was later called. Vs. 9, "sold them": turned them over,
delivered them up. "Sisera": one of the oppressors of Israel
in the days of the judges (Judg., chaps. 4, 5). "Philistines"†:

9 and made them to dwell in this place. But they forgat the Lord their God, and he sold them into the hand of Sisera, captain of the host of Hazor, and into the hand of the Philistines, and into the hand of the king of Moab, and they fought against them. 10 And they cried unto the Lord, and said, We have sinned, because we have forsaken the Lord, and have served the Baalim and the Ashtaroth: but now deliver us out of the hand of our enemies, and we 11 will serve thee. And the Lord sent Jerubbaal, and 2Bedan, and Jephthah, and Samuel, and delivered you out of the hand of your enemies on every side, 12 and ye dwelled in safety. And when ye saw that Nahash the king of the children of Ammon came against you, ye said unto me, Nay, but a king shall reign over us: when the Lord your God was your king.

2 Some ancient authorities read, *Barak*

---

the hereditary enemies of Israel from the occupation of Canaan till the exile. The events of the times of Samson are probably referred to (Judg., chaps. 13–16). "King of Moab"†: the ruler of the people east of the Dead Sea, who oppressed Israel eighteen years (Judg. 3:12–30). "The Baalim† and the Ashtaroth"†: the idols whose worship was practiced by the heathen people living in Canaan. "Jerubbaal† and Bedan† and Jephthah"†: three of the judges who saved Israel at different times in the unsettled period before the days of Samuel. The second name is probably a mistake; "Barak" is the reading in several of the versions, and this is apparently correct. "And Samuel": The prophet includes himself among the men who had brought salvation to the people. This was no mere boasting, but a solemn fact which gave him the right to speak. Vs. 12, "Nahash the king": see the narrative given in Section XXIII. "God was your king":

Now therefore behold the king whom ye have 13
chosen, and whom ye have asked for: and, behold,
the Lord hath set a king over you. If ye will 14
fear the Lord, and serve him, and hearken unto his
voice, and not rebel against the commandment of
the Lord,[3] and both ye and also the king that reigneth
over you be followers of the Lord your God, well: but 15
if ye will not hearken unto the voice of the Lord,
but rebel against the commandment of the Lord, then
shall the hand of the Lord be against you, as it was
against your fathers. Now therefore stand still 16
and see this great thing, which the Lord will do before
your eyes. Is it not wheat harvest to-day? I will 17
call unto the Lord, that he may send thunder and
rain; and ye shall know and see that your wickedness is great, which ye have done in the sight of the
Lord in asking you a king. So Samuel called unto the 18
Lord; and the Lord sent thunder and rain that day:
and all the people greatly feared the Lord and Samuel.

[3] Or, *then
shall both ye
. . . . the Lord
your God; but
etc.*

This was Samuel's chief cause for resentment; it was less his
own rejection as ruler than that of Jehovah, the real king of
Israel.

Vss. 13–18 contain Samuel's appeal to the people to fear and
serve Jehovah, enforced by a sign from heaven. Vs. 15, "against
your fathers": past distresses such as those from which the
judges had delivered their fathers should be warning examples.
Vs. 16, "this great thing": The prophet proposes to show then
a sign, a thunderstorm in midsummer, a most unusual thing
in Palestine. Such a marvel would be the token of God's displeasure that they should wish a king. "Pray for thy servants":

19   And all the people said unto Samuel, Pray for thy
      servants unto the Lord thy God, that we die not:
      for we have added unto all our sins this evil, to ask
20 us a king.   And Samuel said unto the people, Fear
      not: ye have indeed done all this evil: yet turn not
      aside from following the Lord; but serve the Lord
21 with all your heart; [4]and turn ye not aside: for then
      should ye go after vain things which cannot profit
22 nor deliver, for they are vain.   For the Lord will not
      forsake his people for his great name's sake: because
      it hath pleased the Lord to make you a people unto
23 himself.   Moreover as for me, God forbid that I
      should sin against the Lord in ceasing to pray for
      you: but I will instruct you in the good and the
24 right way.   Only fear the Lord and serve him in
      truth with all your heart: for consider how great
25 things he hath done for you.   But if ye shall still do
      wickedly ye shall be consumed, both ye and your
      king.

[4] The Sept. has, *and turn ye not aside after the vanities which,* etc.

The reproof is represented as effective, the sign convincing.   In
terror the people begged for forgiveness, confessing their sin.

Vss. 19–25 relate the people's request that Samuel pray for
them and his comforting reply.   Vs. 21, "vain things": idols
like those which the nations around them worshiped.   The
entire section is a striking statement of Samuel's disinterested and
life-long service in behalf of the people, his sorrow at their desire
for innovation, and his apprehension lest they further weary God
with their complaints, forsake him and perish.

QUESTIONS

(1) What is the subject of this section?   (2)* Where was
this address delivered?   See Section XXII.   (3) At what

time in his life did Samuel deliver this address? (4) Is the appointment of a king spoken of in this address with approval or disapproval? In what previous section is it spoken of in the same way? (5) What is the subject of vss. 3–5? (6)* What does Samuel claim concerning his own conduct as judge? (7) What was the testimony of the people on this point? (8) What is the subject of vss. 6–12? (9) What was Samuel's purpose in recounting these facts? (10)* Name the various deliverers of Israel of whom he speaks in these verses. (11) What is the subject of vss. 13–18? (12) What did Samuel wish to accomplish by this part of his address? (13) What does vs. 19 indicate as to the success of Samuel's address? (14) What is the subject of vss. 20–25, and what was the purpose of these verses?

(15) What does the modern word "statesman" mean? (16)* What is the real work of a statesman? (17) Name some of the great statesmen of the United States living and dead. (18) Does a statesman always hold office? (19) Can Samuel properly be called a statesman? (20) Is a statesman the same as a prophet? Have they anything in common? (21) Who in modern times is most like the prophet of ancient times, the preacher or the statesman? (22) If you regard Samuel as a statesman what do you think of his career as such? (23) Looking at Samuel's address as a statesman's oration, what do you think of it? Characterize it as respects its plan, its dignity, its impressiveness, its persuasiveness. (24) From what source did Samuel draw most of the material for this speech? (25) Could a man who knew nothing of the history of his own or other nations be a great statesman? (26)* What else besides such knowledge must one have to be a statesman?

(27) What seems to you the saddest fact about Samuel's life? (28) How far was that life successful, how far a failure? (29) If a man goes into politics today, what should be his purpose? Would Samuel be a good pattern for such a man?

Can you think of any others whom we might take as an example? (30) If a man becomes a preacher today, what ought to be his aim? (31) Which seems to you to afford the best opportunities for a large and useful life, preaching, teaching, business, or politics?

(32) Samuel maintains that God was constantly active in Israel's history, punishing the sin of the nation and delivering them when they repented and turned to him. * How far is this true of other nations than Israel? (33) Does sin bring disaster to a nation, and does righteousness bring peace and blessing? or is God always on the side of the biggest battalions? Look up Prov. 14:34, and Ps. 144:15, and consider whether you think that applies to modern nations, to the United States, to England, to China, to Japan?

SECTION XXV

SAUL'S SACRIFICE, I SAM. 13:1–15a

Saul was ¹thirty years old when he began to reign; **13** and he reigned two years over Israel. And Saul **2** chose him three thousand men of Israel; whereof two thousand were with Saul in Michmash and in the mount of Beth-el, and a thousand were with Jonathan in ²Gibeah of Benjamin: and the rest of

---

EXPLANATORY NOTES

This section is manifestly a part of the narrative found in 9:1—10:16, and chap. 11, the early Judean account of Saul's life. It therefore follows Section XXIII, showing how after Saul's first victory over the Ammonites he proceeded to break the yoke of the Philistines under which the Hebrews groaned. But a portion of the narrative (vss. 4–15a, especially vss. 7a–15a,) appears to interrupt the account and introduce a strange and unnecessary feature. Can the rejection of Saul have come thus early in his reign? Moreover, does not the offense of Saul seem small in comparison with the denunciation of the prophet? It seems probable that the scene is introduced from a later part of Saul's career, when his disregard of the prophet's commands had become too marked to be endured. As inserted here it is intended to form the sequel to 10:8, which, as was noted in Section XXI, appears out of place. Vs. 1, "thirty years old": As noted in the margin, the text really reads "Saul was [   ] years old when he began to reign, and he reigned [   ] and two years." Several of the versions reject the verse entirely, others supply the conjecture "thirty." But the following verse shows that such a reading is wrong, for there Jonathan his son is old enough to command a section of the army. Vs. 2, "chose him three thousand men": Here at the opening of his reign Saul selected a body of men to serve against

3 the people he sent every man to his tent.   And Jonathan smote the garrison of the Philistines that was
in Geba, and the Philistines heard of it.   And Saul
blew the trumpet throughout all the land, saying,
4 Let the Hebrews hear.   And all Israel heard say that
Saul had smitten the garrison of the Philistines, and
that Israel also was had in abomination with the
Philistines.

And the people were gathered together after Saul

---

the Philistines.   "With Saul in Michmash"†: a rock commanding the northern side of the gorge which ran down from the
highlands to the Jordan valley, a few miles north of Jerusalem.
"Bethel"†: well adapted to purposes of defense, as being high,
and not far from the rest of the army.   "With Jonathan† in
Gibeah": Perhaps the marginal reading "Geba"† is to be preferred.   Geba was a cliff or wall of rock on the south side of the
gorge opposite Michmash.   Gibeah of Benjamin, the home of
Saul, was three or four miles southwest.   "Every man to his
tent": The events just recorded happened at the opening of Saul's
reign.   He kept a few troops for garrison duty, and dismissed the
rest.   Vs. 3, "smote the garrison": the event that started hos-
tilities.   If the proper reading in vs. 2 is "Gibeah," then Jonathan
crossed to Geba, and struck the blow.   If "Geba" is preferred,
then this event was the cause of his having his force at the town
where the Philistines had been.   "Saul blew the trumpet": The
deed of Jonathan in attacking the residents or garrison at Geba
would be sure to rouse the Philistines to revenge.   Saul's forces
must be summoned at once.   Vs. 4, "had in abomination": had
stirred up the anger of the Philistines.

"After Saul to Gilgal": at this point begins the story which
interrupts the sequence of the narrative, and seems out of harmony
with the remaining facts.   Saul would hardly take his forces so
far north as upper Gilgal at such a crisis, much less would he

to Gilgal.   And the Philistines assembled themselves 5
together to fight with Israel, thirty thousand chariots,
and six thousand horsemen, and people as the sand
which is on the sea shore in multitude: and they
came up, and pitched in Michmash, eastward of
Beth-aven.   When the men of Israel saw that they 6
were in a strait (for the people were distressed),
then the people did hide themselves in caves, and
in thickets, and in rocks, and in ³holds, and in ⁴pits.
Now some of the Hebrews had gone over Jordan 7

³ Or, *holes*
⁴ Or, *cisterns*

---

abandon the highlands by retreating to the Gilgal in the Jordan
valley.   Vs. 5, "thirty thousand chariots": Chariots corresponded
to the heavy artillery of modern armies; the numbers are of
course inconceivable.   In fact it would be difficult to use chariots
at all in the rough country north of Jerusalem.   "Beth-aven"†:
not far from Bethel.   Vs. 6, "did hide themselves": The terror of
the Hebrews here described lends color to the suggestion that this
account refers to events late in the reign of Saul, when his kingdom was tottering to its fall.   At first, especially just after the
successful campaign of Jabesh-gilead, matters were much more
hopeful.   "Gad† and Gilead"†: regions east of the Jordan,
where there would be less danger of pursuit by their foes.   Vs. 8,
"Samuel came not": It is apparent that this interpolated section
(vss. 4*b*–15*a*) is intended to follow 10:8 as its sequel and to explain
the rejection of Saul as king.   But its misplacement at the opening of Saul's reign deprives it of its significance as one of the cul-
minating acts of disobedience in a reign which grew increasingly
negligent of the prophet's advice and commands.   Here the conduct of Saul in not waiting for Samuel after the expiration of the
time set by the prophet seems natural and necessary, considering
the hourly loss of soldiers through desertion.   Vs. 9, "he offered
the burnt offering": It appears that his sin as viewed by Samuel
did not consist in offering the sacrifice himself, for David did the

to the land of Gad and Gilead; but as for Saul, he
was yet in Gilgal, and all the people followed him
trembling.

8 And he tarried seven days, according to the set
time that Samuel had appointed: but Samuel came
not to Gilgal; and the people were scattered from

THE RIVER JORDAN

9 him. And Saul said, Bring hither the burnt offering
to me, and the peace offerings. And he offered the
10 burnt offering. And it came to pass that, as soon as
he had made an end of offering the burnt offering,
behold, Samuel came; and Saul went out to meet him
11 that he might salute him. And Samuel said, What
hast thou done? And Saul said, Because I saw that
the people were scattered from me, and that thou

camest not within the days appointed, and that the Philistines assembled themselves together at Michmash; therefore said I, Now will the Philistines come 12 down upon me to Gilgal, and I have not intreated the favour of the Lord: I forced myself therefore, and offered the burnt offering. And Samuel said to 13 Saul, Thou hast done foolishly: thou hast not kept the commandment of the Lord thy God, which he commanded thee: for now would the Lord have established thy kingdom upon Israel for ever. But 14 now thy kingdom shall not continue: the Lord hath sought him a man after his own heart, and the Lord hath appointed him to be prince over his people, because thou hast not kept that which the Lord commanded thee.

And Samuel arose, and gat him up from Gilgal 15 unto Gibeah of Benjamin.

---

same, but in failing to wait till Samuel's arrival. Vs. 12, "have not entreated": the act of solemn consecration before battle. Vs. 14, "thy kingdom shall not continue": That Samuel had ample cause to condemn Saul's conduct in the later years of his reign seems apparent. But unless the present instance was intended to be a mere arbitrary test of exact obedience, the right rather lies with Saul. "After his own heart": These words apply to David, and indicate that already he had been selected, although the reign of Saul continued many years. David was a man "after God's own heart," not in the sense of perfection of character, either then or later in his life, but because of his devotion to the divine purpose to be realized through the nation. The special object of this section is to teach the necessity of obedience; and no doubt in its original setting this part of the narrative gained impressiveness from other features in the life of Saul not included in our records.

QUESTIONS

(1)* What difficulties are found in vs. 1? (2) How large a force did Saul select as a standing army? (3) Where were these forces placed? What did he do with the rest? (4) What exploit was performed by Jonathan? What was its effect upon the Philistines? (5) What did Saul do? Why? (6) Why is it said in vs. 2 that Jonathan smote the garrison, and in vs. 3. that Saul did it? (7) What was the feeling of the Philistines toward Israel as the result of these things?

(8)* What are some of the reasons for regarding 4–15a as a later insertion? What is the scene of these verses? (9) Is there reason to believe that the numbers in vs. 5 are exaggerated? (10) Where did the Philistines encamp? (11) How did this raid of the Philistines affect the Hebrews? What did they do? (12) Does not this terror seem strange after Saul's recent victory over Ammon (11)? (13)* Why did Saul wait seven days for Samuel? (14) How did he finally prepare for battle? (15)* Why did Samuel disapprove of Saul's conduct? (16) What startling announcement did Samuel make to Saul? (17)* Did Saul's conduct on this occasion alone justify such a reproof? (18) May there have been, however, other and more serious acts of wrong-doing, of which this was but the climax? (19)* Who was the "man after God's heart"? (20) Had he been chosen king yet? (21) If not, why did Samuel say, "The Lord hath appointed him"? (22) Setting aside the question whether Saul's conduct on this occasion was sufficient reason for deposing him from the kingship, what is true in general about so-called small faults? May they ruin an otherwise promising life? Can you mention examples? (23) Are there times when seemingly small errors involve grave consequences? (24) Can you state a principle of life that would be always safe to follow?

SECTION XXVI

PHILISTINE OPPRESSION, I SAM. 13:15b-23

And Saul numbered the people that were present
with him, about six hundred men. And Saul, and 16
Jonathan his son, and the people that were present
with them, abode in Geba of Benjamin: but the
Philistines encamped in Michmash. And the 17
spoilers came out of the camp of the Philistines in
three companies: one company turned unto the
way that leadeth to Ophrah, unto the land of Shual:

EXPLANATORY NOTES

This section continues the narrative of 13:1–4a. It describes
the policy of the Philistines in reducing the land by plundering,
and adds a note describing a supposed disarming of the people by
their oppressors, vss. 19–22, which, however, must describe conditions very local to the region of the Philistine garrison. The
narrative as a whole continues the story of Saul's life as begun in
9:1—10:16. Vs. 15, "about six hundred men": This number is
again mentioned in 14:2. "Abode in Geba": In the next chapter
(14:2) Saul is in Gibeah, but the true reading there is probably
"Geba." "Encamped in Michmash": The Philistines had
gathered in sufficient force to compel Saul to leave the place (cf.
13:2). Vs. 17, "spoilers came out": One of the best means of
subduing a country is to devastate it and thus reduce its people
to poverty; on this principle the Philistines were proceeding. "To
Ophra": a place northeast of Bethel, and almost directly north of
Michmash; the land of Shual is not otherwise known. Vs. 18,
"the way to Beth-horon"†: the famous town where Joshua
defeated the Canaanites, east of Michmash. "Toward the wilderness:" This otherwise unknown valley ran from the central ridge
eastward toward the Jordan. Vs. 19, "no smith": This drastic

18 and another company turned the way to Beth-horon:
and another company turned the way of the border
that looketh down upon the valley of Zeboim toward
the wilderness.

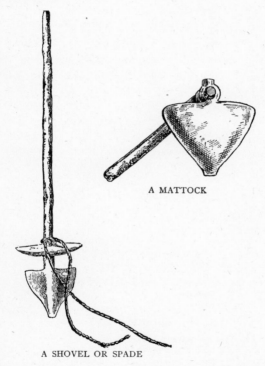

A MATTOCK

A SHOVEL OR SPADE

19 Now there was no smith found throughout all the
land of Israel: for the Philistines said, Lest the
20 Hebrews make them swords or spears: but all the

Israelites went down to the Philistines, to sharpen
every man his share, and his coulter, and his axe,
and his mattock, yet they had a file for the 21
mattocks, and for the coulters, and for the forks,
and for the axes; and to set the goads.   So it came 22
to pass in the day of battle, that there was neither
sword nor spear found in the hand of any of the people that were with Saul and Jonathan: but with
Saul and with Jonathan his son was there found.
And the garrison of the Philistines went out unto the 23
pass of Michmash.

---

method could hardly have been enforced over more than a limited
territory.   Vs. 20, "went down to the Philistines":   The central
ridge of Palestine is much higher than the sea plain on which the
Philistines lived.   Vs. 21, "had a file":   The text of this verse is
very uncertain; this translation is merely a conjecture.   Vs. 22,
"neither sword nor spear":   It seems difficult to understand this
of the early days of Saul's reign, when he chose his forces to watch
the land.   Vs. 23, "unto the pass of Michmash":   This goes back
to describe again the occupation of the crag of Michmash (vs. 16)
after speaking of the raiders.   The section (especially with the
addition of vss. 19–22) emphasizes the difficulty of the Israelite
position, and prepares us to appreciate the providential nature
of the approaching deliverance.

QUESTIONS

(1) How many soldiers did Saul have?   (2) Was he losing
or gaining troops?   (3)* What was the position of the two
armies?   (4) What did the Philistines do in order to reduce
the country?   Do you think it right to destroy trees, crops,
etc., in order to gain advantage over the people who live in the
land?   Are such methods common in war?   As the world

grows more enlightened do you think such ways of injuring an enemy will be abandoned? (5) What directions did the three bands of raiders take? (6)* Why were there no black-smiths? (7) Was "all the land of Israel" a very large region at this time? (8) Where did the Hebrews go to sharpen tools? (9)* What implements needed sharpening? (10) What was the result of this oppressive rule (cf. Judg. 5:8)? (11) How did Saul and Jonathan differ from the rest of the nation? (12)* What place was taken by the Philistine garrison? (13) Would it not be counted a very great deliverance which could rescue Israel from such an unhappy condition? (14) Can you think of other groups of people who have been similarly mis-treated by oppressors? (15) Were the colonies in the time of the Revolution an example? The slaves before the war? Cuba under Spanish rule? (16) What can be done in such a case?

SECTION XXVII

JONATHAN'S EXPLOIT, I SAM. 14:1–16

Now it fell upon a day, that Jonathan the son of 14
Saul said unto the young man that bare his armour,
Come and let us go over to the Philistines' garrison,
that is on yonder side. But he told not his father.
And Saul abode in the uttermost part of Gibeah 2
under the pomegranate tree which is in Migron: and
the people that were with him were about six hundred
men; and Ahijah, the son of Ahitub, Ichabod's 3
brother, the son of Phinehas, the son of Eli, the priest
of the Lord in Shiloh, wearing an ephod. And the

EXPLANATORY NOTES

The section continues the Judean story of Saul's life. Jonathan, the son of Saul, impatient of inactivity, undertakes a hazard-
ous exploit without his father's knowledge and achieves a signal
victory. Vs. 1, "let us go over": The two camps were on opposite sides of the valley, on high ground. Vs. 2, "in Gibeah":
Probably "Geba"† is the better reading. Geba and Michmash
were the two opposing cliffs. "Under the pomegranate": probably a well-known tree, deemed sacred, as trees often were. In
Section XXII Saul sits under a tamarisk. "In Migron": probably "the threshing-floor." Such heights were used for that
purpose. Vs. 3, Ichabod's† brother": This recalls the birth
of Ichabod (4:21) on the day that his father and mother both
died. "The priest of the Lord in Shiloh"†: This refers to Eli†,
not Ahijah, as Shiloh was destroyed at the time the ark was taken
(4:10, 11). "Wearing an ephod"†: This refers to Ahijah; he
was priest at the time. The word translated "wearing" means

4 people knew not that Jonathan was gone. And between the passes, by which Jonathan sought to go over unto the Philistines' garrison, there was a rocky crag on the one side, and a rocky crag on the other side: and the name of the one was Bozez, and the
5 name of the other Seneh. The one crag rose up on the north in front of Michmash, and the other on the
6 south in front of Geba. And Jonathan said to the young man that bare his armour, Come and let us go over unto the garrison of these uncircumcised: it may be that the Lord will work for us: for there is no restraint to the Lord to save by many or by few.
7 And his armourbearer said unto him, Do all that is in thine heart; turn thee, behold I am with thee
8 according to thy heart. Then said Jonathan, Behold, we will pass over unto the men, and we will
9 discover ourselves unto them. If they say thus unto us, Tarry until we come to you; then we will stand
10 still in our place, and will not go up unto them. But

---

also "carrying." If the ephod was an image, as seems probable, the latter is the better translation. Vs. 4, "a rocky crag": The paths on either side that led down from the heights into the valley left between them a crag. "Bozez . . . . Seneh": "Shining" and "thorny" are perhaps the meanings of the two words. Vs. 6, "these uncircumcised": applied only to the Philistines by the Hebrews, as a term of reproach. "No restraint": Mere numbers count for nothing with God. Vs. 9, "tarry until we come": Jonathan proposed to test the probability of success by an omen or sign (cf. Gen. 24:14). If the Philistines started to come down, Jonathan and his companion would understand that it was unwise if they say thus, Come up unto us; then we will go up: for the Lord hath delivered them into our hand: and this shall be the sign unto us. And both of 11 them discovered themselves unto the garrison of the Philistines: and the Philistines said, Behold, the Hebrews come forth out of the holes where they had hid themselves. And the men of the garrison 12 answered Jonathan and his armourbearer, and said, Come up to us and we will shew you a thing. And Jonathan said unto his armourbearer, Come up after me: for the Lord hath delivered them into the hand of Israel. And Jonathan climbed up upon his 13 hands and upon his feet, and his armourbearer after him: and they fell before Jonathan; and his armourbearer slew them after him. And that first slaughter, 14 which Jonathan and his armourbearer made, was ¹ Or, *half an* about twenty men, within as it were ¹half a furrow's *acre of land* length in an acre of land. And there was a trembling 15 in the camp, in the field, and among all the people; the garrison, and the spoilers, they also trembled: and the earth quaked; so there was an exceeding great trembling. And the watchmen of Saul in 16 Gibeah of Benjamin looked; and behold, the multitude melted away, and they went hither and thither.

---

to make the attempt they had in mind. Vs. 11, "out of the holes": The terror felt for the Philistines had caused many to hide in this manner (13:6). Vs. 12, "show you a thing": A taunting, derisive challenge. Vs. 13, "climbed up": The path was very steep. "They fell before Jonathan": Probably there were only a few of the

Philistines out at the edge of the rock, and they were panic-stricken, thinking there must be other Hebrews behind the two. Vs. 14, "that first slaughter": the one before the panic became general. Vs. 15, "in the field": Some of the Philistines were yet in the camp in the early morning; others had gone out on raids. "Earth quaked": This would indicate the author's belief that there was divine assistance to the Hebrew warriors. In the terror of the moment the Philistine force was thrown into confusion.

QUESTIONS

(1) Whom did Jonathan take into his confidence? (2) What did he propose? Was this merely the ambition of youth, or did he believe it was wrong to remain inactive? (3) Was not this plan very dangerous? Was it wise to undertake it? (4)* If it had failed, what would have been thought of it? How can one decide when to take such a risk in the enterprises of life, and when to remain inactive? Is prayer one of the means of deciding such questions? (5) How were the two camps located? (6) Why did not Jonathan tell his father of his purpose? (7) Where was Saul? (8) Who were with him? (9)* Why was he thus inactive? (10) Who was priest? (11) What was the symbol of the priesthood? (12) What is an ephod? (13) Who was Ichabod? (14)* What had happened at Shiloh? (15) Who knew of Jonathan's departure? (16)* Describe the position of the two camps and the ground between them. (17) What were the names of the two rocks? How were they located? (18) What did Jonathan say to his armor-bearer? (19) What was the young man's reply? (20)* What qualities does it show? Do you think such loyalty and courage admirable? (21) What test did Jonathan propose? (22) Was this right? (23)* Could he be sure such a test would work properly? (24) Would it be safe to employ it today? (25) What did the Philistines think when they saw the two men? (26) What was it that determined Jonathan to go up? (27) Was it hard

or easy climbing? (28) What happened when they reached the top? (29)* How do you account for this strange victory? (30) What do you think is the best lesson to be drawn from this section? (31) If the methods of seeking and obtaining divine guidance, illustrated in this section are not such as we should follow today, what better ways are available for us? Cf. for example Jas. 1:5.

AN ANCIENT ALTAR

SECTION XXVIII

SAUL'S DEFEAT OF THE PHILISTINES, I SAM. 14:17-35

17 Then said Saul unto the people that were with him, Number now, and see who is gone from us. And when they had numbered, behold, Jonathan and his
18 armourbearer were not there. And Saul said unto Ahijah, ¹Bring hither the ark of God. For the ark of God was there at that time with the children of
19 Israel. And it came to pass, while Saul talked unto the priest, that the tumult that was in the camp of the Philistines went on and increased: and Saul said
20 unto the priest, Withdraw thine hand. And Saul and all the people that were with him were gathered

¹ The Sept. has, *Bring hither the ephod. For he wore the ephod at that time before Israel*

EXPLANATORY NOTES

The narrative of the early Judean story of Saul is continued in this section. Vs. 17, "Number now": search and see who is absent. The result was the discovery that the only ones who had left Saul's camp were Jonathan and his assistant. Vs. 18, "bring hither the ark"†: The better reading is "ephod"† (see margin). They would be unlikely to take the ark into battle after the events of I Sam., chap. 4. The ephod was used by the priest Ahijah in learning the will of God. Vs. 19, "tumult . . . . increased": On the opposite height Saul could see the growing confusion among the Philistines. "Withdraw thine hand": cease the inquiry. Saul became impatient for action. Vs. 20, "very great discomfiture": Saul and his force rushed down the hill and across the valley to the camp of their enemies on the other hill, where they found everything in confusion, and the Philistines

125

together, and came to the battle: and, behold, every man's sword was against his fellow, and there was a very great discomfiture. Now the Hebrews that 21 were with the Philistines as beforetime, which went up with them ²into the camp from the country round about; even they also turned to be with the Israelites that were with Saul and Jonathan. Likewise all the 22 men of Israel which had hid themselves in the hill country of Ephraim, when they heard that the Philistines fled, even they also followed hard after them in the battle. So the Lord saved Israel that day: and 23 the battle passed over by Beth-aven. And the men 24 of Israel were distressed that day: but Saul adjured the people, saying, Cursed be the man that eateth any food until it be evening, and I be avenged on mine enemies. So none of the people tasted food. And all the people came into the forest; and there 25 was honey upon the ground. And when the people 26 were come unto the forest, behold, the honey dropped: but no man put his hand to his mouth;

² Or, *in the camp round about*

---

bringing about their own defeat (cf. Judg. 7:22). Vs. 21, "turned to be with the Israelites:" The Philistines had forced many of the Hebrews to fight in their army; these now deserted to their brethren when the occasion offered. Vs. 22, "followed hard after them": Many of the Israelites had hid themselves for fear of the Philistines (13:6, 7); these now came out and joined in the pursuit of their enemies (cf. Judg. 7:23). Vs. 23, "by Beth-aven": Some read "Beth-horon," a town on the western border of the highland region. Vs. 24, "Cursed be the man": There were two reasons for Saul's prohibition, (1) that the people might lose

27 for the people feared the oath. But Jonathan heard not when his father charged the people with the oath: wherefore he put forth the end of the rod that was in his hand, and dipped it in the honeycomb, and put his hand to his mouth; and his eyes

28 were enlightened. Then answered one of the people, and said, Thy father straitly charged the people with an oath, saying, Cursed be the man that eateth food this day. And the people were faint.

29 Then said Jonathan, My father hath troubled the land: see, I pray you, how mine eyes have been enlightened, because I tasted a little of this honey.

30 How much more, if haply the people had eaten freely to-day of the spoil of their enemies which they found? [3]for now hath there been no great slaughter among

31 the Philistines. And they smote of the Philistines that day from Michmash to Aijalon: and the people

32 were very faint. And the people flew upon the spoil, and took sheep, and oxen, and calves, and slew them on the ground: and the people did eat them with the

[3] Or, *for had there not been now a much greater slaughter*, etc.?

---

no time in the pursuit of their foes, (2) that their abstinence might be accepted of God as a sacrifice, and so bring complete victory. Vs. 26, "the people feared the oath": Wild honey was found by the Hebrews in their pursuit, but they dared not eat it because of the curse. Vs. 27, "his eyes were enlightened": Jonathan, knowing nothing of his father's prohibition, took some of the honey as he went and gained new strength. Vs. 29, "troubled the land": Jonathan thought his father's curse unnecessary and harmful. The people were suffering and faint, and a little food would have helped them gain a more complete victory. Vs.

blood. Then they told Saul, saying, Behold, the 33
people sin against the Lord in that they eat with the
blood. And he said, Ye have dealt treacherously :
roll a great stone unto me this day. And Saul said, 34
Disperse yourselves among the people, and say unto
them, Bring me hither every man his ox, and every
man his sheep, and slay them here and eat; and sin
not against the Lord in eating with the blood. And
all the people brought every man his ox with him
that night, and slew them there. And Saul built an 35
altar unto the Lord: the same was the first altar
that he built unto the Lord.

31, "from Michmash† to Aijalon"† : from the center of the
highland district down to the lower region west, in the direction
of Philistia. Vs. 32, "with the blood": So hungry were the
people that when the spoil of the enemy fell into their hands, they
did not wait for the sacrificial killing. Vs. 33, "dealt treacherously": disregarded the customs prescribed. "Roll a great
stone": such a stone as would serve as an altar where the animals
could be slain. Vs. 35, "the first altar": The author implies
that Saul built other altars later, but no mention is made of them.

QUESTIONS

(1)* Where was Saul at the opening of this section ? (2)
Why did he conjecture that anyone had left his army ? Or
was he merely anxious to know how strong his forces were ?
(3) Who were found to be missing ? (4) Whom did Saul
summon ? (5)* What was the ephod used for ? (6) Why
did not Saul wait for the answer from the priest ? Was it
because of mere impatience or did he think valuable time
was being lost ? Is this a further indication of Saul's impatient,
head-strong character ? (7) What did Saul and the people

do? (8)* What condition did they find among the Philistines?
(9) What new allies did the Hebrews receive? (10)* What
did those in hiding do? How far did the battle line extend?
(11) What caused the distress of the Hebrews that day?
(12)* What was Saul's motive in forbidding the people to
eat? (13) Was it a wise or unwise measure? (14) What
did they find in the forest? Why did they not eat the honey?
(15) What exception was there to this abstinence? (16)*
Why did Jonathan eat contrary to Saul's orders? (17) What
was the effect upon him? (18) What was his opinion of his
father's command? (19)* Do you think he understood his
father's reasons for the oath? (20) Did Jonathan appear
to think the victory unsatisfactory? (21) How far did the
Hebrews pursue the Philistines? (22) Do you think this
was a smaller victory than might have been expected? (23)
What was the condition of the people? (24)* How did they
satisfy themselves? (25) What was the sin in this conduct?
Was there a law against eating meat which had not been
drained of blood? (26) What did Saul do in this case?
(27) What message did he send to the people? (28) Is the
altar mentioned in vs. 35 the same as the stone of vs. 33?
(29)* What causes contributed to Israel's victory? (30)
Do the events of the lesson reflect credit or discredit upon
Saul? Upon Jonathan? (31) Do you think the sympathy
of the writer was with Saul or with Jonathan? (32) If Jonathan had known of his father's command do you think he
would have been justified in disobeying it under any circumstances? (33) Which is of greater importance, obedience
and the fine discipline that it brings, or success?

SECTION XXIX

JONATHAN'S DELIVERANCE, I SAM. 14:36-46

And Saul said, Let us go down after the Philistines 36
by night, and spoil them until the morning light, and
let us not leave a man of them. And they said, Do
whatsoever seemeth good unto thee. Then said the
priest, Let us draw near hither unto God. And 37
Saul asked counsel of God, Shall I go down after
the Philistines? wilt thou deliver them into the hand
of Israel? But he answered him not that day. And 38
Saul said, Draw nigh hither, all ye chiefs of the
people: and know and see wherein this sin hath
been this day. For, as the Lord liveth, which saveth 39
Israel, though it be in Jonathan my son, he shall
surely die. But there was not a man among all the
people that answered him. Then said he unto all 40
Israel, Be ye on one side, and I and Jonathan my son

EXPLANATORY NOTES

The early Judean narrative of Saul's life is continued in this
section. Vs. 36, "Let us go down": Saul believed that the Philistines, after their defeat of that day, might be completely routed by a
night attack. They were probably encamped on the lower ground
to the west. "Let us draw near": The priest Ahijah† knew that
Saul had not waited for an answer in the morning (vs. 19), and
thought it wise to consult the divine will. Vs. 37, "asked counsel":
The methods of divining permitted in Israel were the sacred lot,
the Urim and Thummim† and the ephod. Vs. 38, "Draw
nigh": Saul was dismayed at receiving no answer and knew there
must have been some error committed. Vs. 39, "not a man . . . .

will be on the other side. And the people said unto
41 Saul, Do what seemeth good unto thee. Therefore
Saul said unto the Lord, the God of Israel, [1]Shew the
right. And Jonathan and Saul were taken by lot:
42 but the people escaped. And Saul said, Cast lots
between me and Jonathan my son. And Jonathan
43 was taken. Then Saul said to Jonathan, Tell me
what thou hast done. And Jonathan told him, and
said, I did certainly taste a little honey with the end
of the rod that was in mine hand; and lo, I must die.
44 And Saul said, God do so and more also: for thou
45 shalt surely die, Jonathan. And the people said unto
Saul, Shall Jonathan die, who hath wrought this
great salvation in Israel? God forbid: as the Lord
liveth, there shall not one hair of his head fall to the
ground; for he hath wrought with God this day.
So the people [2]rescued Jonathan, that he died not.
46 Then Saul went up from following the Philistines:
and the Philistines went to their own place.

[1] Or, *Give a perfect lot*

[2] Heb. *ransomed*

---

answered": The people had followed Saul willingly in the
battle and in his new plan of attack. In the present crisis they
could only follow his suggestion. Vs. 41, "shew the right":
These words were uttered as the priest cast the lot. Saul wanted
to know the truth, no matter what it might be. Vs. 43, "lo, I
must die": It may be supposed that Jonathan spoke these words
either with indignation, condemning his father's vow, or with
noble self-devotion, presenting himself as did the daughter of
Jephthah (Judg. 11:36), ready for death. The latter is more
probable. Vs. 44, "thou shalt surely die": Saul will keep his
vow, although it takes the dearest of his possessions. One can
but admire his Brutus-like constancy. Vs. 45, "the people rescued

Jonathan": In spite of his oath Saul was powerless to execute
sentence against the will of his army. No doubt he was more than
satisfied to have his judgment set aside in this case. Vs. 46, "Saul
went up": It was useless to follow the Philistines farther since no
favorable omen could be gained. The two armies accordingly
went their respective ways.

QUESTIONS

(1) What encouraged Saul to make a night attack on the
Philistines? (2)* What was the condition of the Philistine
army at this time? (3) What did the people say to Saul's
proposal? (4) What did the priest suggest? Why? Who
was the priest? (5)* What was the method of asking counsel
of God? (6) Why was no answer received: was it because
Saul had not waited for a response in the morning (vs. 19)
or because Jonathan had eaten the honey (vs. 27)? (7)*
What effect did this silence have upon Saul? (8) What did
he do? (9) What promise did he make? (10) Did the people
approve his plan? (11)* Did Saul's procedure indicate that
he thought Jonathan might be the cause of the trouble?
How? (12) How was the lot cast? (13) What was the
result? (14)* How do you understand Jonathan felt when
the lot fell upon him? Was he resentful, or angry, or sub-
missive? (15) Did Saul have the power to release Jonathan?
(16) Would it have been natural for him to do so, as a father?
(17)* What was Saul's resolution? Was this heroic or ob-
stinate? (18) What did the people say? (19) Did they
have the right to make Saul break his oath? (20)* Do you
think it would have been right to put Jonathan to death?
(21) Was Saul wrong in making the vow? (22) Do you
think it is right to break a promise or pledge under any condition? (23) What is the lesson here taught on the necessity
of great care in taking oaths or making vows?

SECTION XXX

SAUL'S WARS AND HOUSEHOLD, I SAM. 14:47–52

47 Now when Saul had taken the kingdom over Israel,
he fought against all his enemies on every side:
against Moab, and against the children of Ammon,
and against Edom, and against the ¹kings of Zobah,   ¹ Or, *king*
and against the Philistines: and whithersoever he
48 turned himself, ²he vexed them.   And he did valiant-   ² Or, *he put*
ly, and smote the Amalekites, and delivered Israel   *them to the*
out of the hands of them that spoiled them.   *worse.* The
                                                        Sept. has, *he*
49 Now the sons of Saul were Jonathan, and Ishvi,   *was victorious*

EXPLANATORY NOTES

The section is a summary of Saul's career, standing appro-
priately at the end of the chapters which relate the successful and
glorious events of his reign.   The later chapters tell of his rejection, and such a summary would be less in place in that connection.   Vs. 47, "fought against all his enemies": The picture of
Saul presented in this source, the early Judean story of Saul
(chaps. 9, 10, 11, 13, 14) is noble and kingly.   He was a devoted
ruler and a valiant protector of his land.   All neighboring nations
felt the power of his arms.   "Moab"†: the land lying east of the
northern end of the Dead Sea and the southern end of the Jordan.
"Children of Ammon"†: the people whose land lay north of Moab,
east of the Jordan. "Edom"†: the region south and east of the
Dead Sea. "Kings of Zobah"†: a region north of Ammon. The
margin "king" is to be preferred.   "Philistines"†: These were
the chief enemies of Saul's kingdom, and the power that finally
overthrew it. Vs. 48, "smote the Amalekites"†: a people living
in the south of Judah and in the desert near Kadesh. Vs. 49,
"sons of Saul": Three are named here, Jonathan, Ishvi, and

133

and Malchi-shua: and the names of his two daughters were these; the name of the first-born Merab,
and the name of the younger Michal: and the name 50
of Saul's wife was Ahinoam the daughter of Ahimaaz:
and the name of the captain of his host was Abner
the son of Ner, Saul's uncle.   ³And Kish was the 51
father of Saul; and Ner the father of Abner was the
son of Abiel.

And there was sore war against the Philistines 52
all the days of Saul: and when Saul saw any mighty
man, or any valiant man he took him unto him.

³ According to
some ancient
authorities,
*And Kish the
father of Saul
and Ner . . . :
were the sons
of Abiel*

Malchi-shua; but in I Sam. 31:2 the three who are slain are
Jonathan, Abinadab, and Malchi-shua, while in II Sam. 2:8
Ishbosheth, another son of Saul, is the king.   This last may have
been the same as Ishvi.   In I Chron. 8:33 all four are named.
"Two daughters": The older, Merab, was promised to David, but
was given to another, and Michal, the younger, became his wife.
Vs. 50, "captain of his host": commander in chief; Abner†
was Saul's cousin, the son of Ner, brother of Kish, and grandson
of Abiel, the father of Kish and Ner.   Vs. 5, "sore war": The
entire story of Saul's reign proves this statement.   The Hebrews
were always troubled by the Philistines till the reign of David.
"Any mighty man": Saul was himself tall in stature and wanted
to strengthen his army by the enlistment of all able men.   Like
Frederick the Great he chose the tallest, strongest men he could
find for his guards.

QUESTIONS

Study the lesson carefully, using a map to locate the places.
(1)* How did Saul vindicate his election as king?   (2) Who
were the Moabites?   (3) Where was Ammon?   (4) In
which direction from Palestine was Edom?   (5) Where was
Zobah?   (6)* Describe the relations of Israel with the Phil-

istines. (7) What success did Saul have in war? Does he impress you as a brave, devoted leader? (8)* Where did the Amalekites live? (9) How many sons did Saul have? (10) What were their names? (11) What were the names of his two daughters? (12)* Who was Saul's wife? (13) What was Abner's position? (14) How was he related to Saul? (15)* How were Saul and Abner related to Abiel? (16) Who were Israel's chief enemies? (17) How did Saul choose his soldiers? (18) Does this writer take a favorable view of Saul's reign? (19) Is this in contrast with the attitude of other writers whose narratives are included in I Samuel? (20) Is it probable that both views were right to a certain extent? (21) Would such a man as Saul, tall, soldierly, brave, attract men to himself? (22)* What qualities did Saul possess that every man ought to covet?

SECTION XXXI

SAUL'S CAMPAIGN AGAINST AMALEK, I SAM. 15:1-9

And Samuel said unto Saul, The Lord sent me to 15
anoint thee to be king over his people, over Israel;
now therefore hearken thou unto the voice of the
words of the Lord. Thus saith the Lord of hosts, 2
I have marked that which Amalek did to Israel, how
he set himself against him in the way, when he came
up out of Egypt. Now go and smite Amalek, and 3
[1] utterly destroy all that they have, and spare them

[1] Heb. *devote*

EXPLANATORY NOTES

In this section and the one following the narrative is taken from
the later document of northern Israel which gives special emphasis
to the prophetic work of Samuel and is less favorable to Saul. The
failure of Saul to exterminate Amalek is given as the occasion of
his rejection, without reference to the incidents of 13:8-14, where
the king's deposition has been announced already. The connection of the present account is with chaps. 1-3, 7, 8, 10:17-27 and
12. Vs. 1, "The Lord sent me": The reference is to 10:17-27,
where Saul was chosen by divine lot at the earnest request of the
nation and against the protest of Samuel. From the standpoint
of this writer the election of Saul was always regarded as a mistake, forced by unwise popular clamor, and doomed to end in
failure. Vs. 2, "that which Amalek† did": The reference is to
the events narrated in Exod. 17:8-16, Num. 14:43-45, and Deut.
25:17-19. Vs. 3, "utterly destroy": It is assumed that vengeance
is to be taken on the Amalekites for ancient injuries done to
Israel. We do not have to justify this command, nor the brutal
manner in which it was to be executed. Prophets like Samuel
were devoted heart and soul to the religion of Jehovah, but they

not; but slay both man and woman, infant and suck-
ling, ox and sheep, camel and ass.

4 And Saul summoned the people, and numbered
them in Telaim, two hundred thousand footmen,
5 and ten thousand men of Judah. And Saul came
to the city of Amalek, and ²laid wait in the valley.   ² Or, *strove*
6 And Saul said unto the Kenites, Go, depart, get
you down from among the Amalekites, lest I destroy
you with them: for ye shewed kindness to all the children of Israel, when they came up out of Egypt. So
the Kenites departed from among the Amalekites.
7 And Saul smote the Amalekites, from Havilah as

---

were also the children of a cruel age, and did not hesitate to employ
bloody measures in promoting what they believed to be the right
cause. We need not doubt that Samuel felt confident that he
understood the divine will, but we are also convinced by the whole
spirit of prophecy and the teachings of Jesus that he totally misunderstood the means by which the religion of Jehovah was to be
advanced. Such events in the Old Testament are by some people
held to prove that God was cruel and unjust. But they only
prove that even good men like Samuel were the children of their
age, and did not understand the loving character of the God they
served. Vs. 4, "numbered them in Telaim"†: Saul assembled
his army in a southern town for his campaign against the Amalekites who dwelt in the far south. The numbers given are far too
great for the period (see note on 11:8, section XXIII). Vs. 5, "the
city of Amalek": No name is given, and probably the author
merely means the land in which the Amalekites lived. They
were desert tribes. Vs. 6, "unto the Kenites"†: The friendly
feeling between Israel and these nomads who belonged to the clan
into which Moses had married caused Saul to give them warning.
Vs. 7, "from Havilah": The only region of this name lay east

thou goest to Shur, that is before Egypt. And he 8
took Agag the king of the Amalekites alive, and
utterly destroyed all the people with the edge of the
sword. But Saul and the people spared Agag, and 9
the best of the sheep, and of the oxen, and of the
fatlings, and the lambs, and all that was good, and
would not ³utterly destroy them: but every thing
that was vile and refuse, that they destroyed utterly.

³ Heb. *devote*

---

of Edom.   Probably the writing is a mistake, and the true name
lost.   "As thou goest to Shur"†: a region on the caravan route
from Palestine to Egypt. Vs. 8, "took Agag† the king": as a
trophy of victory, to grace Saul's triumph on the return to Israel.
Vs. 9, "best of the sheep": It was hard to observe the strict injunc-
tion of Samuel to put to death all living things, not because the
warriors of Israel were tender-hearted, but because they longed
to possess the rich spoil of the conquered Amalekites.

QUESTIONS

(1)* What authority had Samuel to command Saul?   Was
the prophet usually regarded as superior to the king in power?
(2) When did Samuel anoint Saul king?   (3) Did Samuel tell
Saul what he had learned from God, or was it what in his own
judgment was God's will?   Is the latter the best explanation
of many difficult narratives of the Old Testament, in which
God is represented as angry, changeable or apparently unjust?
(4) What was the cause of Israel's hostility to Amalek?   (5)*
Who were the Amalekites, and where did they live?   (6)
What was Saul commanded to do?   (7)* Do you think this
was a right command?   (8) Would it be right to exterminate
a nation today?   (9) If not, could it ever have been right?
(10)* Why did Samuel command it?   (11) How complete
was the destruction to be?   (12) What did Saul do?   (13)

What do you think of the number of soldiers mentioned?
(14)* Why are those of Judah mentioned separately from
the rest? (15) What is the meaning of "laid wait"? (16)
What word did Saul send to the Kenites? (17)* Who were
they and why was this warning sent? (18) Did the Kenites
heed the warning? (19) What were the scene and extent of
the campaign? (20)* What was Saul's motive in taking
Agag alive? (21) What else did he and the people spare?
(22)* Was it right or wrong to spare the king and the beasts?
(23) Was it because Saul was more merciful than Samuel that
he spared the king? (24) Can we judge Samuel in this
instance by the enlightened principles of Christianity? (25)
Would not the conduct of the Hebrews in destroying the
Amalekites be rightly regarded as savage and without excuse?
(26) May we see in this fact the measure of the growth which
the world has enjoyed in morality and mercy, through the
teachings of the prophets and Jesus?

SECTION XXXII

SAMUEL'S REBUKE OF SAUL, I SAM. 15:10-35

Then came the word of the Lord unto Samuel, 10
saying, It repenteth me that I have set up Saul to be 11
king: for he is turned back from following me,
and hath not performed my commandments.   And
Samuel was wroth; and he cried unto the Lord all
night.   And Samuel rose early to meet Saul in the 12
morning; and it was told Samuel, saying, Saul came
to Carmel, and, behold, he set him up a ¹monument,
and is gone about, and passed on, and gone down to

¹ Heb. *hand*

EXPLANATORY NOTES

In this section we continue with the document which gives the
story of Samuel's career as told by the prophetic writer of the
northern kingdom.   In it the reign of Saul is regarded as a mistake, the result of popular demand, but destined to failure.   Samuel
who always occupies the place of importance in the thought of
this writer, denounces Saul for his departure from the prophet's
commands regarding Amalek.   Vs. 11, "it repenteth me":
The prophets proclaimed the will of God as they understood it,
and used such forms of speech as their hearers could understand.
They felt that they understood the will of God for their generation,
and did not hesitate to announce what they felt to be for the best
interest of religion and the state as the divine word.   Our means
of knowing that it lacked something of expressing the mind of
Jehovah is to compare it with the teachings of Jesus.   "Samuel
was wroth": angry; partly at Saul who had disappointed him
by his conduct, and partly at the unhappy turn of events by which
his plans for the king, whom he loved, were frustrated.   Vs. 12,
"set him up a monument": a trophy, or stone commemorating

13 Gilgal.   And Samuel came to Saul: and Saul said
  unto him, Blessed be thou of the Lord: I have per-
14 formed the commandment of the Lord.   And Samuel said, What meaneth then this bleating of the
  sheep in mine ears, and the lowing of the oxen which
15 I hear ?   And Saul said, They have brought them
  from the Amalekites: for the people spared the best
  of the sheep and of the oxen to sacrifice unto the
  Lord thy God; and the rest we have ²utterly de-   ² Heb. *devoted*
16 stroyed.   Then Samuel said unto Saul, Stay, and I
  will tell thee what the Lord hath said to me this
17 night.   And he said unto him, Say on.   And Samuel
  said, Though thou wast little in thine own sight, wast
  thou not made the head of the tribes of Israel ?   And
18 the Lord anointed thee king over Israel; and the
  Lord sent thee on a journey, and said, Go and utterly
  destroy the sinners the Amalekites, and fight against
19 them until they be consumed.   Wherefore then

---

his victory.   Carmel† was on the way home from the south.
"Down to Gilgal"†: From the high region of Hebron one would
descend somewhat in going northward to the district of Shiloh in
which Gilgal lay.   Vs. 15, "best of the sheep": Saul and the
army were not willing to miss the chance of taking home some
of the Amalekite spoil; but the king pretended that it was only
taken as a sacrifice.   Vs. 17, "little in thine own sight": recalling
Saul's modest estimate of himself when he hid at the time of his
election (10:22).   Vs. 18, "the Lord sent thee": It was Samuel
who sent Saul on this mission of destruction, but he believed he
was obeying the will of God.   Vs. 19, "fly upon the spoil": The
spoil belonged to God and was to be "devoted," i.e., destroyed

didst thou not obey the voice of the Lord, but didst
fly upon the spoil, and didst that which was evil in
the sight of the Lord? And Saul said unto Samuel, 20
Yea, I have obeyed the voice of the Lord and have
gone the way which the Lord sent me, and have
³Heb. *devoted* brought Agag the king of Amalek, and have ³utterly
destroyed the Amalekites. But the people took of 21
the spoil, sheep and oxen, the chief of the devoted
things, to sacrifice unto the Lord thy God in Gilgal.
And Samuel said, Hath the Lord as great delight in 22
burnt offerings and sacrifices, as in obeying the voice
of the Lord? Behold, to obey is better than sacrifice, and to hearken than the fat of rams. For rebel- 23
⁴Heb. lion is as the sin of ⁴witchcraft, and stubbornness is
divination as idolatry and teraphim. Because thou hast rejected the word of the Lord, he hath also rejected

---

like a sacrifice. They had taken it for themselves. Vs. 20, "I
have obeyed": Saul finds no wrong in his conduct. The fact
that he and the people kept some of the spoil, and brought back
Agag the king to add to their triumph, seems to him a small matter
in comparison with their obedience in the principal item, the
destruction of Amalek. Vs. 22, "hath the Lord . . . . delight?"
This is one of the great verses of the Old Testament. In it
Samuel's doctrine of obedience to God is made known. God
cares little for sacrifices†, or any other outward service, as compared with love and obedience. "Fat of rams": The fat was
regarded as one of the most desirable parts of the animal, and was
therefore set aside as God's part, and burned on the altar. Vs. 23,
"witchcraft† . . . . idolatry† and teraphim"†: three forms of
superstition which were recognized as immoral and forbidden.
Samuel tells the king that disobedience and stubbornness are just

24 thee from being king.   And Saul said unto Samuel,
I have sinned: for I have transgressed the commandment of the Lord, and thy words: because I feared
25 the people, and obeyed their voice.   Now therefore,
I pray thee, pardon my sin, and turn again with me
26 that I may worship the Lord.   And Samuel said
unto Saul, I will not return with thee: for thou hast
rejected the word of the Lord and the Lord hath
27 rejected thee from being king over Israel.   And as
Samuel turned about to go away, he laid hold upon
28 the skirt of his robe, and it rent.   And Samuel said
unto him, The Lord hath rent the kingdom of Israel
from thee this day, and hath given it to a neighbour
29 of thine, that is better than thou.   And also the
5Strength of Israel will not lie nor repent: for he is   5 Or, *Victory*
30 not a man, that he should repent.   Then he said, I   Or, *Glory*

---

as wrong as these in the sight of God.   Vs. 24, "I have sinned":
When Saul saw the fixed purpose of Samuel, he tried to escape
by partial confession and by putting most of the blame on the
people.   Vs. 25, "that I may worship": As Samuel was the
recognized prophet in Israel, Saul thought that he could only
perform the acts of worship through him.   Strictly speaking,
however, this was the function of the priests.   He begs the prophet
not to desert him.   Vs. 27, "laid hold upon the skirt": Saul
tried to detain Samuel by seizing his cloak or outer garment; but
when it tore, the prophet made that fact the symbol of the kingdom torn from him.   "A neighbor of thine": David is meant of
course.   We do not know whether Samuel yet knew who the next
king would be.   But he knew that another would be chosen in
place of the rejected Saul.   Vs. 29, "strength of Israel": a name
applied by the prophet to God.   Jehovah was Israel's true glory

have sinned: yet honour me now, I pray thee, before
the elders of my people, and before Israel, and turn
again with me, that I may worship the Lord thy God.
So Samuel turned again after Saul; and Saul wor- 31
shipped the Lord.

Then said Samuel, Bring ye hither to me Agag the 32
king of the Amalekites. And Agag came unto him
6 Or, *trembling* ⁶delicately. And Agag said, Surely the bitterness of
death is past. And Samuel said, As thy sword hath 33
made women childless, so shall thy mother be childless among women. And Samuel hewed Agag in
pieces before the Lord in Gilgal.

Then Samuel went to Ramah; and Saul went up 34
to his house to Gibeah of Saul. And Samuel came 35
7 Or, *but* no more to see Saul until the day of his death; ⁷for
Samuel mourned for Saul.

---

and victory (see margin). God had determined that another
king must be chosen, and he would not change his mind regarding
the matter. Vs. 30, "before the elders"†: The king begs Samuel
not to leave him, as this would ruin his credit with the men of
influence and the people generally. Vs. 31, "so Samuel turned":
The prophet was unwilling to swerve from his severe condemna-
tion of Saul's disobedience, although personally he was fond of
him. But to save the king from too sudden a loss of prestige he
consented to treat him as king still. Vs. 32, "Agag came unto
him delicately": The rendering "trembling" is to be preferred.
The king of the Amalekites saw in the stern face of the prophet the
certainty of his doom. "The bitterness of death is past": These
words are not very clear. They cannot mean that the king
expected any mercy from Samuel. Perhaps the rendering, "the
bitterness of death is great," would be preferable. Vs. 33, "hewed

Agag in pieces": The rough and uncompromising nature of Samuel appears in this act. It seems very terrible to picture this man of God executing vengeance on this king with such unbending severity. Yet it reveals his stern idea of what God required. Vs. 35, "Samuel mourned": His affection for the king never wavered. The writer of this narrative holds the view that Samuel thought Saul's choice as king a mistake, but he still liked the man.

QUESTIONS

(1)* In what sense can it be said that God repents? (2) In what sense can the command to destroy the Amalekites be regarded as God's command? (3) How did Samuel feel when he saw that Saul had to be rebuked and dethroned? (4) What did Saul do at Carmel? Where was this place? (5)* What was the king's purpose in setting up the monument? Did it indicate pride on his part? (6) Where did Samuel meet Saul? (7) What was Saul's attitude when they met? (8)* What evidence did Samuel have that Saul had not obeyed his command? (9) On whom did Saul lay the blame of bringing home the spoil? (10) Was this the fact, or was Saul evading responsibility? (11) What would be the value of a sacrifice taken by violence from another, and costing the worshiper nothing? It is not probable, however, that the Hebrews ever stopped to reason about the matter in this manner. (12)* Why does Saul say "the Lord *thy* God" and not "the Lord *our* God"? Had he abandoned the worship of Jehovah, or did he think of Samuel as having a special right to call God his own? (13) What exaltation had Saul enjoyed? (14) To whom does Samuel attribute the command to destroy the Amalekites? In what sense could it be said to be God's command at all? (15) To what extent had the king obeyed? (16)* To what extent did he confess that he had failed? (17) What great principle does Samuel state in vs. 22? (18)* What were witchcraft, idolatry, and teraphim? (19) What was the consequence of Saul's incomplete obedience? (20) Does the penalty visited upon Saul seem greater than is demanded by his conduct? (21)* If so, what is the justification for Samuel's view of the case? (22) Do you think that Saul was sincere in his repentance and confession? (23) What was Samuel's answer to Saul's appeal to forgive him? (24) How did Saul try to detain him? (25)* What startling announcement did Samuel make about the kingdom? (26) What final request did Saul make of Samuel? (27) Did the prophet consent to remain with the king? (28)* Why had Saul spared Agag? (29) What did Samuel command regarding him? (30) What were the feelings of Agag as he was brought to Samuel? (31) What did Samuel do with him? (32)* How can you account for this terrible treatment of a foe by a prophet? (33) Is it ever right to take a human life? (34) Where did Saul and Samuel go? (35) How did Samuel feel toward Saul? (36)* What is the great lesson of this section? (37) What application can be made of the principle of vs. 22 at the present time? Is obedience of greater importance than any outward act of worship? Is it harder to render?

* REVIEW QUESTIONS

(Answers to these questions are to be written)

(1) Why did the people of Israel ask for a king?

(2) What two views do the narratives present regarding Samuel's feeling about a king?

(3) Under what circumstances did Samuel and Saul first meet?

(4) What were the incidents connected with Saul's public choice as king?

(5) What heroic deed did Saul perform soon afterward?

(6) What was the character of Samuel's conduct as prophet and judge?

(7) What was the occasion of Samuel's first recorded rebuke of Saul?

(8) What were the relations between the Hebrews and the Philistines in the days of Saul?

(9) What heroic exploit did Jonathan perform?

(10) What prohibition did Saul place upon the people, and what were its results?

(11) Against what nations did Saul conduct campaigns?

(12) What criticism did Samuel offer on Saul's campaign against Amalek?

(13) What were the elements of strength in Saul's character? Of weakness?

SECTION XXXIII

SAMUEL'S CHOICE OF DAVID, I SAM. 15:35*b*—
16:13

And the Lord repented that he had made Saul king over Israel.

And the Lord said unto Samuel, How long wilt 16 thou mourn for Saul, seeing I have rejected him from being king over Israel? fill thine horn with oil, and go, I will send thee to Jesse the Bethlehemite: for I have provided me a king among his sons. And Samuel said, How can I go? if Saul 2

EXPLANATORY NOTES

With the present section the second general division of the Book of I Samuel begins (see Introduction, 3). The appearance of David in the history is the new feature, and henceforth everything centers in him. Hitherto the narrative has vibrated between the early Judean record of Saul's life and the north Israel account of Samuel, the partiality of each author for his hero being strongly marked. From this point onward the interest centers in David, and all our sources unite in his honor. In this section a prophetic story of David's selection as king by Samuel is given. Vs. 35, "the Lord repented": As in 15:11 God is represented in language which ascribes to him human emotions. Vs. 1, "fill thine horn with oil": Oil was used to anoint kings, priests and prophets to office; it was carried in a horn (I Kings 1:39). "Jesse the Bethehemite": Jesse was the father of David. The town of Bethlehem†, south of Jerusalem, became famous as the "city of David" and later as the birthplace of Jesus. Vs. 2, "he will kill me": Saul was not a man to let others plot against him without an effort to save his throne. "Take an heifer": By making a sacrificial

148

hear it, he will kill me. And the Lord said, Take an heifer with thee, and say, I am come to sacrifice to
3 the Lord. And call Jesse to the sacrifice, and I will shew thee what thou shalt do: and thou shalt anoint
4 unto me him whom I name unto thee. And Samuel did that which the Lord spake, and came to Bethlehem. And the elders of the city came to meet him trembling, and said, Comest thou peaceably?
5 And he said, Peaceably: I am come to sacrifice unto the Lord: sanctify yourselves, and come with me to the sacrifice. And he sanctified Jesse and his sons,
6 and called them to the sacrifice. And it came to pass, when they were come, that he looked on Eliab, and said, Surely the Lord's anointed is before him.
7 But the Lord said unto Samuel, Look not on his countenance, or on the height of his stature; because I have rejected him: for the Lord seeth not as man seeth; for man looketh on the outward appearance,
8 but the Lord looketh on the heart. Then Jesse

---

feast the excuse for his journey, no suspicions would be excited. Samuel was accustomed to make such journeys to several places every year (I Sam. 7:10, 17). Vs. 3, "call Jesse to the sacrifice": The man and his household were invited to the feast; this would insure David's presence. Vs. 4, "trembling": Samuel was a man of great importance and authority, and the elders† of Bethlehem were alarmed at his unexpected coming. Vs. 5, "sanctify yourselves": by washing and putting on their best garments. The sacrifice was of course a feast (I Sam. 9:13). Vs. 6, "looked on Eliab": Jesse's oldest son was tall and handsome, and Samuel thought at first that he was the proper man for king. Vs. 7,

called Abinadab, and made him pass before Samuel.
And he said, Neither hath the Lord chosen this.
Then Jesse made Shammah to pass by. And he 9
said, Neither hath the Lord chosen this. And Jesse 10
made seven of his sons to pass before Samuel. And
Samuel said unto Jesse, The Lord hath not chosen
these. And Samuel said unto Jesse, Are here all 11
thy children? And he said, There remaineth yet
the youngest, and, behold, he keepeth the sheep.
And Samuel said unto Jesse, Send and fetch him:
for we will not sit [1]down till he come hither. And 12
he sent, and brought him in. Now he was ruddy,
and withal [2]of a beautiful countenance, and goodly
to look upon. And the Lord said, Arise, anoint him:
for this is he. Then Samuel took the horn of oil, 13
and anointed him in the midst of his brethren; and
the spirit of the Lord came mightily upon David from
that day forward. So Samuel rose up, and went to
Ramah.

[1] Heb. *around*

[2] Heb. *fair of eyes*

"looketh on the heart": the inner character, disposition, and
prospects of a man. Vs. 10, "seven of his sons": One after
another, beginning with the oldest, the sons of Jesse were brought
for Samuel's inspection. Vs. 11, "he keepeth the sheep": Jesse
had not thought it worth while to bring the youngest boy. But
he was as important as any member of the family at the feast, and
as it happened, the one on whom the prophet's choice would fall.
Vs. 12, "Arise, anoint him": Samuel had been pleased by the
appearance of the older sons, but David fulfilled his ideal at once.
The appeal which the youth made to his heart he accepted as the
voice of God. Vs. 13, "anointed him": It is difficult to explain

this semi-public anointing of David to kingship in the face of the later ignorance of David and his family that any such an honor was to be his. Perhaps they interpreted the action as merely appointment to membership in one of the "schools of the prophets;" or this may be merely a late tradition intended to give to David's rule the sanction of Samuel's authority. "Spirit† of the Lord": It is the purpose of the writer to say that from this time forth David showed himself worthy of the kingship by his deeds.

QUESTIONS

(1)* What is meant by the words "the Lord repented"? (2) Why did Samuel mourn for Saul? (3) What was the purpose of the horn of oil? For what was oil used? (4) Where was Samuel directed to go? (5)* Where is Bethlehem? What events occurred there? What event in the life of Jesus occurred there? (6) Why did Samuel fear to go? (7) How did he conceal his true purpose? (8) Who especially was to be invited to the sacrifice? (9)* Why were the elders of Bethlehem troubled at the coming of the prophet? (10) How were the people to prepare for the sacrificial feasts? (11) Which of Jesse's sons did Samuel think would make a suitable king? (12)* Who is meant by the words "the Lord's anointed"? Was a king usually spoken of in this way? (13) What is the contrast between men's choice and God's? (14) Describe the inspection and rejection of others of the sons of Jesse. (15)* Why had Jesse left one of his sons at home? (16) What directions did Samuel give regarding the youngest of the boys? (17) Do you not suppose the prophet equally insisted on the presence of the children from other families? (18) Would it be possible or advisable for a minister to insist that all the children of his congregation should be present before the service proceeded? Is any congregation complete which lacks children? (19)* Describe David's appearance in your own words. (20) How was Samuel impressed with David? (21) What was God's will regarding

David as understood by Samuel? (22)* What do you suppose David and his family understood the anointing to mean? (23) What indications are there that they did not understand what it really meant? (24) What is meant by the spirit of the Lord coming upon David? (25) Where did Samuel go after the feast? (26) What does this section teach regarding God's choice of David as king? Do you suppose its purpose was to point out the connection of the great prophet Samuel with the choice of David? Would this give the sanction of Samuel's authority to David's reign? (27)* What does it teach regarding family worship at the sanctuary? Does it imply that people ought to attend church service as families and not merely as individuals? (28) What is its suggestion regarding the human and divine estimate of men's fitness for important work? (29) Did David prove in his later life that he was the fittest of the brothers for the place he was to fill? Is it often the case that the young, immature, and unpromising member of a family may attain the highest and most useful place?

SECTION XXXIV

DAVID BROUGHT TO SAUL, I SAM. 16:14–23

14 Now the spirit of the Lord had departed from
Saul, and an evil spirit from the Lord ¹troubled   ¹ Or, *terrified*
15 him.   And Saul's servants said unto him.   Behold
16 now, an evil spirit from God troubleth thee.   Let
our lord now command thy servants, which are
before thee, to seek out a man who is a cunning player
on the harp: and it shall come to pass, when the

EXPLANATORY NOTES

With this section the early Judean narrative of David's career
begins.   Two striking accounts of his introduction at the court
of Saul are given, quite different in character.   This is the opening of the first or main narrative.   In it King Saul is troubled with
a malady and David is brought as a minstrel to cheer him, and
becomes his armor-bearer.   Vs. 14, "departed from Saul": In
Saul's conversation with Samuel at their first interview he had
been told that the spirit† of God would come upon him and he
should become another man (10:6).   When he met the band of
prophets (10:10), and again when the news from Jabesh-gilead
reached him (11:6) it is said the spirit of the Lord came mightily
upon him.   Now that spirit of strength and courage had left him,
he was no longer like his former self.   Happiness and contentment,
the qualities of a quiet and successful life, had forsaken the king.
"Evil spirit from the Lord": All endowments, good and evil,
were believed by the Hebrews to come from God as the one source
of all things.   Saul was troubled by periods of depression, melan-
choly, unreasoning terror.   These were ascribed to an evil spirit.
Vs. 15, "a cunning player on the harp"†: Music was believed by
the ancients to be a means of soothing the spirits of troubled or

evil spirit from God is upon thee, that he shall play
with his hand, and thou shalt be well. And Saul 17
said unto his servants, Provide me now a man that
can play well, and bring him to me. Then answered 18
one of the young men, and said, Behold, I have seen
a son of Jesse the Beth-lehemite that is cunning in
playing, and a mighty man of valour, and a man of
war, and ²prudent in ³speech, and a comely person,
and the Lord is with him. Wherefore Saul sent 19
messengers unto Jesse, and said, Send me David thy
son, which is with the sheep. And Jesse took an ass 20

² Or, *skilful*
³ Or, *business*

---

frenzied men. Vs. 18, "mighty man of valour": This refers not
to military skill, as do the following words "man of war," but to
David's position as a man of good family and wealth, worthy of a
place at the court (see note on 9:1). "Lord is with him": He
had qualities of success and popularity, and was a God-fearing
man. Contrast this description of David as mature and experienced with the picture presented from the other source in vss.
11, 12. Vs. 19, "send me David": Saul as king had the right to
summon any man to his service (14:52). Jesse as a well-to-do
farmer of Bethlehem would willingly send his son for the royal
service. Vs. 20, "ass laden": It was courtesy to send a present
for the king, and this Jesse does. Bread, a bottle† or skin of wine,
and a young goat dressed would be a suitable gift. Saul's court
at Gibeah was a very simple one, and probably he welcomed such
tokens of good-will from his subjects, many of whom must have
been as rich as he. Vs. 21, "loved him greatly": There was
instant good will toward David. Saul's unreasoning jealousy of
him was a later development. "Armor-bearer": attendant in
war, and body servant at home. Vs. 22, "stand before me":
remain at court. Vs. 23, "Played with his hand": Saul's malady
came on him only at certain periods; then David quieted and
cheered him with his music.

laden with bread, and a ⁴bottle of wine, and a kid,   ⁴ Or, *skin*
21 and sent them by David his son unto Saul. And
David came to Saul, and stood before him: and he
loved him greatly; and he became his armourbearer.
22 And Saul sent to Jesse, saying, Let David, I pray
thee, stand before me; for he hath found favour in

ANCIENT HARPS

23 my sight. And it came to pass, when the evil spirit
from God was upon Saul, that David took the harp,
and played with his hand; so Saul was refreshed, and
was well, and the evil spirit departed from him.

QUESTIONS

(1)* What change came over Saul? (2) How does the
author describe this malady? (3) Did Saul's servants think
that God was afflicting the king? What is meant by Saul's
servants? (4) What remedy did they suggest? (5)* What
was the effect of music in such cases? Is it now so used?
(6) What was a harp? How was it used? On what occasions? (7) How did Saul receive the suggestion? (8)* Tell
all you can of Jesse as to his home, position, and family. (9)
Put in other terms the six statements made concerning David

by Saul's young man. (10) What message did Saul send to Jesse? (11) Would Jesse regard the king's command as an honor to himself and David? (12) What present did he send to Saul? (13) Who took this present? How far did he have to go? (14) How was Saul pleased with David? (15) What position was given David? (16)* What was Saul's second message to Jesse? Was this sent at once or some time after? (17) How did David help the king? (18) Which of the two men, Saul or David, do you think the author of this account admired the more? (19)* What bearing has it upon the story of David's life? (20) Is there any encouragement for young men who are looking for a useful career in the story of David's promotion at Saul's court? (21) What qualities win young men respect and advancement today?

SECTION XXXV

GOLIATH'S CHALLENGE, I SAM. 17:1-11

17   Now the Philistines gathered together their armies
to battle, and they were gathered together at Socoh,
which belongeth to Judah, and pitched between
2 Socoh and Azekah, in Ephes-dammim. And Saul
and the men of Israel were gathered together, and
pitched in the vale of ¹Elah, and set the battle in
3 array against the Philistines. And the Philistines
stood on the mountain on the one side, and Israel
stood on the mountain on the other side: and there
4 was a valley between them. And there went out a
champion out of the camp of the Philistines, named
Goliath, of Gath, whose height was six cubits and a

¹ Or, *the
terebinth*

EXPLANATORY NOTES

In this section the early Judean or main narrative of David's
life is continued from Section XXXIV. A Philistine giant defies
the Hebrews to send a man to fight with him. Vs. 1, "gathered
their armies": In 7:13, 14, which is taken from the north-Israel
record of Samuel's life, it is said that the Philistines were subdued
and no more disturbed Israel in the days of the prophet. Such a
statement, made by an earnest admirer of Samuel, was not quite
accurate, as the present narrative shows. "Between Socoh†
and Azekah"†: two towns west of Bethlehem on the frontier of
the highland region of Judah. Between them ran the valley of
Elah†, where Saul's camp occupied the high valley side. Vs. 4,
"a champion": a warrior who represented his people, and
offered to settle the conflict in single combat with some Hebrew.
"Six cubits† and a span": The cubit was about a foot and a

span.   And he had an helmet of brass upon his head, 5
and he was clad with a coat of mail: and the weight
of the coat was five thousand shekels of brass.   And 6
he had greaves of brass upon his legs, and a javelin
of brass between his shoulders.   And the staff of his 7
spear was like a weaver's beam; and his spear's
head weighed six hundred shekels of iron: and his
shield-bearer went before him.   And he stood and 8

² Heb. *ranks*

cried unto the ²armies of Israel, and said unto them,
Why are ye come out to set your battle in array?
am not I a Philistine, and ye servants to Saul? choose
you a man for you, and let him come down to me.
If he be able to fight with me, and kill me, then will 9
we be your servants: but if I prevail against him,
and kill him, then shall ye be our servants, and serve

³ Or, *reproach*

us.   And the Philistine said, I ³defy the armies of 10
Israel this day; give me a man, that we may fight
together.   And when Saul and all Israel heard those 11
words of the Philistine, they were dismayed, and
greatly afraid.

---

half; the span a handbreadth.   Goliath† came from a race of
giants.   Vs. 5, "coat of mail": a shirt made of overlapping
scales of brass (bronze).   The garment would weigh perhaps
a hundred and fifty pounds.   Vs. 7, "weaver's beam": the
shaft of a loom with which cloth was woven by hand.   The giant
was fully protected, and his weapons were in keeping with his
immense size.   He was an object of terror.   Vs. 8, "Why are ye
come?": why bring out an army when the issue of battle can be
decided in single combat?   The giant was willing to let all the
campaign depend upon the result of his fight.   Vs. 10, "I defy":

He attempted by scornful and taunting words to anger the Hebrews so that some one of them would rush out against him. Vs. 11, "greatly afraid": The enormous size and equipment of the giant left no hope of victory against him. The chiefs of Israel would hardly consent to let their king try such an unequal contest; the king would be unlikely to allow Jonathan to venture into such danger, and for the rest, no man offered to go.

QUESTIONS

(1)* Who were the Philistines? (2) What was their object in fighting against Israel? Were they usually engaged in raids into the land of Israel? (3) Where did they gather? (4) Who came out to oppose them? (5) Where did the Hebrews camp? (6)* How were the two camps placed? (7) Why did the two armies not fight? Were they afraid or were they waiting to see if there would not be some single combats first? (8)* Describe the champion of the Philistines, giving ten particulars from the text. (9) What was his purpose in appearing before the Hebrew lines? (10) What did he challenge the Hebrews to do? Are such challenges common in modern warfare? (11)* What offer did he make? (12) How did he try to arouse them to fight him? (13) Why did no one offer to accept the challenge? (14) Do you think the Hebrews were cowards or were the odds too great to be ventured? (15)* If in these desperate circumstances someone were to volunteer to fight Goliath, what would be thought of him? (16) Did the writer apparently feel that no better place could be found to introduce David to public life than this? (17) Do you not think that the Philistine giant is a very good symbol of great wrongs and abuses in the world, bold, strong, insolent, insulting?

SECTION XXXVI

DAVID IN THE CAMP, I SAM. 17:12–31

Now David was the son of that Ephrathite of 12
Beth-lehem-judah, whose name was Jesse; and he
had eight sons: and the man was an old man in the
days of Saul, stricken in years among men. And 13
the three eldest sons of Jesse had gone after Saul to
the battle: and the names of his three sons that
went to the battle were Eliab the first-born, and next
unto him Abinadab, and the third Shammah. And 14
David was the youngest; and the three eldest followed Saul. Now David went to and fro from 15
Saul to feed his father's sheep at Beth-lehem. And 16

EXPLANATORY NOTES

In the account of David's arrival at the camp and introduction
to Saul as presented in this section we have a very different picture
from that given in the Judean narrative of David's life as given in
Section XXXIV. There he was an experienced warrior selected
as a minstrel to relieve Saul's malady, and was taken to court and
became Saul's friend and armor-bearer. Here he is unknown to
Saul, is a shepherd boy sent with provisions to his brothers, is
treated by them with superiority and disdain and only finds out
the possibility of advancement by inquiring what reward awaits
the overthrow of the giant. Clearly this story comes from a
different source. It was no doubt a popular tradition regarding
David. We need not be disturbed by the variations in the stories.
A hero like David drew about him many recitals of his exploits,
told differently as they were known in different parts of the land.
This section is omitted entirely in the Septuagint†. Either its

the Philistine drew near morning and evening, and
presented himself forty days.

17 And Jesse said unto David his son, Take now for
thy brethren an ephah of this parched grain, and
these ten loaves, and carry them quickly to the camp
18 to thy brethren; and bring these ten cheeses unto
the captain of their thousand, and look how thy
19 brethren fare, and take their pledge. Now Saul,
and they, and all the men of Israel, ¹were in the vale   ¹ Or, *are*
20 of Elah fighting with the Philistines. And David rose

---

translators did not find it in the Hebrew text which they used, or
they omitted it to avoid the difficulties which its variations from
the other narratives presented. Vs. 12, "that Ephrathite"†:
dweller in Ephrathah, or Bethlehem†. Vs. 13, "gone after Saul":
The father was too old for war, and David too young. The names
of the sons are the same as those given in 16:6–9. Vs. 15, "went
to and fro": This verse is evidently the work of the compiler,
who attempted thus to harmonize the two stories. It is clear,
however, that David could not at the same time have been the
warrior-minstrel of the court of Saul and the shepherd lad in
Bethlehem. Moreover, 16:22 contradicts this statement. Vs. 16,
"Philistine drew near": This is added to explain the condition
when David arrived at the camp. Vs. 17, "an ephah of this
parched grain": about a bushel of browned barley or wheat. Vs.
18, "the captain of their thousand": The army was divided by
hundreds and thousands, or companies and regiments. The
people within reach sent in provisions, both to their own kinsmen
and to others of the army. Cheeses were some preparation of
thickened milk. "Take their pledge": This may mean take a
receipt for the provisions, or bring back some token agreed upon.
Vs. 19, "vale of Elah"†: the place described in 17:2, about
twelve miles from Bethlehem. This verse is perhaps a part of
Jesse's direction to David (note the margin). Vs. 20, "place of

up early in the morning, and left the sheep with a
keeper, and took and went, as Jesse had commanded him; and he came to the ²place of the wagons
as the host which was going forth to the ³fight
shouted for the battle.   And Israel and the Philis- 21
tines put the battle in array, army against army.
And David left his baggage in the hand of the keeper 22
of the baggage, and ran to the army and came and
saluted his brethren.   And as he talked with them, 23
behold, there came up the champion, the Philistine
of Gath, Goliath by name, out of the ranks of the
Philistines, and spake according to the same words:
and David heard them.   And all the men of Israel, 24
when they saw the man, fled from him, and were sore
afraid.   And the men of Israel said, Have ye seen 25
this man that is come up? surely to ⁴defy Israel is
he come up: and it shall be, that the man who
killeth him, the king will enrich him with great
riches, and will give him his daughter, and make his
father's house free in Israel.   And David spake to 2

margin notes:
² *barricade*
³ *battle ground*
⁴ *reproach*

the wagons": the entrenchment within which the soldiers remained
at night.   Vs. 23, "the same words": the words of defiance and
insult with which he taunted Israel.   Vs. 25, "make his father's
house free": exempt from payments of tax or public service.   Vs.
26, "What shall be done?": David had a boy's keen curiosity
regarding all the details of the king's offer.   "This uncircumcised
Philistine": Circumcision was the mark of the Hebrew and other
Semitic races.   The Philistines are the only people in Palestine
whom the Hebrews called "uncircumcised" (Judg. 14:3; I Sam.
14:6).   Vs. 28, "Eliab's anger was kindled": He thought David

the men that stood by him, saying, What shall be done to the man that killeth this Philistine, and taketh away the reproach from Israel? for who is this uncircumcised Philistine, that he should [5]defy   [5] *reproach*
27 the armies of the living God? And the people answered him after this manner, saying, So shall it be done to the man that killeth him.

28 And Eliab his eldest brother heard when he spake unto the men; and Eliab's anger was kindled against David, and he said, Why art thou come down? and with whom hast thou left those few sheep in the wilderness? I know thy pride and the naughtiness of thine heart: for thou art come down
29 that thou mightest see the battle. And David said,
30 What have I now done? Is there not a cause? And he turned away from him toward another, and spake after the same manner; and the people answered
31 him again after the former manner. And when the words were heard which David spake, they rehearsed them before Saul; and he sent for him.

---

was only a curious and inquisitive boy. It is plain that the author of this narrative is unaware of David's anointing as king, or of his position as Saul's armor-bearer. Vs. 29, "is there not a cause?": is it not a matter of moment? Vs. 30, "spake after the same manner": David refused to give up his inquiries till he had satisfied himself regarding the facts. Vs. 31, "which David spake": his words of contempt for the Philistine; no one else had talked thus, and when his boldness was reported to the king, he sent for him to see if he might be able to fight Goliath.

QUESTIONS

Read the lesson and the notes carefully.

(1)* How does this narrative differ from the story of David's entrance into public life in 16:14–23? (2) What is said of Jesse? (3) Who were the sons with Saul in the army? (4)* How is David's presence in Bethlehem explained by the com piler? (5) What direction did Jesse give his son? What provisions was he to take? (6) What was he to do on arrival at the camp? (7)* Where were Saul and his army at this time? How far did David have to travel? (8) What did David do with his sheep while he was away? (9) What did he find when he reached the camp? (10)* What constituted the camp? (11) Do you understand that both armies came out and faced each other for forty days while the giant made his defiance? (12) What is meant by David's "baggage"? What did he do with it? (13) Who was Goliath? (14)* What did he say? (15) Does it seem likely that an entire army would fly from one man, even though he were a giant? (16) What was the talk that David heard in the ranks regarding the giant? (17)* What rewards had Saul offered to the man who would kill him? (18) What is meant by making a house free? (19)* Why did David ask again about the rewards? (20) How did David speak about the Philistine? (21) What did Eliab think of David's conduct? (22) How did he try to humiliate him? (23)* Can you reconcile this attitude of Eliab with the knowledge that David was to be king? (24) Would he have treated an armor-bearer of the king in this manner? (25) Was it not natural that David should wish to see the battle? (26) What was David's response? (27) Did he resent his brother's words? (28)* How did Saul hear of David? (29) Why did he summon him? (30)* What is the most important teaching of this section? (31) In what way does it indicate the great popular regard in which David was held? (32) Recall the exploit of Jonathan (Section XXVII) and consider whether the unhesitating courage of both these young men was justified? Is a man who goes forward impetuously in a moment of peril or opportunity more likely to win success than one who waits, considers the dangers, and makes no effort?

A MOABITE WARRIOR

SECTION XXXVII

DAVID'S VICTORY OVER GOLIATH, I SAM. 17:32-54

¹ Or, *within him*

And David said to Saul, Let no man's heart fail 32
¹because of him; thy servant will go and fight with
this Philistine. And Saul said to David, Thou art 33
not able to go against this Philistine to fight with him:

EXPLANATORY NOTES

In this section the early Judean narrative of David's life is
resumed from 16:14—17:11 (Sections XXXIV, XXXV). There
it will be remembered David is brought by Saul as a minstrel to his
court, and is found to be a man of war and experience, even though
only a youth in years. He becomes Saul's armor-bearer. In time
of war Goliath of Gath defies Saul's army and challenges any
man in it to single combat. In the present section David accepts
the challenge, and assures Saul, who is alarmed for his safety,
that even though he is young, he has fought harder battles than
contests with men, and is not afraid of the giant. Saul attempts
to protect him with his own armor, but David cannot wear it and
conquers the Philistine with his sling. Vs. 32, "let no man's
heart fail": David alone is full of courage, as the writer wishes
to make clear. The words that follow may be rendered as in the
text (referring to Goliath) or as in the margin. Vs. 33, "thou art
but a youth": Even though David was "a man of war and prudent
in speech" (16:18), he was a young man with no such strength or
experience as the giant. Vs. 34, "there came a lion": there
would come. The form of the verb shows that it was repeated.
Lions frequented the jungles along the Jordan, and might stray
up to the highlands in search of prey (II Sam. 23:20) The bears
from the mountains were even fiercer, as the tradition regarding
the fate of the young men at Bethel indicates (II Kings 2:24).
The beasts named were the most dreaded enemies of the flocks
(Hos. 13:7, 8; Amos 3:12). Vs. 36, "shall be as one of them":

166

34 for thou art but a youth, and he a man of war from his youth.   And David said unto Saul, Thy servant kept his father's sheep; ²and when there came a lion, or a bear, and took a lamb out of the ² Or, *and there came a lion and a bear . . . and I went out,* etc.

HEAD OF DAVID—MICHELANGELO

35 flock, I went out after him, and smote him, and delivered it out of his mouth: and when he arose against me, I caught him by his beard, and smote him, and

36 slew him.   Thy servant smote both the lion and the bear: and this uncircumcised Philistine shall be as

³ Or,
reproached

one of them, seeing he hath ³defied the armies of the living God. And David said, The Lord that de- 37 livered me out of the paw of the lion, and out of the paw of the bear, he will deliver me out of the hand of this Philistine. And Saul said unto David, Go, and the Lord shall be with thee. And Saul clad 38 David with his apparel, and he put an helmet of brass upon his head, and he clad him with a coat of mail. And David girded his sword upon his apparel, and 39 he assayed to go; for he had not proved it. And David said unto Saul, I cannot go with these; for I have not proved them. And David put them off him. And he took his staff in his hand, and chose 40 him five smooth stones out of the ⁴brook, and put them in the shepherd's bag which he had, even in his scrip; and his sling was in his hand: and he drew near to the Philistine. And the Philistine came on 41

⁴ Or, torrent
bed

---

not more to be dreaded than the foes David had met and defeated. Vs. 37, "he will deliver me": David's trust was not in his own strength, but in the help of God. Vs. 38, "with his apparel": Saul had the best, perhaps the only armor in the camp (cf. 13: 19–23). Vs. 39, "his sword": apparently David's own sword. As an armor-bearer of Saul he would have such arms as befitted his station. "He assayed to go": made a vain effort to walk in the armor. Saul was much taller, and David "had not proved," i.e., was not accustomed to, any kind of armor. Vs. 40, "took his staff": the shepherd's club. In the emergency he preferred to use the weapons of his shepherd life. He even laid aside the sword he wore as Saul's lieutenant. "His scrip": the bag in which a shepherd would carry his food. "His sling": made of leather and whirled about the head to gain velocity. Vs. 41, "the man

and drew near unto David; and the man that bare
42 the shield went before him.   And when the Philistine
looked about, and saw David, he disdained him;
for he was but a youth, and ruddy, and withal of a
43 fair countenance.   And the Philistine said unto David,
Am I a dog, that thou comest to me with staves?
44 And the Philistine cursed David by his gods.   And the
Philistine said to David, Come to me, and I will
give thy flesh unto the fowls of the air, and to the
45 beasts of the field.   Then said David to the Philistine, Thou comest to me with a sword and with a
spear, and with a javelin: but I come to thee in the
name of the Lord of hosts, the God of the armies of
46 Israel, which thou hast ⁵defied.   This day will the   ⁵ Or,
Lord deliver thee into mine hand: and I will smite   *reproached*
thee, and take thine head from off thee; and I will
give the carcases of the host of the Philistines this day
unto the fowls of the air, and to the wild beasts of the
earth; that all the earth may know that there is a

---

that bare the shield": The equipment of Goliath, including an
armor-bearer, was most imposing.   Vs. 42, "disdained him":
thought him no worthy opponent.   Vs. 43, "Am I a dog?": Such
weapons as David bore would do to drive off dogs, but not to
fight with warriors.   For David's staff, the only weapon he saw,
he had only contempt, and felt himself insulted.   "By his gods":
the deities of Gath and of all Philistia.   Vs. 44, "to the fowls of the
air": The boasting of a confident fighter before the battle.   Vs.
45, "Lord of hosts": the name given to Jehovah by the Hebrews,
signifying his leadership of their armies.   Vs. 46, "I will smite
thee": David can equal the giant in boastings, only he has con-

God in Israel; and that all this assembly may know 47
that the Lord saveth not with sword and spear: for
the battle is the Lord's and he will give you into our
hand. And it came to pass, when the Philistine 48
arose, and came and drew nigh to meet David, that
David hastened, and ran toward the army to meet
the Philistine. And David put his hand in his bag, 49
and took thence a stone, and slang it, and smote the
Philistine in his forehead; and the stone sank into
his forehead, and he fell upon his face to the earth.
So David prevailed over the Philistine with a sling 50
and with a stone, and smote the Philistine, and slew
him; but there was no sword in the hand of David.
Then David ran, and stood over the Philistine, and 51
took his sword, and drew it out of the sheath thereof,
and slew him, and cut off his head therewith. And
⁶ Or, *mighty* when the Philistines saw that their ⁶champion was
man dead, they fled. And the men of Israel and of 52

---

fidence in the help of God. Vs. 47, "saveth not with sword and
spear": the great truth that all the Bible impresses. Vs. 48, "ran
toward the army": the Philistine host. Vs. 49, "took thence a
stone": One recalls Michelangelo's David, tense, watchful,
holding the sling over his shoulder, ready to hurl the stone. "He
fell": The battle was over as soon as it began; one stone accomplished the purpose. Vs. 51, "took his sword": He used the
giant's own sword to cut off his head as a trophy. Vs. 52, "pursued the Philistines": The death of the giant and at the hands of
a youth struck terror into the hearts of Israel's enemies, and
fired the Hebrews with fierce courage. "Gai . . . . Ekron"†:
Probably Gath† and Ekron, the two well-known Philistine cities

Judah arose, and shouted, and pursued the Philis-
tines, until thou comest to [7]Gai, and to the gates of   [7] The Sept.
Ekron.   And the wounded of the Philistines fell   has, *Gath*
down by the way to [8]Shaaraim, even unto Gath,   [8] Or, *the two
53 and unto Ekron.   And the children of Israel   gates*
returned from chasing after the Philistines, and
54 they spoiled their camp.   And David took the head
of the Philistine, and brought it to Jerusalem; but
he put his armour in his tent.

---

are meant.   Shaaraim (Josh. 15:36) was a town near these cities.
Vs. 53, "spoiled their camp": showing the completeness of the
rout.   Vs. 54, "brought it to Jerusalem": an evident error, as
Jerusalem was not a Hebrew city at this time.   David and Saul
returned with the spoil to Gibeah, Saul's home and the location of
the court.   "In his tent": Here David is thought of as having a
tent, in harmony with his position on Saul's staff.   Later on the
sword of Goliath was deposited in the sanctuary at Nob (I Sam.
21:8, 9).

QUESTIONS

(1)* What was David's position, according to this section?
(2) What was his word to Saul regarding Goliath?   (3) Is
there an intentional contrast between the attitude of David
and that of Saul?   (4)* Why was Saul afraid to have David
go to the contest?   (5) What proof did David give of his fitness to fight?   (6) Did he refer to a single occasion of conflict
or to frequent experiences?   (7) On what did David rely for
his victory?   (8)* What do you think Saul's feeling was
regarding David's chances of success?   Even should he fail,
was it worth while to send him?   (9) How did he prepare
David for the battle?   (10) Why did not David, as Saul's
armor-bearer, have armor of his own?   (11)* How did David

feel in Saul's armor? (12) What did he take instead? (13) Why did he take *five* stones? Was it well to be prepared for a long conflict? (14) Describe the two men, David and Goliath, as they faced each other. (15) How did Goliath treat David? (16) Why was he angry? Did he have a right to feel that David was no fit antagonist for him? (17) What was his threat? (18) How did David reply? (19)* Do you think David was confident of victory or was he merely anxious to save Israel's credit? (20) To whom did he look for help? (21) Describe the battle. (22)* How did the downfall of Goliath affect the Philistines? the Hebrews? (23) What became of the Philistines? (24) What advantage did the Hebrews take of their victory? (25) What did David do with his spoils? (26) What error is there in vs. 54? (27) What is the chief purpose of this section? (28) Would a romantic interest always attach to one who had performed such an exploit?

SECTION XXXVIII

DAVID AT SAUL'S COURT, I SAM. 17:55—18:5

55 And when Saul saw David go forth against the Philistine, he said unto Abner, the captain of the host, Abner, whose son is this youth? And Abner said, As thy soul liveth, O king, I cannot tell.
56 And the king said, Inquire thou whose son the
57 stripling is. And as David returned from the slaughter of the Philistine, Abner took him, and brought him before Saul with the head of the Philis-
58 tine in his hand. And Saul said to him, Whose son art thou, thou young man? And David answered, I am the son of thy servant Jesse the Beth-lehemite.
18 And it came to pass, when he had made an end of speaking unto Saul, that the soul of Jonathan was knit with the soul of David, and Jonathan loved him

---

EXPLANATORY NOTES

In this section occurs another of the popular stories about David. It follows the line of 17:12–31 (Section XXXVI), in which David is unknown to Saul, but arrives at the camp at the right time to defeat the Philistine. In the other narrative, the early Judean story of David, there would be no need of an introduction of David to Saul after the death of Goliath, for he was already well known at the court as Saul's minstrel and armorbearer. Vs. 55, "whose son is this youth?": Saul did not know him, having but met him that day for the first time. Even Abner† knows nothing of him. Vs. 57, "the head of the Philistine": David kept the bloody trophy in his hand. Vs. 1, "soul of Jona-

as his own soul. And Saul took him that day, and 2
would let him go no more home to his father's house.
Then Jonathan and David made a covenant, be- 3
cause he loved him as his own soul. And Jonathan 4
stripped himself of the robe that was upon him, and
gave it to David, and his apparel, even to his sword,
and to his bow, and to his girdle. And David went 5
¹ Or, *prospered* out whithersoever Saul sent him, and ¹behaved
himself wisely: and Saul set him over the men of
war, and it was good in the sight of all the people, and
also in the sight of Saul's servants.

---

than† was knit": Some conversation between Saul and David,
not recorded here, is implied in this verse. It made its impression
on Jonathan, so that he was completely fascinated by David.
The character of Jonathan is one of the finest in the Old Testament. If friendship ever helped to make a man, surely David
was immensely ennobled by his intimacy with the son of Saul. Of
the two, Jonathan was superior, although the writers of the narratives magnify David at every point. Vs. 2, "Saul took him":
According to the other document (16:22) Saul had already made
David his constant attendant some time before. We need not
attempt the useless task of "reconciling" the two accounts. Our
purpose is to ascertain just what each one has to say of David.
Vs. 3, "made a covenant": a solemn agreement. They promised
eternal friendship to each other. Vs. 4, "gave it to David":
Jonathan's love made him want to give David all he had. As
Saul had given David his armor to wear, so Jonathan now gave
him his mantle and arms. Did the writer, in his warm admiration for David, feel that these acts of Saul and his son were significant of David's succession to the honor of kingship? "His
bow": This was Jonathan's characteristic weapon (II Sam. 1:18,
22). Vs. 5, "behaved himself wisely": The word means also to
prosper (see margin). He was now made captain by Saul.

"Over the men of war": This would be likely to make the older soldiers jealous; but so popular was David that people and warriors alike approved his promotion.

QUESTIONS

Read over the text carefully, and study the comments.

(1) What did Saul ask of Abner? (2)* What does this question imply as to Saul's acquaintance with David? Could David have been Saul's armor-bearer, and yet be unknown to him? (3) Did Abner know him? (4)* What does "as thy soul liveth" mean? (5) What was the captain ordered to do? (6) Where was David taken by Abner? (7) What was he carrying? (8) What conversation took place between David and the king? (9)* What indications are there that more was said than is reported? Do we usually have in the Bible more than fragments of the conversations or addresses reported? (10) Who was Jonathan? (11) How many sons had Saul? (12)* What did Jonathan think of David? (13) Would it seem that they had ever met before? (14) What mark of honor did Saul show David? (15) What kind of an agreement did Jonathan and David make? (16) Did Jonathan foresee that David would be king? (17)* How did Jonathan show his love for David? (18) Do you suppose David gave Jonathan his garments and weapons? (19) What weapons did Jonathan give David? (20)* What services did David render Saul? (21) How did he conduct himself? (22) What high place did the king give him? (23) Why did not the older warriors complain of his rapid promotion? (24)* What elements in David's character are prominent in this section? (25) Do you suppose Jonathan's admiration for David may have been awakened by the deed which he himself would like to have performed, but was not permitted by his father to attempt?

SECTION XXXIX

SAUL'S JEALOUSY OF DAVID, I SAM. 18:6–16

And it came to pass as they came, when David 6
returned from the slaughter of the [1]Philistine, that
the women came out of all the cities of Israel, singing and dancing, to meet king Saul, with timbrels,
with joy, and with [2]instruments of music.

And the women [3]sang one to another as they 7
played, and said,

> Saul hath slain his thousands,
> And David his ten thousands.

And Saul was very wroth, and this saying dis- 8
pleased him; and he said, They have ascribed unto

[1] Or,
Philistines

[2] Or, *triangles*
or *three-
stringed
instruments*

[3] Or, *answered*

EXPLANATORY NOTES

With this section we return once more to the main line of the
narrative told by the early Judean writer. The praise of the
women of Israel for David's exploit rouses all of Saul's former
moodiness, and adds to it the rage of jealousy. Vs. 6, "as they
came": Saul, David, and the army. "Women came out": The
welcome of a warrior or the celebration of a victory was often the
work of the dancing and singing women (Judg. 11:34; Exod.
15:20). "Timbrels": tambourines. "Instruments": It is not
clear what they were; they were apparently instruments with three
parts, either sides (like triangles) or strings. Vs. 7, "thousands
. . . . ten thousands": The two lines may have been sung as an
antiphonal chant by two groups of women. There was no desire
to slight Saul, but David was the hero of the moment. Probably
neither had slain many victims in person, but David had made the
victory possible. Vs. 8, "very wroth": It seemed to the king like

David ten thousands, and to me they have ascribed but thousands: and what can he have more but the kingdom?

9   And Saul eyed David from that day and forward.

10   And it came to pass on the morrow, that an evil spirit from God came mightily upon Saul, and he [4]prophesied in the midst of the house: and David

[4] Or, *raved*

11 played with his hand, as he did day by day. And Saul had his spear in his hand; and Saul cast the spear; for he said, I will smite David even to the wall. And David avoided out of his presence twice.

12 And Saul was afraid of David, because the Lord

13 was with him, and was departed from Saul. Therefore Saul removed him from him, and made him his captain over a thousand; and he went out and

14 came in before the people. And David [5]behaved himself wisely in all his ways; and the Lord was

[5] Or, *prospered*

---

a deliberate slight. Vs. 9, "Saul eyed David": regarded him with suspicion and malice. Vs. 10, "an evil spirit"†: a fit of madness like his former attacks, so that he raved (margin). The use of the word "prophesied" for Saul's conduct shows how frenzied must have been the conduct of the rough, gypsy-like "prophets" of the age at times (I Sam. 10:6, 10; 19:18–24). Vs. 11, "cast the spear": Vss. 10, 11 seem to be out of place, as it was hardly time as yet for Saul to grow violent toward David till he had tried milder measures. The passage is a duplicate of 19:9, 10, probably inserted here by mistake. Vs. 12, "Saul was afraid": This also shows that it joins immediately to vs. 9. Vs. 13, "removed him": gave him a place among the soldiers in the field and thus banished him from his presence. Vs. 14, "the Lord was with him": an expression emphasizing his genial and

with him. And when Saul saw that he behaved 15
himself very wisely, he stood in awe of him. But 16
all Israel and Judah loved David; for he went out
and came in before them.

---

friendly nature, as well as his success. Vs. 15, "stood in awe":
His position as captain in the field gave him opportunities which
only increased his popularity. Vs. 16, "Judah and Israel":
south and north. "Loved David": From II Sam. 21:19 some
have supposed that "Elhanan" was David's real name, and that
"David" ("beloved") was the popular name applied to him
in the period of his rising power. "Went out and came in":
discharged the duties of his public office.

QUESTIONS

Study carefully the material of the section. Try to master
its ideas.

(1) How were Saul and David greeted on their return from
the campaign? (2) What instruments did the women carry?
(3)* On what other occasion had women celebrated victories
in this manner? (4) What was their song? (5) Did they
intend any discourtesy to Saul? (6)* Was Saul liked by the
people? (7) How did the words of the women affect the king?
(8) Do you think Saul's feelings were natural and pardonable?
(9) Did Saul's words imply that he already feared David's
popularity? (10) How did Saul treat David from this time?
(11)* What difficulties occur in placing vss. 10, 11 in their
present position? (12) What kind of a malady is described?
(13)* What connection was there between "prophesying"
and "raving"? (14) What did David do to relieve Saul?
(15) What did Saul do? (16) How did David escape? (17)
Is it probable that this scene belongs to a later time? (18)*
What qualities in David made Saul afraid of him? (19) Do
you think David at this time aspired to be king? (20) How

did Saul get rid of David? (21) Why did he not dismiss him entirely from his service? (22)* What caused David to gain such popularity? (23) Do you think the people thought of making David king? (24) If not, how could he affect Saul's prosperity? (25)* Would you say the king's jealousy was groundless? (26) What does this section teach on the subject of jealousy?

SECTION XL

DAVID MARRIES MICHAL, I SAM. 18:17-30

And Saul said to David, Behold, my elder daughter 17
Merab, her will I give thee to wife: only be thou
valiant for me, and fight the Lord's battles.   For
Saul said, Let not my hand be upon him, but let
the hand of the Philistines be upon him.   And David 18
said unto Saul, Who am I, and [1]what is my life, or
my father's family in Israel, that I should be son-in-
law to the king?   But it came to pass at the time 19

[1] Or, *who are my kinsfolk*

EXPLANATORY NOTES

In this section two separate stories of marriage proposals
between Saul and David are given.   The first from a popular
source is contained in vss. 17-19.   Saul offers Merab to David,
encouraging him to fight the Philistines, and hoping that he will
fall in battle.   That he did not intend to allow David to marry
his daughter is shown by his unscrupulous bestowal of her upon
another.   The second story from the main Judean narrative is
found in vss. 20-30 and is quite independent of the other.   Michal
is in love with David, and Saul thinks this a good occasion to
entrap him.   He proposes to him that he marry Michal on condition that he bring the proofs of his having slain 100 Philistines.
This he does, to the king's surprise and disappointment, and
the marriage is concluded.   Vs. 17, "only be thou valiant":
The offer of Merab as David's wife appears to be the fulfilment of
the offer to give his daughter to any man who should kill Goliath
(17:25), an offer mentioned in this same source.   By further
insistence that David shall fight in his behalf he hopes to procure
his death before his marriage.   Vs. 18, "my father's family":
David was needlessly modest, exhibiting characteristic oriental

180

when Merab, Saul's daughter, should have been
given to David, that she was given unto Adriel the
20 Meholathite to wife.   And Michal, Saul's daughter,
loved David: and they told Saul, and the thing
21 pleased him.   And Saul said, I will give him her,
that she may be a snare to him, and that the hand of
the Philistines may be against him.   Wherefore
Saul said to David, Thou shalt this day be my son-
in-law a second time.

22   And Saul commanded his servants, saying, Commune with David secretly, and say, Behold, the
king hath delight in thee, and all his servants love
23 thee: now therefore be the king's son-in-law.   And

---

politeness. His family was quite as good as Saul's. Vs. 19,
"given unto Adriel": a studied affront to David. By an error in
the text of II Sam. 21:8 Adriel is called the husband of Michal.

The second story, vss. 20–30, is apparently a duplicate of the
first, with the incidents slightly different. Vs. 20, "Michal†
. . . . loved David": This is continued directly from vs. 10,
which describes the love of the nation for David. Saul was
pleased, thinking it an excellent snare to entice David to endanger
his life. Vs. 21, "a second time": The words are obscure in the
Hebrew. If they are to be translated as here they are probably
added by the compiler to harmonize the paragraph with vss.
17–19. They may, however, be translated "on two conditions"
(not named) or "after two years" (unlikely). Probably the last
part of the verse is an interpolation. It is inconsistent with the
next verse where Saul approaches David not personally but
through his servants. Vs. 22, "commune with David": Saul
could hardly make the proposal to David, as it would be unbe-
coming. He puts the members of the court to work suggesting
the subject to David. Vs. 23, "a poor man": The customs of the

Saul's servants spake those words in the ears of
David. And David said, Seemeth it to you a light
thing to be the king's son-in-law, seeing that I am
a poor man, and lightly esteemed? And the servants 24
of Saul told him, saying, On this manner spake
David. And Saul said, Thus shall ye say to David, 25
The king desireth not any dowry, but a hundred
foreskins of the Philistines, to be avenged of the
king's enemies. Now Saul thought to make David
fall by the hand of the Philistines. And when his 26
servants told David these words, it pleased David
well to be the king's son-in-law. And the days were
not expired; and David arose and went, he and his 27

---

age required the young man who asked for a wife to make a considerable present, here called "dowry," to her father. In the
case of the king's daughter this would need to be large. Vs. 25,
"desireth not any dowry": This was exactly the plan that Saul
had meditated all the time to secure David's death. Saul would·
ask only for the proofs that David had killed a hundred Philistines,
not doubting that in the attempt David would be killed. The
mutilation of the bodies of enemies, living (Judg. 1:7; I Sam.
11:2) or dead (I Sam. 31:9; II Sam. 4:7), a custom brutal and
disgusting to us, was not infrequent in that age. Many nations
have practiced the cutting off of heads, hands, ears, or other portions of the bodies of their slain enemies as trophies of victory
(cf. the Indian custom of taking scalps). Josephus, the Jewish
historian, says that David was to bring six hundred heads. Vs.
26, "it pleased David well": The daughter of Saul was attractive,
the honor was great, the danger he held as a small thing, and he
supposed Saul sincere. "Not expired": No time limit is mentioned for the exploit, but this expression implies it. David lost
no time. Vs. 27, "two hundred": The Septuagint† has "one

men, and slew of the Philistines two hundred men; and David brought their foreskins, and they gave them in full number to the king, that he might be the king's son-in-law. And Saul gave him Michal his 28 daughter to wife. And Saul saw and knew that the Lord was with David; and Michal, Saul's daughter, 29 loved him. And Saul was yet the more afraid of David; and Saul was David's enemy continually.

30   Then the princes of the Philistines went forth: and it came to pass, as often as they went forth, that David ²behaved himself more wisely than all the ᵃ Or, *prospered* servants of Saul; so that his name was much ³set by. ᵇ Heb. *precious*

---

hundred" which agrees with vs. 25. "Gave him Michal": It is clear from both stories that the king had no intention of giving David his daughter. But after the fulfilment of the conditions there was no excuse for further delay. Vs. 28, "Saul saw and knew": His plans to kill David had failed, and his own daughter was the contented and happy wife of the man he hated. He could not fail to see the favorable issue of all David's affairs. Vs. 30, "Philistines went forth": to battle or on raids; this gave opportunity for fighting in which David was always the most successful of the Hebrew leaders. His popularity increased constantly. The contrast between Saul and David is heightened. Saul grew more envious, jealous, suspicious, and vengeful; David more valiant, skilful, successful, and popular.

QUESTIONS

(1)* What two accounts of marriage arrangements are given in this section? (2) What previous statement had led David to expect the king's daughter in marriage? (3) Was Saul's offer of Merab in fulfilment of an earlier promise or the result of good-will toward David? (4)* What conditions did he impose in the marriage with Merab? (5) What was Saul's motive in this offer? Was it the most promising way of seeking David's death? (6) Did David receive it in good faith? (7) What did he say of himself? (8)* Was David right in thinking himself unworthy of marriage with Saul's daughter? (9) How was the marriage prevented? (10) Did Saul intend at any time that it should take place? (11) To whom was Merab married? (12)* What are the indications that vss. 20-30 are from another source than vss. 17-19? (13) What is the name of Saul's daughter in the second narrative? (14) What made it easy for Saul to plot against David?. (15)* Do you suppose that Saul's knowledge that Michal loved David was pleasant when he first learned it? (16) How did he plan to take advantage of it? (17) What are the reasons for regarding vs. 21b as an interpolation? (18) Why did Saul use his servants in influencing David? Is there here an indication that Saul and David were not on easy terms of friendship? (19)* What objection did David raise to the proposal? (20) What was the custom in reference to a payment for a bride? (21) Do you think Saul's servants knew that he was plotting against David? (22) Why was Saul willing to give up a marriage gift and take in exchange the killing of the Philistines? (23)* What two advantages would Saul gain by this plan? (24) How was David pleased by the proposal? (25) Give the reasons why he found it satisfactory. Would it remove all difficulties in the way of his marriage with the king's daughter? (26) How did David show his promptness? (27) How many Philistines did he kill? (28) Was it a time of war between Israel and the Philistines? (29) Do you think Saul was glad when David fulfilled the conditions? What would have pleased him most? (30)* How does this account differ from that of Merab's proposed marriage? (31) How did these things affect Saul? (32) What events gave David fresh opportunities for public approval? (33) What is the leading idea of this section? (34) Do you not think Saul's nature has changed greatly since he became king? (35) What new and unpleasant elements are now seen in his character? (36) Is it ever possible for one who shows himself insincere and designing to be loved and trusted?

MODERN ARABS

SECTION XLI

SAUL'S PLOTS AGAINST DAVID, I SAM. 19:1-17

And Saul spake to Jonathan his son, and to all his 19
servants, that they should slay David. But Jonathan, Saul's son, delighted much in David. And 2
Jonathan told David, saying, Saul my father seeketh
to slay thee: now therefore, I pray thee, take heed to
thyself in the morning, and abide in a secret place,
and hide thyself: and I will go out and stand beside 3
my father in the field where thou art, and I will commune with my father of thee; and if I see aught, I
will tell thee. And Jonathan spake good of David 4

EXPLANATORY NOTES

The narrative of the Judean writer of David's life is continued
in this section from Section XL. It falls into three divisions: (1)
Saul's command to put David to death, and Jonathan's successful
intercession (vss. 1–7); (2) David's increasing popularity and
Saul's attempt upon his life (vss. 8–10); (3) Michal's rescue of
David from Saul's plot (vss. 11–17). Vs. 1, "should slay David":
Saul's plans to dispose of David by strategem having failed, he
no longer conceals his hatred, but orders the assassination of the
young man. "Delighted much in David": The other writer
described this affection of Jonathan† for David, but the present
narrative mentions it here for the first time. Vs. 2, "take heed to
thyself in the morning": Jonathan warns David at night of
his father's purpose to kill him the next day. Vs. 3, "beside my
father in the field": David was to hide where he could overhear
the conversation of Saul and Jonathan. In this way David would
know just how Saul felt, and if there was anything else that he
needed to know, Jonathan would tell him Vs. 4, "Let not the

186

unto Saul his father, and said unto him, Let not the
king sin against his servant, against David; because
he hath not sinned against thee, and because his
5 works have been to thee-ward very good: for he put
his life in his hand, and smote the Philistine, and the
Lord wrought a great ¹victory for all Israel: thou   ¹ Heb.
sawest it, and didst rejoice; wherefore then wilt   *salvation*
thou sin against innocent blood, to slay David with-
6 out a cause? And Saul hearkened unto the voice of
Jonathan: and Saul sware, As the Lord liveth, he
7 shall not be put to death. And Jonathan called
David, and Jonathan showed him all those things.
And Jonathan brought David to Saul, and he was
in his presence, as beforetime.

8   And there was war again: and David went out,
and fought with the Philistines, and slew them with
9 a great slaughter; and they fled before him. And
an evil spirit from the Lord was upon Saul, as he sat
in his house with his spear in his hand; and David

---

king sin": Jonathan pleads earnestly for his friend. David, he
says, has done nothing but good, and has risked his life in the
king's service. Vs. 6, "Saul sware": This solemn oath assured
the young man that the king would change his attitude toward
David. Vs. 7, "brought David to Saul": Perhaps it is meant
that Jonathan called David from his hiding place while Saul was
still there, and effected their reconciliation on the spot. Vs. 9,
"an evil spirit"†: A fresh outburst of mad fury followed the new
victory of David and the consequent public rejoicing, of which he
was the hero. It is not unlikely that this is a duplicate of 18:10,
11, which, as we saw in Section XXXIX, seemed to be out of

was playing with his hand. And Saul sought to 10
smite David even to the wall with the spear; but he
slipped away out of Saul's presence, and he smote
the spear into the wall: and David fled, and escaped
that night. And Saul sent messengers unto David's 11
house, to watch him, and to slay him in the morning:
and Michal, David's wife, told him, saying, If thou
save not thy life to-night, to-morrow thou wilt be
slain. So Michal let David down through the 12
window: and he went, and fled, and escaped. And 13
Michal took the teraphim, and laid it in the bed, and
put a ²pillow of goats' hair at the head thereof, and
covered it with the clothes. And when Saul sent 14
messengers to take David, she said, He is sick.
And Saul sent the messengers to see David, saying, 15
Bring him up to me in the bed, that I may slay him.
And when the messengers came in behold, the tera- 16
phim was in the bed, with the ²pillow of goats' hair at
the head thereof. And Saul said unto Michal, Why 17
hast thou deceived me thus, and let mine enemy go,
so that he is escaped ? And Michal answered Saul,
He said unto me, Let me go: why should I kill thee ?

² Or, *quilt*

---

place. Vs. 10, "fled and escaped": David avoided the danger,
and probably went to his house. The words, "that night," seem
to belong to the following verse, which then reads, "and that
night Saul sent messengers," etc. Vs. 11, "unto David's house":
Some commentators connect this directly with 18:27, and understand it to have been David's wedding night when he would be
least suspicious of Saul's intentions. Michal†, his wife learned

of the plot, or observed Saul's men about the place, and warned
him.   Vs. 12, "through the window": The escape of the spies
from Jericho (Josh. 2:15) and of Saul of Tarsus from Damascus
(Acts 9:25), will be recalled.   Vs. 13, "took the teraphim"†:
The image was probably life-size.   By laying it in David's bed
lifting the head slightly with a pillow or roll, and covering it, as
the Arabs cover their heads to sleep, Michal made it resemble a
human form.   Vs. 14, "she said, He is sick": Probably the better
reading is "they said."   Saul's men waited about the house till
morning, then they entered to take David and found him sick, as
they supposed.   Thinking thus, and remarking it to one another,
they returned to Saul.   Vs. 15, "bring him up": Sick or well the
king wants him brought up as he is at once.   Vs. 16, "behold the
teraphim": When Saul's men returned to David's house to take
him, they discovered the fraud.   Vs. 17, "why should I kill
thee?": Michal asserts that David threatened her.   Of course
she did so to deceive Saul still further.   Her devotion to David
is apparent.   This entire section shows Saul's insane hatred of
David, and his desperate efforts to put him to death.   It must be
remembered that it is written with strong bias toward David.   If
we had the whole of the life of Saul told by a friendly writer it
might modify somewhat our judgment based on these narratives.

QUESTIONS

Read attentively the material of the lesson and the notes.

(1) What command did Saul give his son and servants?
(2)* How does this differ from his previous conduct toward
David?   (3) How did Jonathan feel toward David?   (4)
What advice did Jonathan give David?   (5)* How was David
to secure information regarding Saul's purpose?   (6) What
arguments did Jonathan use in David's favor?   (7) Would
such praise of David be likely to pacify or anger Saul?   (8)*
What effect did Jonathan's words have on the king?   (9)
What promise did he make?   What does this indicate as to
Saul's regard for Jonathan?   (10) How was reconciliation
effected?   (11) Why were the Philistines the most constant
enemies of Israel?   (12) What did David accomplish in the

campaign? (13)* What connection is there between the victory of David and the madness of Saul? Would the popular praise of David be likely to inflame Saul's anger again? (14) Where was Saul's house? Would Saul's house probably be a royal palace, or the home in which he had always lived at Gibeah? Was there any "royal" house before David's reign? (15) How was David seeking to relieve the king's trouble? (16)* Why was Saul armed? (17) How was David's life placed in peril at that time? (18) What other attempt did Saul make to kill David? If this was on David's wedding night, would it not further prove Saul's determination not to have David joined to his family? (19) What warning did Michal give David? (20) How do you suppose she learned of the danger? (21)* In what manner did she aid him to escape? (22) What other persons in Bible history escaped from danger in a similar way? (23) How did Michal deceive the men of Saul? (24) What is meant by teraphim? (25) How did Saul further reveal his hatred for David when he learned that he was sick? (26) When was it that the men of Saul found out the deception? (27) Were Michal's sympathies with Saul or with David? (28)* Why did she tell Saul that David had threatened her life? (29) What is the purpose of this section? (30) In what light does Saul appear in it? (31) Was Michal justified in the deception she practiced? (32) Do you admire her devotion to David?

SECTION XLII

DAVID'S FLIGHT TO SAMUEL, I SAM. 19:18-24

18 Now David fled, and escaped, and came to Samuel to Ramah, and told him all that Saul had done to him. And he and Samuel went and dwelt in
19 Naioth. And it was told Saul, saying, Behold,
20 David is at Naioth in Ramah. And Saul sent messengers to take David: and when they saw the company of the prophets prophesying, and Samuel standing as head over them, the spirit of God came upon the messengers of Saul, and they also prophe-

---

EXPLANATORY NOTES

This section contains one of the popular traditions regarding David, of which the purpose seems to be an explanation of the origin of the proverb noted in vs. 24, which has a different explanation in 10:12. It is not the true continuation of 19:1-17 (Section XLI), which is found in 21:1 f. David takes refuge with Samuel at Ramah, the prophet's home and the chief sanctuary.* Here Saul attempts to take him, first by sending troops to arrest him, and finally by coming in person. But he is drawn into the circle of prophets in the exercise of their ecstatic rites, and falls overpowered to the earth. Vs. 18, "to Samuel to Ramah": This is the first mention of the prophet since 16:13 when he returned to Ramah from Bethlehem after anointing David. "Dwelt in Naioth"†: a place in Ramah, probably near the sanctuary or high place. Vs. 20, "sent messengers": Saul was determined to arrest David wherever he might be. "Prophets prophesying"†: performing the enthusiastic and unrestrained rites of their religious order. It is one of the chief virtues of Samuel, a saner and wiser man, that he did not despise these ignorant and often fanatical

sied. And when it was told Saul, he sent other 21
messengers, and they also prophesied. And Saul
sent messengers again the third time, and they also
prophesied. Then went he also to Ramah, and came 22

¹ The Sept. has
the well of the
threshing floor
that is, etc.
² Or, cistern

to ¹the great ²well that is in Secu: and he asked and
said, Where are Samuel and David? And one said,
Behold, they be at Naioth in Ramah. And he went 23
thither to Naioth in Ramah: and the spirit of God
came upon him also, and he went on, and prophesied,
until he came to Naioth in Ramah. And he also 24
stripped off his clothes, and he also prophesied

³ Or, fell

before Samuel, and ³lay down naked all that day and
all that night. Wherefore they say, Is Saul also
among the prophets?

---

men, but drew them to him and gradually made of them aids in
the spread of a higher type of prophecy. "Spirit† of God": the
messengers of Saul were seized with the emotion which dominated
the prophets, and forgot their errand. Vs. 21, "they also prophesied": The contagion of prophetic frenzy overpowered them also.
It is the purpose of the story to show that among the means by
which the life of David was saved from so many dangers, was this
strange influence of the prophets engaged in their sacred rites,
which was like a wall of protection to the persecuted man. Vs. 22,
"came to the great well": At last Saul, angry that none of his
messengers had secured David, came himself to make sure of his
prey. What follows may perhaps be rendered "he came to the
cistern of the threshing-floor which is in the height." The word
Secu is unknown as a place-name and probably signifies the upper
part of Ramah. Vs. 23, "went thither to Naioth": On inquiry
he learned the whereabouts of the man he was seeking and started
to find him. Vs. 24, "stripped off his clothes": the act of one
possessed of a controlling influence too strong to be resisted. Like

the messengers he had sent, Saul fell under the spell of the prophetic religious exercises. The end of the verse supplies an explanation of the proverb as originating in this incident.

QUESTIONS

(1) What explanation does this story give of David's flight from his house at night? (2) Why would David be likely to find Samuel in Ramah? (3)* Where was Ramah? How far from Gibeah? (4) Why did David go to Samuel, for counsel or safety? (5) In what place in Ramah did Samuel and David live? (6) How did Saul learn where David was? (7) How did he attempt to arrest him? (8) What prevented the success of the plan? (9)* Describe in your own words what occurred to the messengers. (10) What was Samuel's relation to the prophets at Ramah? (11) Do you suppose he practiced these forms of "prophesying"? (12)* What did Saul do when he heard what had happened? (13) How often did he attempt to take David? (14) What final effort did Saul make? (15)* To what place in Ramah did he go? (16) What happened to Saul on his arrival? (17) What evidence of a disordered mind did Saul give? (18) How long did he continue in his trance or sleep? (19)* Was this the same sort of madness that had seized him in his own home (18:10)? (20) What proverb is said to have originated in this incident? (21) Is any other explanation of its origin given? (22) How do you explain the two stories regarding the proverb?* (23) What do you understand to be the purpose of this section? (24) With whom are the sympathies of the writer strongly enlisted, Saul or David? May it have been part of his purpose to show that no combination of forces can be successful finally against a good man?

SECTION XLIII

THE FRIENDSHIP OF DAVID AND JONATHAN
I SAM. 20:1-23

And David fled from Naioth in Ramah, and came 20
and said before Jonathan, What have I done? what
is mine iniquity? and what is my sin before thy
father, that he seeketh my life? And he said unto 2
him, God forbid; thou shalt not die: behold, my
father doeth nothing either great or small, but that
he discloseth it unto me: and why should my father

EXPLANATORY NOTES

This section resumes the main narrative of the Judean account
of David's life. Yet it seems to have stood originally at some
earlier point in the growing hostility of Saul toward David. In
this section Jonathan hardly believes that his father means harm
to his friend, whereas the events of 19:1-17 (to say nothing of
19:18-24, from the other source) show all too plainly that Saul
was jealous of David beyond all enduring of his presence. If the
scenes at David's house (19:11-17) and at Ramah (19:18-24)
had actually taken place at this time, David would not have
needed to ask counsel of Jonathan. He would have known that
his only safety lay in instant flight. The section probably stood
originally at an earlier place in the narrative. Vs. 1, "fled from
Naioth": These words were probably supplied by the compiler
to join together the two narratives. "What have I done?":
The two young men are such close friends that David trusts
Jonathan even in a matter which so closely concerns his father.
Unconscious of evil, David only feels that Saul's attitude is
increasingly hostile. Vs. 2, "he discloseth it unto me": Jonathan
is astonished to learn of David's apprehension, for he has seen

3 hide this thing from me? it is not so. And David
sware moreover, and said, Thy father knoweth
well that I have found grace in thine eyes; and he
saith, Let not Jonathan know this, lest he be grieved:
but truly as the Lord liveth, and as thy soul liveth
4 there is but a step between me and death. Then
said Jonathan unto David, [1]whatsoever thy soul
5 [2]desireth, I will even do it for thee. And David said
unto Jonathan, Behold, to-morrow is the new moon,
and I should not fail to sit with the king at meat: but
let me go that I may hide myself in the field unto the
6 third day at even. If thy father miss me at all, then
say, David earnestly asked leave of me that he might
run to Beth-lehem his city: for it is the yearly sacri-
7 fice there for all the family. If he say thus, It is
well; thy servant shall have peace: but if he be
wroth, then know that evil is determined by him.
8 Therefore deal kindly with thy servant; for thou hast
brought thy servant into a covenant of the Lord with
thee: but if there be in me iniquity, slay me thyself;
for why shouldest thou bring me to thy father?

[1] Or, *What doth thy soul desire, that I should do it for thee?*
[2] Heb. *saith*

---

nothing to indicate Saul's hatred of his friend. Surely, he thinks
the king would have spoken to him if such were the case. Vs. 3,
"let not Jonathan know": David thinks Saul may purposely
conceal his designs from his son, knowing his affection for David;
but he is very certain that his life is in the greatest danger. Vs. 5
"the new moon": The beginning of the month was regarded as a
festal time. The king's household would be expected to be present
at the feast on that day. Vs. 6, "yearly sacrifice": This was to
be the excuse offered for David's absence. If the king noticed

And Jonathan said, Far be it from thee: for if I 9
should at all know that evil were determined by my
father to come upon thee, then would I not tell it
thee? Then said David to Jonathan, Who shall 10
tell me if perchance thy father answer thee roughly?
And Jonathan said unto David, Come and let us go 11
out into the field. And they went out both of them
into the field.

And Jonathan said unto David, The Lord, the 12
God of Israel, be witness; when I have sounded
my father about this time to-morrow, or the third
day, behold, if there be good toward David, shall I
not then send unto thee, and disclose it unto thee?
The Lord do so to Jonathan, and more also, should 13
it please my father to do thee evil, if I disclose it not
unto thee, and send thee away, that thou mayest
go in peace: and the Lord be with thee, as he hath
been with my father. And thou shalt not only 14
while yet I live shew me the kindness of the Lord

---

the vacant place, and was angry, they would know that it was no
passing mood. Family feasts were held on the birthday of the
father or the oldest son (Job. 1:4). Vs. 9, "would I not tell
thee?": There could be no concealments between two such
friends. Vs. 10, "who shall tell me?": In case Saul was angry
with David Jonathan might find it hard to get word to him. Vs.
11, "into the field": They could arrange their plan of communication better away from the court. Vs. 13, "The Lord do so":
a form of making a very solemn promise. It invoked God's
wrath upon the man who made the pledge, in case he should not
fulfil it. "Be with thee": The meaning of these words seems

15 that I die not: but also thou shalt not cut off thy
kindness from my house for ever: no, not when the
Lord hath cut off the enemies of David every one
16 from the face of the earth. So Jonathan made a
covenant with the house of David, saying, And the
Lord shall require it at the hand of David's enemies.
17 And Jonathan caused David to swear again,[3]for the
love that he had to him: for he loved him as he loved
18 his own soul. Then Jonathan said unto him, To-
morrow is the new moon: and thou wilt be missed,
19 because thy seat will be empty. And when thou
hast stayed three days, thou shalt go down quickly,
and come to the place where thou didst hide thyself
[4]when the business was in hand, and shalt remain
20 by the stone Ezel. And I will shoot three arrows
on the side thereof, as though I shot at a mark.
21 And, behold, I will send the lad, saying, Go, find the
arrows. If I say unto the lad, Behold, the arrows
are on this side of thee; take [5]them, and come; for

[3] Or, *by his love toward him*

[4] Heb. *in the day of the business*

[5] Or, *him*

---

clearly to be that Jonathan believes David will be king. Vs. 15,
"from my house": The writer recalls David's kindness to the
son of Jonathan (II Sam. 9:1 f.), and traces its motive to this
interview between the friends. Vs. 16, "at the hand of David's
enemies": The covenant of love and kindness between the two
men and their families was not to be broken; and if it were broken
by David, God would see that David's enemies punished him for
his faithlessness. Vs. 19, "where thou didst hide": By the third
day Jonathan would certainly know the mind of his father. At
that time David was to take his place at the spot designated, where
another event, not here named, had taken place. It is possible

there is peace to thee and ⁶no hurt, as the Lord
liveth.   But if I say thus unto the boy, Behold, the 22
arrows are beyond thee;   go thy way;   for the Lord
hath sent thee away.   And as touching the matter 23
which thou and I have spoken of, behold, the Lord
is between thee and me for ever.

---

that the reference is to 19: 2 f. "By the stone Ezel": No such place
is known.   It may be better rendered "by the side of the stone
heap yonder."   Vs. 22, "the arrows are beyond thee": They
thus arranged a plan of communication in case Jonathan should
not be able to come alone to David.

QUESTIONS

Read over the text and notes with care.

(1) With what is the first part of vs. 1 intended to connect
this section?   (2)* In his distress what did David do?   (3)
Why was Jonathan astonished at David's questions?   (4)
What gave him confidence that David was mistaken?   (5)*
To what did David attribute Jonathan's ignorance of his
father's intentions?   (6) How did David express his sense of
danger?   (7) What offer did Jonathan make?   (8) What
was the feast of the new moon?   (9)* Why would David be
expected to be in his place especially at that time?   (10) What
would be the object of his hiding?   (11) What explanation
of David's absence was Jonathan to give?   (12) Was this
true?   Did the men of that age feel that a falsehood of this
kind was wrong?   Do you think that falsehood is ever right?
Even in this case could not some better way have been found
to ascertain the facts?   (13)* What was a yearly sacrifice?
(14) Where did David's family live?   How far was it from
Saul's home?   (15) How was Jonathan to know whether
Saul was angry with David or not?   (16)* What did David

beg from his friend? (17) Was he afraid Jonathan would deceive him? (18) What did Jonathan promise? How does this close and trusting friendship of the two young men impress you? Is it an easy thing to secure such a friend? (19) What might arise to prevent the two friends from communicating? (20)* Why did they go into the field to arrange their plan? (21) Why did Jonathan need so much time to learn his father's feeling? (22)* If Saul was unfriendly to David, would he show it more the longer David was away? (23) What form of pledge did Jonathan make to David (vs.13)? (24) Did Jonathan appear to think that David would become king? Why? Do you think he was glad to believe that David would be king? Is not this a rare example of an unselfish nature? (25)* Did he mean to imply that God was no longer with his father? (26) What is meant by "the kindness of the Lord"? (27) For whom did Jonathan ask David's care? (28) Does this imply that he did not expect to live as long as David? (29)* What future glory did Jonathan predict for David (vs. 15)? (30) What warning did Jonathan give David in case he should not keep the covenant? (31) By what did Jonathan ask David to swear (vs. 17 margin)? (32)* What plan did Jonathan propose for letting David know Saul's attitude? (33) What were the signals agreed upon? (34) What is the purpose of this section? (35) Do you remember any other conspicuous cases of close friendship in the Bible or in history?

SECTION XLIV

PARTING OF DAVID AND JONATHAN, I SAM.
20:24–42

So David hid himself in the field: and when the 24
new moon was come, the king sat him down to eat
food. And the king sat upon his seat, as at other 25
times, even upon the seat by the wall; and Jonathan
stood up, and Abner sat by Saul's side: but David's
place was empty. Nevertheless Saul spake not any- 26
thing that day: for he thought, Something hath
befallen him, he is not clean; surely he is not clean.
And it came to pass on the morrow after the new 27
moon, which was the second day, that David's
place was empty: and Saul said unto Jonathan his
son, Wherefore cometh not the son of Jesse to meat,
neither yesterday, nor to-day? And Jonathan 28

EXPLANATORY NOTES

This section, continuing the story of the parting of David and
Jonathan, is from the early Judean life of David. Saul gives
unmistakable tokens of anger at David's absence from the feast
of the new moon, and rebukes Jonathan for his friendship with the
son of Jesse. Thereupon Jonathan gives David the sign to depart,
and bids him farewell. Vs. 24, "new moon was come": The
feast was eaten on the evening on which the moon was first seen.
Vs. 25, "the king sat": It was a sacrificial feast, and the four
chief members of Saul's household were supposed to be present—
Saul, Jonathan, Abner, and David. Vs. 26, "he is not clean":
Any accident might have rendered David unfit for a feast of this
kind, which required that all participants should be ceremonially

answered Saul, David earnestly asked leave of me to
29 go to Beth-lehem: and he said, Let me go, I pray
thee; for our family hath a sacrifice in the city; and
my brother, he hath commanded me to be there, and
now, if I have found favor in thine eyes, let me get
away, I pray thee, and see my brethren.   Therefore
he is not come unto the king's table.

30   Then Saul's anger was kindled against Jonathan,
and he said unto him, Thou son of a perverse rebellious woman, do not I know that thou hast chosen
the son of Jesse to thine own shame, and unto the
31 shame of thy mother's nakedness?   For as long as
the son of Jesse liveth upon the ground, thou shalt
not be established, nor thy kingdom.   Wherefore
now send and fetch him unto me, for he ¹shall surely
32 die.   And Jonathan answered Saul his father, and
said unto him, Wherefore should he be put to death?
33 what hath he done?   And Saul cast his spear at him

¹ Or, *is worthy
to die.* Heb. *is
a son of
death*

---

clean.   Vs. 29, "my brother": David's father was still living
(22:3), but the eldest brother might summon the clan.   Vs. 30,
"perverse rebellious woman": The most common method of
insulting a man in the Orient is to speak slightingly of his mother.
This Saul does, even though Jonathan's mother is his own wife.
His language is coarse and rude.   Of course a mother could
be disgraced by the evil conduct of her son; but Jonathan had
done nothing unworthy.   Vs. 31, "thou shalt not be established":
His care is for Jonathan's future as king, although he now treats
him with severity and contempt.   Saul is confident that David
is plotting to gain the throne.   "Send and fetch him": Saul thus
assumes that Jonathan knew where David was.   Vs. 33, "cast

to smite him; whereby Jonathan knew that it was determined of his father to put David to death.   So 34 Jonathan arose from the table in fierce anger, and did eat no food the second day of the month; for he was grieved for David, because his father had done him shame.

And it came to pass in the morning, that Jonathan 35 went out into the field ²at the time appointed with David, and a little lad with him.   And he said unto 36 his lad, Run, find now the arrows which I shoot. And as the lad ran, he shot an arrow ³beyond him. And when the lad was come to the place of the arrow 37 which Jonathan had shot, Jonathan cried after the lad, and said, Is not the arrow beyond thee? And 38 Jonathan cried after the lad, Make speed, haste, stay

² Or, *to the place*

³ Heb. *making it pass over him*

his spear," or "raised the spear at him": This was sufficient evidence that the king's intentions were only evil concerning David. Vs. 34, "in fierce anger": He felt his father's jealousy to be so unreasonable that it angered him intensely, and he could eat nothing. Vs. 36, "beyond him": While the boy picked up one, Jonathan shot an arrow over his head. Vs. 37, "cried after the lad": Of course the words were intended for the ears of David, whom he wanted to warn not to remain near the place but to fly at once. Vs. 41, "David arose": These verses, 41, 42, are quite evidently a later insertion. If David and Jonathan could meet and talk, there was no need of arranging signals and shooting arrows. "Toward the south": Probably the reading should be "from beside the mound," i.e., of stones (see note on 20:19). "Bowed himself three times": This ceremonious politeness in the circumstances seems out of place between the friends. "Kissed one another": Men kiss in the east in salutation and for affection's sake. "Until David exceeded": Perhaps the meaning

not. And Jonathan's lad gathered up the arrows,
39 and came to his master. But the lad knew not anything: only Jonathan and David knew the matter.
40 And Jonathan gave his weapons unto his lad, and
41 said unto him, Go, carry them to the city. And as
soon as the lad was gone, David arose [4]out of a
place toward the South, and fell on his face to the
ground, and bowed himself three times: and they
kissed one another, and wept one with another, until
42 David exceeded. And Jonathan said to David, Go
in peace, forasmuch as we have sworn both of us in
the name of the Lord saying, the Lord shall be
between me and thee, and between my seed and thy
seed, for ever. And he arose and departed: and
Jonathan went into the city.

[4] Heb *from beside the South.* Sept. *from beside the mound*

---

was "until the evening;" or some other point of time. The
present reading is uncertain. Vs. 42, "he arose and departed":
The last clause of vs. 42 probably joined vs. 40 directly. When
Jonathan had gathered up his arrows, he returned to the city
and David went his way.

QUESTIONS

(1)* At whose direction and where did David hide? (2)
Of what kind of a meal did Saul partake that night? Were
such feasts important events in Hebrew households? Would
they correspond to our Christmas or Thanksgiving gatherings?
(3) Describe the sitting at the king's feast. (4) What reason
occurred to Saul in explanation of David's absence? (5)*
What circumstances would keep a man from a sacred feast?
(6) Why did Saul notice David's absence on the second day?
(7) What explanation did Jonathan offer? Was this true?

(8)* Of what nature was a family sacrifice? (9) What is meant by "in the city"? Where was Bethlehem? (10) Why did David say his brother had commanded him, rather than his father? (11)* Why was Saul angry with Jonathan? (12) Why did he use such coarse language about Jonathan's mother? (13) Why did Saul fear David? (14) What was Jonathan ordered to do? (15)* What qualities in Jonathan are revealed by his defense of David? Was not Jonathan's position a most difficult one, loving both his father and David as he did? Do you think he hoped up to the very last to be able to reconcile the two? (16) What act of violence warned Jonathan of his father's true feelings? (17) How did Jonathan manifest his indignation at his father's conduct? (18) How did he prepare to warn David? (19)* What was the signal which informed David what to do? (20) To whom did he really address the words "make speed, haste"? (21) Did the boy understand the actions of his master? (22) What did he order the boy to do with his weapons? (23) What difficulty arises from vss. 42, 43? (24) Describe the conduct of the two men as related in these verses. (25) How did they renew their compact of friendship? (26)* What is the best lesson to be drawn from this section? (27) Is there any more precious possession in life than true friendship?

SECTION XLV

DAVID'S VISIT AT NOB, I SAM. 21:1-9

21 Then came David to Nob to Ahimelech the priest:
and Ahimelech came to meet David trembling, and
said unto him, Why art thou alone, and no man with
2 thee? And David said unto Ahimelech the priest,
The king hath commanded me a business, and hath
said unto me, Let no man know anything of the
business whereabout I send thee, and what I have
commanded thee: and I have appointed the young

EXPLANATORY NOTES

In this section, which is taken from the main narrative, the
Judean story of David's life, there is presented a continuation of
the account in 19:1-17, which tells of Saul's attempt to arrest
David in his house. The compiler has followed that incident with
David's journey to Samuel at Ramah (19:18-24) from a different
source. But it seems probable that originally the present section
was the true sequel. David, compelled to fly from his home at
night, perhaps his wedding night as was there pointed out (cf.
Section XLI), makes his way to Nob, just north of Jerusalem,
where he appears without attendants and unarmed and begs for
food and weapons. Vs 1, "to Nob† to Ahimelech"†: David
probably was on the way to his own clan at Bethlehem, the safest
place for him, and Nob was on the road. "Trembling": If David
had left his house in the haste of instant escape the night before
(19:12), he would be likely to arrive at Nob early in the morning,
without weapons or food, and with all the signs of flight. This
astonished the priest, who had been accustomed to think of David
as the chief friend of Saul and a man of power Vs. 2, "commanded me a business": David explains his appearance and lack
of preparation as due to an important and secret mission on which

men to such and such a place. Now therefore what 3 is under thy hand? give me five loaves of bread in my hand, or whatsoever there is present. And 4 the priest answered David, and said, There is no common bread under my hand, but there is holy bread; if only the young men have kept themselves from women. And David answered the priest, and 5 said unto him, Of a truth women have been kept from us about these three days; when I came out, the vessels of the young men were holy, ¹though it was but a common journey; how much more then to-day shall their vessels be holy? So the priest 6 gave him holy bread; for there was no bread there but the showbread, that was taken from before the

¹ Or, *and it may be used as common bread*

---

he had been sent by Saul. He was alone because the troops were ordered to meet him at a designated place. Of course this entire story of David's was false. He was a fugitive, unarmed and alone, flying from a king he feared. Vs. 3, "give me five loaves": He needed bread and knew of no other way to get it than to implore it of his friend the priest. Vs. 4, "no common bread": The showbread of the tabernacle was holy. The priest had no other sort. The sacred bread could only be eaten by the priests and those who had prepared themselves by washing and abstinence. In the later law it could be eaten only by the priests and in the sanctuary (Lev. 24:9). The priest said that he could give him the sacred bread in the emergency, provided the attendants, of whom David had just spoken, were ceremonially clean. Vs. 5, "how much more": David insists that the whole mission on which he and his (imaginary) troops are sent is so sacred that it is sufficient to make their persons and weapons holy. Vs. 6, "gave him holy bread": The scruples of Ahimelech were satisfied by the insistent words of David, and he gave him the holy bread. This

Lord, to put hot bread in the day when it was taken away.

7 Now a certain man of the servants of Saul was there that day, detained before the Lord; and his name was Doeg the Edomite, the ²chiefest of the herdsmen that 8 belonged to Saul. And David said unto Ahimelech, And is there not here under thy hand spear or sword? for I have neither brought my sword nor my weapons with me, because the king's business required haste. 9 And the priest said, The sword of Goliath the Philistine, whom thou slewest in the vale of ³Elah, behold, it is here wrapped in a cloth behind the ephod: if thou wilt take that, take it; for there is no other save that here. And David said, There is none like that; give it me.

² Or, *mightiest*

³ Or, *the terebinth*

---

was placed on the table of showbread every week. The priest gave him the loaves which were just being taken from the table to make room for the fresh bread. Vs. 7, "Doeg the Edomite"†: Saul was a man of some wealth, and this foreigner was employed by him as a herdsman to care for his mules or cattle. Some errand probably kept him at the sanctuary for a time. His presence there was a sad thing for David and the priests, as they later found to their cost (22:9). Vs. 8, "spear or sword": David had no weapons, on account of his hasty flight. He tried to explain this fact to the priest on the ground of urgent business for the king, and then begged some kind of weapons. Vs. 9, "the sword of Goliath": The trophy of David's victory hung in the sanctuary. Heavy as it must have been, it was better than nothing. David professed to be greatly pleased with it. "Behind the ephod"†: The ephod here is hardly a garment, more likely it was an image which the ideas of the time did not regard as idolatrous, and permitted even in the sacred tent.

QUESTIONS

Read carefully the text and what is said about it in the notes.

(1)* With what event is this arrival of David at Nob most satisfactorily connected? Does it seem to follow his escape from his house? (2) Where was Nob? (3) In what condition was David on his arrival? What would account for this fact? (4) Who was the priest? (5)* Have we met him in any former lesson? (6) Why did the priest tremble? Was David's coming a matter of great importance? (7) How did David explain his appearance? (8)* Who did he say were with him? Was it true that he had a body of followers? Why did he say this? (9) What was his need? (10) Why was this request for food perplexing to the priest? (11) What did the priest give David? Do you think the priest did the right thing in giving David what he requested? Would you say that human need ought to be more important than the forms of religion? Was this the view Jesus took of the matter? (cf. Mark 2:23–28). (12) Do you think David was justified in telling the falsehood? What do you suppose he gave as an excuse to his conscience for telling the lie? Do you think any excuses are sufficient in such a case? (13) What servant of Saul's was present at Nob? (14)* Why is he mentioned? (15) What was his business at the sanctuary? (16) What additional request did David make of the priest? (17) What excuse did he offer for having no weapons? (18)* What did Ahimelech suggest? (19) Where was the sword of Goliath? (20) What is meant by the ephod? (21) Was David glad to have this sword? (22)* Would it have been better for David to tell the simple truth to the priest? (23) What do you think is the most impressive lesson of this section?

*REVIEWED QUESTIONS
(Answers to these questions are to be written)

(1) What part did Samuel have in the choice of David as king?

(2) What was the occasion of David's introduction to the court of Saul?

(3) What great exploit of David's made him a popular hero?

(4) What were the causes of Saul's growing hatred of David?

(5) What attempts did he make to secure David's death?

(6) What were the relations of David and Jonathan? Give particulars.

(7) What took place at Nob on David's flight from Saul?

SECTION XLVI

DAVID AT THE COURT OF ACHISH
I SAM. 21:10-15

And David arose, and fled that day for fear of 10
Saul, and went to Achish the king of Gath. And 11
the servants of Achish said unto him, Is not this
David the king of the land? did they not sing one
to another of him in dances, saying,

> Saul hath slain his thousands,
> And David his ten thousands?

And David laid up these words in his heart, and 12

EXPLANATORY NOTES

The story of David among the Philistines given in this section
was probably a late popular tradition. It anticipates the real
facts as set down in 27:1 f., and is inconsistent with those facts.
It cannot be supposed that David would go back to the court of
Achish after the events of this section, or that he would have dared
to present himself in Gath with the sword of Goliath in his possession, or that the Philistines would have called him "king of the
land." The story is probably related to that giving the account
of David at Ramah (19:18-24). Vs. 10, "Achish the king of
Gath"†: This king is named in 27:2 f. as the one in whose service
David was enlisted for a considerable time. Vs. 11, "Is not this
David?": This question would be very strange in the mouths
of men as familiar with Saul's rule as were the Philistines at this
time. Perhaps the author of this late narrative wished to dis-
prove the fact that David ever served the Philistines, as discredit-
able alike to him and to Israel. This story would indicate that
David's stay in Gath was very short, and was not connected with
military service. The proverb is the familiar one of 18:7. The

13 was sore afraid of Achish the king of Gath.   And
he changed his behavior before them, and feigned
himself mad in their hands, and ¹scrabbled on the   ¹ Or, *made
doors of the gate, and let his spittle fall down upon   marks*
14 his beard.   Then said Achish unto his servants,
Lo, ye see the man is mad; wherefore then have ye
15 brought him to me ?   Do I lack madmen, that ye
have brought this fellow to play the madman in my
presence ?   shall this fellow come into my house ?

---

citizens of Gath would be far more likely to bring against David
the charge of Goliath's death.   Vs. 13, "changed his behavior":
David was terrified that he had been discovered, though how he
could expect to keep his identity secret in Gath is not easy to understand.   As the insane were regarded as sacred, under the direct
care of deity, he played the part of a madman.   It was the common belief of antiquity, and still prevails in the east, that the
demented are under the special power and protection of deity,
their minds are with God; hence they are reverenced and left
to wander about as they choose.   Vs. 15, "do I lack madmen?":
The king with rough humor indicates that he was not making a
collection of lunatics at his court.   David thus gained the opportunity of escape.   The account is intended to magnify the risks
and perils of David's career, his hair-breadth escapes, and the
divine favor by which he survived.

QUESTIONS

Read over the section and the explanatory notes.

(1)* What difficulties are there in regarding this section as
the continuation of the last?   (2) What seem to be its origin
and character?   (3) Where did David go according to this
account?   (4)* Who had lived in Gath?   (5) What did the
servants of Achish call David?   How did they know him?
(6) What proverb did they recall?   (7)* What incident in

David's history would they be most likely to remember?
(8) How did these reports affect David? (9) How did he try
to protect himself? What made it possible to use this method
successfully? Would you regard this as a clever ruse, or a
needless deception? (10) What was the reason for thinking
such conduct would insure his safety? (11) How did this
conduct impress Achish? (12)* Why did he not imprison or
kill David? (13) What opportunity did this attitude of the
king afford David? (14)* What did David intend to do in
Gath, according to this narrative? Would he have felt safe
if he could have secured a place in Achish's service? (15)
What do you think is the purpose of this section? (16) Can
you think of other leaders in history who have gone through
great personal perils?

SECTION XLVII

DAVID AT ADULLAM AND IN MOAB, I SAM.
22:1–5

22 David therefore departed thence, and escaped to the cave of Adullam: and when his brethren and all his father's house heard it, they went down thither 2 to him. And every one that was in distress, and every one that was in debt, and every one that was ¹discontented, gathered themselves unto him; and he became captain over them: and there were with him about four hundred men.

3 And David went thence to Mizpeh of Moab; and

¹ Heb. *bitter of soul*

EXPLANATORY NOTES

The narrative here continues the main story given in the Judean account of David's career. It seems to follow 21:9 (Section XLV), the record of David's interview with Ahimelech the priest at Nob. Vs. 1, "departed thence": If the relation just suggested is the true one, David had just left the sanctuary at Nob. "Cave of Adullam"†: "Stronghold" is a better rendering than "cave." The town was in David's tribe of Judah, and a natural refuge in his distress. "Went down thither to him": David's family would not be safe in Bethlehem after he was outlawed from the court, and so took refuge with him in the stronghold. Vs. 2, "became captain": David's popularity won him many friends in his flight from Saul. Many others who were inclined to the outlaw life for various reasons rallied around him. Debtors would welcome the opportunity to escape being sold for debt. From these sources he soon found himself with a considerable following. Such a company gathered about Jephthah, (Judg. 11:3). Later David's 400 grew to 600 (30:9). Vs. 3, he said unto the king of Moab, Let my father and my mother, I pray thee, come forth, and be with you, till I know what God will do for me. And he 4 brought them before the king of Moab: and they dwelt with him all the while that David was in the stronghold. And the prophet Gad said unto David, 5 Abide not in the stronghold; depart, and get thee into the land of Judah. Then David departed, and came into the forest of Hereth.

"Mizpeh of Moab"†: The place is unknown. "Mizpeh" means "watchtower." There were many places of that name in Palestine. It may have been the "stronghold" mentioned in vss. 4, 5. It would seem that David deemed himself insecure on the soil of Israel, in spite of the force at his command. It has been supposed that he was led to choose Moab as a refuge because of his own descent from Ruth the Moabitess (Ruth 4:18–22; Matt. 1:5, 6). Vs. 5, "prophet Gad": one of several prophets who advised David at various times. His advice here was to return to Judah, probably because it was wiser not to leave the sacred land, and also to remain with his own people in hope of better days. The "forest of Hereth" is unknown. It was probably not far from Adullam.

QUESTIONS

Carefully read the text and the notes.

(1)* From what place did David go in vs. 1? (2) Where was Adullam? (3) To what place in Adullam did David go? Is "cave" or "stronghold" the better translation? (4) Who came to him here? (5)* Why did his family come? (6) What became of the family possessions in Bethlehem? Do you suppose Saul seized them? (7) What other classes joined David? (8)* Why did they come to him? What had he to offer them? (9) How many were there of them?

(10) Why did not David remain in Adullam? (11) Where did he go? (12) Why did he go to Moab? (13) What request did he make of the king of that land? Is not his care of his aged parents a beautiful feature in David's life? Would not a true man regard this as his first duty? (14) Where was Moab? (15)* Did David leave his 400 followers in Adullam, or take them to Moab? Could they easily care for themselves after he left them? (16) How long did his parents remain in Moab? (17) Who advised David to return? (18)* What were the reasons for this? Was it always better for a leader to be near his people? (19) To what place did he go? (20) What is the value of this narrative in the life of David? (21) What religious significance did the advice of the prophet have? (22) Was the prophet Gad anxious to see David made king?

SECTION XLVIII

SAUL'S SLAUGHTER OF THE PRIESTS, I SAM.
22:6-23

And Saul heard that David was discovered, and 6
the men that were with him: now Saul was sitting
in Gibeah, under the tamarisk-tree [1]in Ramah, with
his spear in his hand, and all his servants were standing about him. And Saul said unto his servants 7
that stood about him, Hear now, ye Benjamites; will
the son of Jesse give every one of you fields and
vineyards, will he make you all captains of thousands
and captains of hundreds, that all of you have con- 8
spired against me, and there is none that discloseth
to me when my son maketh a league with the son of
Jesse, and there is none of you that is sorry for me,
or discloseth unto me that my son hath stirred up
my servant against me, to lie in wait, as at this day?

[1] Or, *on the
height*

EXPLANATORY NOTES

This section is from the principal source, the early Judean life
of David. Vs. 6, "David was discovered": Nothing is said as
to how Saul learned this or whether he knew where David was.
"Sitting in Gibeah"†: The court was in Saul's own town. He
sat on the height under a tree that was probably held sacred
(Judg. 4:5). It was the place where he administered justice.
His spear he held in place of a sceptre and his officers stood about
him. Vs. 7, "fields and vineyards": It appears that Saul had
chosen his officers from his own tribe of Benjamin. His question
is ironical, "Has David offered you a higher price, that you seem
to favor him?" Vs. 8, "conspired against me": To the diseased

9 Then answered Doeg the Edomite, who ²stood by
the servants of Saul, and said, I saw the son of Jesse
coming to Nob, to Ahimelech the son of Ahitub.

10 And he inquired of the Lord for him, and gave him
victuals, and gave him the sword of Goliath the
Philistine.

11   Then the king sent to call Ahimelech the priest,
the son of Ahitub, and all his father's house, the
priests that were in Nob: and they came all of them

12 to the king.   And Saul said, Hear now, thou son of
Ahitub.   And he answered, Here am I, my lord.

13 And Saul said unto him, Why have ye conspired
against me, thou and the son of Jesse, in that thou
hast given him bread, and a sword, and hast inquired
of God for him, that he should rise against me, to lie

14 in wait, as at this day?   Then Ahimelech answered
the king, and said, And who among all thy servants

² Or, was set
over

---

fancy of the king all his court was in league with David.   The
charge is really against Jonathan, whom Saul accuses of urging
David on against him.   Vs. 9, "Doeg the Edomite"†: the herd-
man of Saul, who was at Nob when David visited Ahimelech
(21:7).   He was probably not "over" (margin), but "beside"
the officers of Saul, being a hired foreigner.   He tells of the gifts
of bread and the sword, and adds that the priest inquired of God
for David.   All this was fresh fuel on the flame of the king's
insane anger.   Vs. 11, "sent to call Ahimelech"†: From Gibeah
to Nob was but a short distance.   The entire company of the
priests was summoned.   Vs. 13, "Why have ye conspired?":
The king charges them directly with disloyalty to himself and
secret assistance to David.   "To lie in wait": Of course David
had done nothing of the kind.   Vs. 14, "who . . . . is so faithful

is so faithful as David, who is the king's son-in-law, and is taken into thy council, and is honorable in thy house? Have I to-day begun to inquire of God for 15 him? be it far from me: let not the king impute anything unto his servant, nor to all the house of my father; for thy servant knoweth nothing of all this, less or more. And the king said, Thou shalt surely 16 die, Ahimelech, thou, and all thy father's house. ³Heb. *runners* And the king said unto the ³guard that stood about 17 him, Turn, and slay the priests of the Lord; because their hand also is with David, and because they knew that he fled, and did not disclose it to me. But the servants of the king would not put forth their hand to fall upon the priests of the Lord. And the 18 king said to Doeg, Turn thou, and fall upon the priests. And Doeg the Edomite turned, and he

---

as David?": The priest was astounded at the charge, but with rare courage defended David. Vs. 15, "Have I to-day begun to inquire?": "Have I not many times before made inquires for him with your approval?" The priest marveled that he should now be blamed for doing what had always been his duty. Vs. 16, "Thou shalt surely die": No one but a mad tyrant would have treated a company of innocent men so brutally. Here the character of Saul is shown in its most repulsive form. Vs. 17, "would not put forth their hand": The sacredness of the priest's office, as well as the terrible injustice of the command made them hesitate. Vs. 18, "he fell upon the priests": Doeg had no scruples. The priests were men of peace, unarmed, and appalled at the sentence of the king. Allowing for all exaggeration in the numbers and details, it was a massacre that must have done much to weaken the loyalty of Saul's friends. Vs. 19, "the city of the priests": It hardly seems possible that Saul would dare to destroy

fell upon the priests, and he slew on that day four-
score and five persons that did wear a linen ephod.
19 And Nob, the city of the priests, smote he with the
edge of the sword, both men and women, children
and sucklings, and oxen and asses and sheep, with
the edge of the sword.

20   And one of the sons of Ahimelech, the son of
Ahitub, named Abiathar, escaped, and fled after
21 David.   And Abiathar told David that Saul had
22 slain the Lord's priests.   And David said unto
Abiathar, I knew on that day, when Doeg the Edomite was there, that he would surely tell Saul: I
have occasioned the death of all the persons of thy
23 father's house.   Abide thou with me, fear not; for
he that seeketh my life seeketh thy life: for with me
thou shalt be in safeguard.

---

a Hebrew city, the site of a local sanctuary.   This is perhaps a
later addition to the story.   Vs. 20, "Abiathar† escaped": Perhaps he had been left in charge of the sanctuary.   He fled to David
as the only means of saving his life.   Vs. 22, "I have occasioned
the death": David must have felt the weight of this fact, for he had
deceived the priest with a falsehood regarding his own condition
and relations to Saul (chap. 21).   Vs. 23, "thou shalt be in
safeguard": David could only compensate for his former deception and its terrible consequences by doing his utmost for the last
survivor of the family of Ahimelech.   The purpose of the narrative is apparently to show why it was that the priestly aid and
sympathy passed from Saul to David.

QUESTIONS

Study the text of the lesson and the notes upon it.

(1) What news came to Saul concerning David?   (2)
Where was Saul in the scene described?   (3) What was the

purpose of holding court in this manner? (4)* What accusation did Saul bring against his officers? (5) What did he call them? Why? (6) Were his charges true? Do you think several of the officers may have liked David better than the king himself? (7)* What two things did he charge against Jonathan? (8) What ground was there for such insinuations? (9) What do such words indicate regarding Saul's frame of mind? (10)* Why did not Saul's officers answer the charge? May it be possible that we have only an incomplete report of the conversation? (11) Who volunteered information? (12) What did Doeg know? (13) What three charges did he make against the priest? Whom did Saul summon? (14)* Why did he send for all the priests? (15) What did Saul say to Ahimelech? (16) How did the latter receive the king's words? (17)* What good things did he have to say of David? (18) Would this argument please or anger the king? (19) What did he say about his inquiries of God in behalf of David? (20)* How did he protest his innocence? Do you think the conduct of the priest manly and noble in his frank truthfulness and his courageous defense of David? (21) What effect did this have upon Saul? (22) What sentence did Saul pronounce? Did he have the right to kill these men? (23)* Why did he include the other priests in the order? (24) Why would not Saul's guard put the priests to death? Was a priest held in awe? (25)* Why should Saul think that Doeg would do what the rest had refused to do? (26) What is meant by "wear a linen ephod"†? (27) How did Saul complete the tragedy? (28)* What is the difficulty about this verse (vs. 19)? (29) How did Abiathar have a chance to escape? (30) Where did he go? (31)* What did David say regarding the tragedy? (32) Do you think he felt remorse for his own part in the death of the priests? Would not a man feel a life-long regret for his part in such an event? (33) What promise did he make to Abiathar? (34) How

would you describe the character of Doeg? (35) What new
light is thrown by this study on the nature of Saul? Is not
this a terrible picture of Saul, cruel, suspicious of all, even his
own son, vindictive, unjust? (36) What do you think to be
the chief purpose of this section? How does it illustrate the
mad rage and bitter consequences of jealousy?

SECTION XLIX

DAVID AT KEILAH, I SAM. 23:1-14

And they told David, saying, Behold, the Philis- **23** tines are fighting against Keilah, and are robbing the threshing-floors. Therefore David inquired of the **2** Lord, saying, Shall I go and smite these Philistines? And the Lord said unto David, Go, and smite the Philistines, and save Keilah. And David's men said **3** unto him, Behold, we are afraid here in Judah: how much more then if we go to Keilah against the armies of the Philistines? Then David inquired of the **4** Lord yet again. And the Lord answered him, and said, Arise, go down to Keilah; for I will deliver

---

EXPLANATORY NOTES

This section is taken from the main narrative of David's life, the early Judean account. David rescues Keilah, a city of Judah, from an attack by the Philistines, and remains there until Saul hears of his whereabouts and determines to pursue him. The people of Keilah will not offer to protect him, and he and his men make their escape to the wilderness. Vs. 1, "fighting against Keilah"†: One of the Philistine raids, so common in the time, was spoiling the region. "Robbing the threshing-floors"†: As these were high and conspicuous, it was easy to discover them, drive away the farmers and secure the grain. Vs. 2, "David inquired": by means of the ephod† which Abiathar the priest had. Vs. 3, "we are afraid": David's men thought it folly to attempt such an exploit as the relief of Keilah, since they were hardly safe even in the stronghold at Adullam. Vs. 5, "brought away their cattle": the beasts of burden which the Philistines had taken to carry away the spoil. Vs. 6, "fled to David": This verse, introduced here

5 the Philistines into thy hand. And David and his
men went to Keilah, and fought with the Philistines,
and brought away their cattle, and slew them with

WINNOWING GRAIN

6 a great slaughter. So David saved the inhabitants
of Keilah. And it came to pass, when Abiathar
the son of Ahimelech fled to David to Keilah, that
he came down with an ephod in his hand.

And it was told Saul that David was come to
Keilah. And Saul said, God hath ¹delivered him 7
into my hand; for he is shut in, by entering into a
town that hath gates and bars. And Saul summoned all the people to war, to go down to Keilah to 8
besiege David and his men. And David knew that
Saul was devising mischief against him; and he 9
said to Abiathar the priest, Bring hither the ephod.
Then said David, O Lord, the God of Israel, thy
servant hath surely heard that Saul seeketh to come 10
to Keilah, to destroy the city for my sake. Will the
men of Keilah deliver me up into his hand? will 11
Saul come down, as thy servant hath heard? O

¹ Sept. has *sold*

---

rather than at 22:23, shows how David was able to inquire of
God, having a priest with him. The practice of securing answers
from oracles was common in that age. An inquiry made through
a priest by means of an ephod was supposed to have the divine
sanction and to receive an answer from God. Later ages have
learned that the will of God is ascertained less by such magical
devices than by open-minded study of the divine program for the
age, aided by all the disclosures of past prophetic teaching. Vs.
7, "he is shut in": David was living in Keilah since his relief of
the place. Saul could count on the loyalty of its citizens to himself, so he was certain of capturing David. Vs. 10, "to destroy
the city": Saul would hope to secure David from the men of
Keilah, but if they were not willing to surrender him as prisoner,
Saul was prepared to destroy the place in order to accomplish his
purpose. Vs. 12, "They will deliver thee": The oracle assured
David that Saul would come, and that in spite of all David had
done for them, the men of Keilah would give him up to Saul.
Vs. 13, "departed out of Keilah": David and his warriors (600
here, but 400 in 22:2) escaped from the town before Saul started

Lord, the God of Israel, I beseech thee, tell thy servant. And the Lord said, He will come down.
12 Then said David, Will the men of Keilah deliver up
me and my men into the hand of Saul? And the
13 Lord said, They will deliver thee up. Then David
and his men, who were about six hundred, arose
and departed out of Keilah, and went whithersoever
they could go. And it was told Saul that David was
escaped from Keilah; and he forbare to go forth.
14 And David abode in the wilderness in the strongholds, and remained in the hill-country in the
wilderness of Ziph. And Saul sought him every
day, but God delivered him not into his hand.

---

out, and dispersed so that it was difficult to follow them. Vs. 14,
"wilderness of Ziph"†: It is probable that the reference to this
particular locality is a mistake, due to the later allusion to the
place. David probably roamed about in the district west of the
Dead Sea, called "The Wilderness" or "The Wilderness of
Judah."

QUESTIONS

Read carefully the section, and the notes upon it.

(1) Who told David about the danger to Keilah? (2)
Where was Keilah? (3)* Why did the Philistines fight
against it? (4) What was David's motive in wishing to fight
the Philistines in behalf of a Hebrew city? (5) Do you suppose he thought his help might be remembered with gratitude later? (6) How did David make inquiry of God?
Were such oracles common in that day? How do men
ascertain the will of God today? Which method do you
think the more satisfactory? (7) What answer did he receive? (8)* What objection did David's men make? (9)

What was the result of the expedition? (10) What naturally would be the sentiments of the people of Keilah toward David? (11)* What is the purpose of vs. 6 at this point? (12) What were Saul's feelings when he heard that David was in Keilah? Is it not singular that both Saul and David, though enemies to each other, should trust God for guidance, each believing his cause the right one? (13) What preparations did Saul make? (14)* How did David learn Saul's plans? (15) Was David troubled over the report of Saul's purpose? (16) What inquiries did he make of God? (17) What answer did he receive? (18)* Why should the men of Keilah think they were justified in giving up David to Saul? (19) What did David do on learning of their probable action? (20) How many companions did he have? (21) Where did they go? (22) What change did this make in Saul's plans? (23) What kind of life did David lead in this period? (24) To whom is David's safety attributed in the text?

SECTION L

JONATHAN'S VISIT TO DAVID, I SAM. 23:15-18

15 And David saw that Saul was come out to seek his life: and David was in the wilderness of Ziph in 16 ¹the wood. And Jonathan, Saul's son, arose, and went to David into ¹the wood, and strengthened his ¹ Or, *Horesh* 17 hand in God. And he said unto him, Fear not; for the hand of Saul my father shall not find thee; and thou shalt be king over Israel, and I shall be next unto thee; and that also Saul my father knoweth. 18 And they two made a covenant before the Lord: and David abode in ¹the wood, and Jonathan went to his house.

EXPLANATORY NOTES

This short section appears to be an insertion from a source external to the main narrative. It was doubtless one of the popular stories regarding David which had its rise in Judah, and was intended to strengthen David's claim to the throne by its statement that Jonathan foresaw and approved his choice as king. It was perhaps intended as a parallel to 20:35-42. Vs. 15, "David saw": "Feared" is a better translation. David's position was alarming, for the country in which he could find refuge was small, and it was unsafe for any of the people to afford him assistance against Saul's will. "In the wood": The marginal reading "Horesh" is only a conjecture. No place of that name is known with certainty. It was perhaps some wooded spot in the wilderness of Ziph† in the south of Judah. Vs. 16, "strengthened his hand in God": assured him that he had the divine protection. Vs. 17, "Fear not": Four things were mentioned by Jonathan as reasons why David should take courage.   The fact that David was to be king could only be inferred by Jonathan from David's character and ability.   Saul had feared such a result from the first.   Vs. 18, "made a covenant": Such an agreement had already been mentioned (18:3; 20:8).   It was a pledge that they would be true to each other, whatever happened.

QUESTIONS

Read and consider carefully the text and notes.

(1)* What is the purpose of this brief section?   (2) Where was David at this time?   (3) Did he have his men with him?   (4) What was the danger that he feared?   (5) By whom was he visited?   (6)* How far, and in what direction, did Jonathan travel to see David?   (7) What is meant by "strengthened his hands in God"?   Did Jonathan's visit give David courage as indicating that the sympathies even of Saul's friends were with him?   (8) What command did he give to David?   (9)* What assurance did he give regarding David's danger from Saul?   (10) How did he know this?   Was the statement the result of his feeling that David would succeed at last in spite of all that might happen?   (11) What led him to believe David would be king?   (12)* May this part of Jonathan's message have been supplied by the writer, in the light of the later facts?   (13) What position did Jonathan assign himself in the anticipated court of David?   (14) Why should Jonathan say that Saul knew David was to be king?   (15) What agreement did the two men make?   (16)* What do you regard as the most significant feature of this interview?   (17) What bearing would it have upon David's claims to the throne in later days?   (18) How does it illustrate the strong and beautiful friendship of Jonathan and David?

SECTION LI

DAVID PURSUED BY SAUL, I SAM. 23:19-29

19 Then came up the Ziphites to Saul to Gibeah,
saying, Doth not David hide himself with us in the
strongholds in ¹the woods, in the hill of Hachilah,   ¹ Or, *Horesh*
20 which is on the south of ²the desert? Now there-   ² Or, *Jeshimon*
fore, O king, come down, according to all the desire
of thy soul to come down; and our part shall be to
21 deliver him up into the king's hand. And Saul said,
Blessed be ye of the Lord; for ye have had compas-

EXPLANATORY NOTES

Several accounts are preserved telling of Saul's pursuit of David
and of the latter's escape. Whether these are different incidents
or variations of the same tradition is a matter of doubt. One has
already been given, the story of David's rescue of Keilah and his
escape from it at the approach of the king (I Sam. 23:1-14,
Section XLIX). The present section is perhaps a parallel of this,
having its origin in popular stories of David's exploits preserved
in Jewish traditions. It recounts the rescue of David from the
hands of Saul by reason of a Philistine raid in Judah, which
recalled the king to the north. It has been suggested that it was
a local tradition attempting to account for the name of a rock in
the region. Vs. 19, "Doth not David hide?": These Ziphites
belonged in the country to the south of Hebron, called the
wilderness of Ziph†. "In the hill of Hachilah": Some height
in the vicinity of Ziph. The place is not known. "South of the
desert": "Jeshimon," as the margin reads, was the desert region
west of the Dead Sea. Vs. 20, "come down": They pledged
themselves to capture David for Saul if the latter would come to
take him. Vs. 21, "have had compassion": Perhaps Saul's
friends showed so little zeal in attempting to rid him of David's

sion on me. Go, I pray you, make yet more sure, 22
and know and see his place where his ³haunt is, and
who hath seen him there; for it is told me that he
dealeth very subtly. See therefore, and take 23
knowledge of all the lurking-places where he hideth
himself, and come ye again to me ⁴of a certainty, and
I will go with you: and it shall come to pass, if he
be in the land, that I will search him out among all
the ⁵thousands of Judah.

And they arose, and went to Ziph before Saul: but 24
David and his men were in the wilderness of Maon,
in the Arabah on the south of ⁶the desert. And Saul 25
and his men went to seek him. And they told David:
wherefore he came down to the rock, and abode in

³ Heb. *foot*

⁴ Or, *with the certainty.*

⁵ Or, *families*

⁶ Or, *Jeshimon*

---

presence that he welcomed any sign of devotion. Vs. 22, "dealeth
very subtly": They would find it hard to take David by any
stratagem. Vs. 23, "of a certainty": When they had made sure
of David's whereabouts they were to return and tell the king.
Vs. 24, "wilderness of Maon, in the Arabah": Maon was a village
directly south of Ziph. The Arabah is the name of the entire
trench of the Jordan, especially the southern end, beyond the Dead
Sea. Vs. 25, "down to the rock": some well-known mountain
in that region. Vs. 26, "on this side . . . . on that side": The
pursuit of Saul was fierce, and in David's rapid flight around the
side of the mountain Saul and his men were but a little way behind.
Vs. 27, "Philistines have made a raid": The news called Saul
away just in time to save David from capture. The king had to
return to defend his land against the raiders. Vs. 28, "Sela-
hammahlekoth": From this incident the rock received this name,
"rock of divisions" or "separations" or "escape." Vs. 29,
"En-gedi"†: a place on the west shore of the Dead Sea, about
halfway along its side.

the wilderness of Maon.   And when Saul heard that, he pursued after David in the wilderness of Maon.
26 And Saul went on this side of the mountain, and David and his men on that side of the mountain: and David made haste to get away for fear of Saul; for Saul and his men compassed David and his men
27 round about to take them.   But there came a messenger unto Saul, saying, Haste thee and come; for the Philistines have made a raid upon the land.
28 So Saul returned from pursuing after David, and went against the Philistines: therefore they called
29 that place [7]Sela-hammahlekoth.   [8]And David went up from thence, and dwelt in the strongholds of En-gedi.

[7] That is, *The rock of divisions* or *escape*
[8] Chap. 24:1 in Heb.

QUESTIONS

(1) Read the lesson and the notes upon it, look up the names in the dictionary, and locate the places on the map.   (2)* Why did the people of Ziph inform Saul regarding David's retreat? Did they wish to injure David, or please Saul, or merely to make trouble on general principles?   (3) If they thought David a rebel and a dangerous man, was it their duty to help capture him?   Is it the duty of all citizens to help enforce law, or only the duty of the police?   (4)* How did Saul feel when he received their offer?   Did he seem to feel that it would require their help to capture David?   (5) Tell what Saul did in his effort to secure his enemy?   (6) Does it seem to have been by mere chance that David evaded Saul by getting on the opposite side of the mountain?   (7)* Why did not Saul continue the chase until he caught David?   (8) Would you call it a "providential escape," when a person is thus saved from a very great peril?   (9) In what ways does God help people in times of peril?

SECTION LII

DAVID'S MAGNANIMITY, I SAM. 24:1-22

And it came to pass, when Saul was returned from 24
following the Philistines, that it was told him, saying, Behold, David is in the wilderness of En-gedi.
Then Saul took three thousand chosen men out of all 2
Israel, and went to seek David and his men upon

EXPLANATORY NOTES

The story of David's escape from Saul's pursuit, which was
begun in 23:19 (Section LI) is continued in the present section.
It is apparently one of the popular Judean traditions regarding
David's wonderful preservation. It is much like the narrative
found in 23:1-14 (Section XLIX, the escape from Keilah) which is
completed in chap. 26 (Section LV, David's refusal to kill Saul in
the barricade). In both the Ziphites were the informants, and
in both David spares Saul's life. The two accounts are perhaps
variations of the same story. Vs. 1, "returned from following
the Philistines": In 23:27 (Section LI) Saul is recalled from the
pursuit of David by news of a Philistine raid. Nothing is said of
the outcome. It is merely assumed that the king was successful
in expelling his foes from the highlands. On his return he takes
up again the pursuit of David. "The wilderness of En-gedi"†:
on the west shore of the Dead Sea, near the center. Vs. 2, "three
thousand": Saul also had three thousand men with him at the
beginning of his rule (13:2). "Rocks of the wild goats": haunts
of the ibex, still found in that rough region. Vs. 3, "sheepcotes":
shelters for sheep; probably caves with walls built around the
entrance. "Saul went in": for privacy; the Septuagint says
"to sleep." "David and his men": Of course only a few of
David's men could have been in the cave, which was probably
not large. They had taken refuge there from Saul's soldiers no

3 the rocks of the wild goats. And he came to the sheepcotes by the way, where was a cave; and Saul went in to cover his feet. Now David and his men were ¹abiding in the innermost parts of the cave. ¹ Or, *sitting*

4 And the men of David said unto him, Behold, the day of which the Lord said unto thee, Behold, I will deliver thine enemy into thy hand, and thou shalt do to him as it shall seem good unto thee. Then David arose, and cut off the skirt of Saul's robe

5 privily. And it came to pass afterward, that David's heart smote him, because he had cut off

6 Saul's skirt. And he said unto his men, the Lord forbid that I should do this thing unto my lord, the Lord's anointed, to put forth my hand against him,

7 seeing he is the Lord's anointed. So David checked his men with these words, and suffered them not to rise against Saul. And Saul rose up out of the cave and went on his way.

8 David also arose afterward, and went out of the cave, and cried after Saul, saying, My lord the king.

---

doubt. Vs. 4, "Behold, the day": Saul, coming in from the light, could not see the men sitting about the cave. They felt that the advantage David had must not be lost. It was the moment they had waited for. "Cut off the skirt": David would not injure Saul, however. He only cut off a part of his garment as a proof that the king was in his power. Vs. 5, "David's heart smote him": Even this small act seemed presumptuous. He felt that the king's person, anointed of God, was sacred. Vs. 6, "should do this thing": It is the answer to their insistence that he should kill Saul. Vs. 8, "cried after Saul": David had no

And when Saul looked behind him, David bowed
with his face to the earth, and did obeisance. And 9
David said to Saul, Wherefore hearkenest thou to
men's words, saying, Behold, David seeketh thy
hurt? Behold, this day thine eyes have seen how 10
that the Lord had delivered thee to-day into my
hand in the cave: and some bade me kill thee; but
mine eye spared thee; and I said, I will not put forth
my hand against my lord; for he is the Lord's
anointed. Moreover, my father, see, yea, see the 11
skirt of thy robe in my hand; for in that I cut off the
skirt of thy robe, and killed thee not, know thou and
see that there is neither evil nor transgression in my
hand, and I have not sinned against thee, though
thou ²huntest after my life to take it. The Lord 12
judge between me and thee, and the Lord avenge
me of thee; but my hand shall not be upon thee.
As saith the proverb of the ancients, Out of the 13
wicked cometh forth wickedness; but my hand shall

> Or, *layest
wait for*

---

intention of missing his chance to impress upon the king the cause-
less nature of his hatred, and his own generous and loyal feelings
toward the king. Vs. 9, "hearkenest to men's words": Here for
the first time it is intimated that Saul's courtiers used their influence to embitter their lord against David. "The Lord had delivered thee": David boldly claimed that God was on his side in
the strife with Saul. Vs. 12, "the Lord avenge me of thee":
The words are not a call for vengeance, but a cry for justification
and vindication. Only God could know how little he wished
injury to the king, whom he reverenced and even called "my
father." Vs. 13, "Out of the wicked": Proverbs were very
common among the Hebrews (compare I Sam. 10:12; Ezekiel

14 not be upon thee. After whom is the king of Israel
   come out? after whom dost thou pursue? after a
15 dead dog, after a flea. The Lord therefore be judge,
   and give sentence between me and thee, and see,
   and plead my cause and ³deliver me out of thy hand.   ³ Heb. *give*
     sentence for me
16 And it came to pass, when David had made an
   end of speaking these words unto Saul, that Saul
   said, Is this thy voice, my son David? And Saul
17 lifted up his voice, and wept. And he said to David,
   Thou art more righteous than I; for thou hast rendered unto me good, whereas I have rendered unto
18 thee evil. And thou hast declared this day how that
   thou hast dealt well with me, forasmuch as when
   the Lord had delivered me up into thy hand, thou
19 killedst me not. For if a man find his enemy, will
   he let him go well away? wherefore the Lord reward thee good for that which thou hast done unto
20 me this day. And now, behold, I know that thou
   shalt surely be king, and that the kingdom of Israel

12:23; Luke 4:23). The meaning is that one naturally expects
evil from an evil-minded man, and that in the end a bad man
brings disaster upon himself (does David mean Saul?), but that
for himself he has no purpose to do the king any injury. Vs. 14,
"after a dead dog, after a flea": By such comparisons, David
would persuade Saul that it was not worth while for the king to
hunt down so obscure a man. Vs. 16, "Saul . . . . wept":
His better nature was appealed to, and he saw, with self-reproach,
the injury he was doing to David. Vs. 17, "thou hast rendered
unto me good": The contrast between David's conduct and his
own brought him to repentance and grief. Vs. 20, "thou shalt
surely be king": In the strong emotion of the moment, Saul

shall be established in thy hand.   Swear now there- 21
fore unto me by the Lord, that thou wilt not cut off
my seed after me, and that thou wilt not destroy my
name out of my father's house.   And David sware 22
unto Saul.   And Saul went home; but David and
his men gat them up unto the stronghold.

---

insists that David's conduct has made him deserving of the kingship, and that God will bestow it upon him.   This was of course
very far from the king's usual thought, and the writer probably
intends us to understand it merely as the momentary result of
David's generous action and words.   Vs. 21, "Swear now":
Saul begs David to promise kindness to the king's family.   The
writer no doubt had in mind David's later consideration for the
house of Saul.

QUESTIONS

(1) Read the lesson over carefully, making sure that you
understand the terms, and find the scene of these events on
the map.   (2)* Why was Saul pursuing David?   (3) Was it
natural that David's men should want to kill Saul when they
had the opportunity?   Would you call it weakness on David's
part that he refused to harm the king?   Does it require more
heroism at times to keep from doing a mean thing than at
other times to do a noble one?   (4)* How many reasons can
you give for David's refusal to harm Saul?   In II Kings
6:8–23 there is another story of generous treatment to an
enemy.   Such was the conduct of Saladin toward Richard of
England in the Crusades.   (5) What use did David want to
make of the strip of cloth he cut from Saul's robe?   (6) What
did David say to Saul, when he called to him after he left the
cave?   Repeat his words as well as you can.   (7)* What
effect did David's speech have upon Saul?   How do we
know that he was affected by it?   (8) Do you think that kind-

ness and generosity are usually more powerful than severity? What does the proverb say about "a soft answer" (Prov. 15:1)? What does Paul mean by "heaping coals of fire" on the head of an enemy (Rom. 12:20)? (9) Is this rule of kindness in return for evil to be followed in all cases? Name some cases if you can, in which you think it would be right to return evil for evil. (10)* Suppose David had killed Saul here when he had the chance, what difference would it have made in his own career?

A NATIVE OF SYRIA

SECTION LIII

DAVID AND NABAL, I SAM. 25:1–22

And Samuel died; and all Israel gathered them- 25
selves together, and lamented him, and buried him
in his house at Ramah.   And David arose, and went
down to the wilderness of Paran.

¹ Or, *business was*

And there was a man in Maon, whose¹ possessions 2
were in Carmel; and the man was very great, and he
had three thousand sheep, and a thousand goats:

EXPLANATORY NOTES

This story of David's outlaw life, showing his method of
getting provision for his men by compelling the farmers of the
region to contribute, is from the early Judean narrative of David's
life.   It is very vivid, and admirably describes the border life of
the age, the self-indulgence and heedlessness of Nabal, and the
prompt, fierce anger of David when insulted.   It appears to follow the story of David's escape from Saul in chap. 26, which is a
variant of 24:1–22 (Section LII).   The opening words regarding Samuel's death are not connected in any manner with the
context.   They are taken apparently from 28:3.   They do not
belong to this narrative.   Vs. 1, "Samuel died": The last reference to the prophet was in the story of David's flight to Ramah
(19:18–24).   This verse may have followed immediately after
that account.   In 28:3 it forms the appropriate introduction to
the scene at En-dor.   "The wilderness of Paran"†: a region
some fifty miles south of Beersheba.   If the word is read "Maon"
with the Greek translation (the Septuagint†) the difficulty of so
long a journey is removed.   Vs. 2, "in Maon": a village lying
five miles south of Ziph.   It was mentioned in 23:24, 25 (Section
LI), as the region in which David took refuge from Saul's pursuit.
"In Carmel"†: a town between Ziph and Maon.   The sheep-

3 and he was shearing his sheep in Carmel. Now
the name of the man was Nabal; and the name of
his wife Abigail; and the woman was of good understanding, and of a beautiful countenance: but the
man was churlish and evil in his doings; and he was
4 of the house of Caleb. And David heard in the
5 wilderness that Nabal was shearing his sheep. And
David sent ten young men, and David said unto the
young men, Get you up to Carmel, and go to Nabal,
6 and greet him in my name: and thus shall ye say[2]
to him that liveth in prosperity, Peace be unto thee,
and peace be to thy house, and peace be unto all that
7 thou hast. And now I have heard that thou hast
shearers: thy shepherds have now been with us,
and we [3]did them no hurt, neither was there aught
missing unto them, all the while they were in Carmel.
8 Ask thy young men, and they will tell thee: wherefore
let the young men find favor in thine eyes; for we
come in a good day: give, I pray thee, whatsoever
cometh to thy hand, unto thy servants, and to thy son
David.

[2] Or, *All hail!
and peace be,*
etc.

[3] Heb. *put
them not to
shame*

---

shearing time was like a festival, in which great provisions were
made for generous hospitality. Vs. 3, "Nabal . . . . and
Abigail": The beauty and discretion of the woman are contrasted with the surly and selfish disposition of her husband.
"House of Caleb": the leader of the clans of Judah in the times
of the conquest, and the possessor of the Hebron district
(Num. 14:24; Josh. 14:6–14). Vss. 4–8, David had been for some
time near Nabal's property, on good terms with his shepherds, and
in a measure guarding his flocks. It was customary for men living

And when David's young men came, they spake 9
to Nabal according to all those words in the name
of David, and ⁴ceased. And Nabal answered 10
David's servants, and said, Who is David? and who
is the son of Jesse? there are many servants now-a-
days that break away every man from his master.
Shall I then take my bread, and my water, and my 11
flesh that I have killed for my shearers, and give it
unto men of whom I know not whence they are?
So David's young men turned on their way, and 12
went back, and came and told him according to all
these words. And David said unto his men, Gird 13
ye on every man his sword. And they girded on
every man his sword; and David also girded on his
sword; and there went up after David about four
hundred men; and two hundred abode by the baggage.

But one of the young men told Abigail, Nabal's 14
wife, saying, Behold, David sent messengers out of
the wilderness to salute our master; and he railed

⁴ Or, *remained
quiet*

a roving life like David's to depend on the gifts of the farmers and
to exercise some care over their property in return. At the shearing festival when David knew that there was plenty of provision
prepared, he sent to ask for whatever Nabal chose to give him.
Vs. 10, "servants that break away": Nabal refused to give anything. He said he had not asked David to guard his flocks, and
did not propose to pay him by giving him food. Any runaway
slave, he said, might make such a demand. Vs. 13, "Gird ye
on": David's wrath knew no bounds at this refusal. While he
had no legal right to demand this present from Nabal, it was so
much in harmony with the custom of the times that he was in-

15 at them. But the men were very good unto us, and
we were not ⁵hurt, neither missed we anything, as
long as we went with them, when we were in the

⁵ Heb. *put to shame*

16 fields: they were a wall unto us both by night and by
day, all the while we were with them keeping the

17 sheep. Now therefore know and consider what thou
wilt do; for evil is determined against our master,
and against all his house: for he is such a worthless
fellow, that one cannot speak to him.

18 Then Abigail made haste, and took two hundred
loaves, and two ⁶bottles of wine, and five sheep ready
dressed, and five measures of parched grain, and a
hundred clusters of raisins, and two hundred cakes

⁶ Or, *skins*

19 of figs, and laid them on asses. And she said unto
her young men, Go on before me; behold, I come
after you. But she told not her husband Nabal.

20 And it was so, as she rode on her ass, and came down
by the covert of the mountain that, behold, David
and his men came down toward her; and she met

21 them. Now David had said, Surely in vain have I

---

sulted at Nabal's conduct. He and two-thirds of his men started
at once to deal with the landowner as they thought he deserved.
Vs. 17, "evil is determined": One of Nabal's servants warned
his master's wife, Abigail, of their danger. Evidently the household had but small respect for Nabal. Vs. 18, "two hundred
loaves": The present prepared by Abigail for David was propor-
tioned to the size of his band. The loaves were flat, thin cakes;
the skins of wine would hold several gallons each; the *seah*, here
translated "measure," was about one and one-half pecks. Vs. 19,
"go on before me": The present was sent first, that David might
be somewhat pacified before Abigail met him. Vs. 21, "David had

kept all that this fellow hath in the wilderness, that nothing was missed of all that pertained unto him: and he hath returned me evil for good. God 22 do so [7]unto the enemies of David, and more also, if I leave of all that pertain to him by the morning light so much as one man-child.

[7] Some authorities read *unto David*

LOAVES OF BREAD

said": As he led his men toward the home of Nabal he was in an angry mood, reflecting on what he regarded as his friendly and helpful conduct toward Nabal, and the latter's ungracious disdain. Vs. 22, "unto the enemies of David": The margin "unto David" is much more natural. He called down imprecations on himself in case he should fail to avenge the insult.

QUESTIONS

(1) Read over the lesson until all of its details are clear. Look up the scene on the map. Read carefully the notes

for explanation of text, and consult the dictionary for any names or words not understood. (2)* How did the death of Samuel affect the people? How did they honor him? With what American statesman could you compare Samuel, in the greatness of his influence and the public esteem in which he was held? (3) Give as complete a picture of Nabal as you can as to his home, his social position, and his disposition. Would the term "wealthy farmer" or "ranchman" best describe his business? (4) What sort of wife did he have? What is the writer's object in describing Abigail's character? (5)* What did David and his men do in the vicinity of Nabal's estate? What would we think today of a man who got his living by doing work nobody asked him to perform, and then demanding pay for it? What justification was there for this conduct in David's case? Was it probable that bands of robbers and outlaws, like David's, often levied this kind of "blackmail" on the landowners of Palestine? (Compare Scott's character "Rob Roy" for a man who followed a similar vocation). (6) At what favorable time did David make his request for compensation? What made him think he would be certain to obtain his request? (7) How did Nabal treat David's messengers? Do you think he really did not know that David's men had guarded his flocks, or was he merely evading his obligations, or did he resent the system of demanding gifts of this sort, or was he simply a surly and unsocial man? (8)* Do you think David's anger arose from Nabal's refusal to give him provisions, or from the surly and insulting manner in which the request was scorned? (9) What bearing has the story of Nabal upon the question of courtesy in one's treatment of others? Do you think it is usually possible to estimate one's real character by his politeness, deference, and regard for others? What would be your definition of a "gentleman"? (10) How did Nabal's wife learn of her husband's treatment of David? (11) What means did she use to save the household from danger? What would have happened had she not taken prompt action? What qualities in Abigail are especially desirable in our own day? (12)* What do you think was the purpose of this story?

SECTION LIV

DAVID AND ABIGAIL, I SAM. 25:23–44

23 And when Abigail saw David, she hasted, and
alighted from her ass, and fell before David on her
24 face, and bowed herself to the ground. And she fell
at his feet, and said, Upon me, my lord, upon me be
the iniquity; and let thy handmaid, I pray thee,
speak in thine ears, and hear thou the words of thy
25 handmaid. Let not my lord, I pray thee, regard
this worthless fellow, even Nabal; for as his name
is so is he; [1]Nabal is his name, and folly is with him: [1] That is *Fool*
but I thy handmaid saw not the young men of my
26 lord, whom thou didst send. Now therefore, my

EXPLANATORY NOTES

The narrative of this section is continued from the early
Judean story of David's life. It follows immediately after 25:1–22
(Section LIII). In the present study the purpose of the entire
account is given—the manner in which David secured his wife,
Abigail. Her beauty and goodness of heart, as well as her wisdom
in dealing with a delicate and dangerous situation, led David to
desire to marry her. Vs. 23, "fell before David": prostrating
herself, as was the custom before superiors. Vs. 24, "upon me
be the iniquity": Abigail assumes the responsibility for the insult
to David, though she had not known what had happened. Vs.
25, "this worthless fellow": She insists that no heed must be
paid to the conduct of her husband, who is reckless, foolish,
deprived of reason by his habits of drinking. Nabal's name,
(folly) seemed fitting. For herself, she had known nothing of
David's request. Vs. 26, "let thine enemies . . . . be as Nabal":

lord, as the Lord liveth, and as thy soul liveth, seeing the Lord hath withholden thee [2] from blood-guiltiness, and from avenging thyself with thine own hand, now therefore let thine enemies, and them that seek evil to my lord, be as Nabal. And now this 27 present which thy servant hath brought unto my lord, let it be given unto the young men that follow my lord. Forgive, I pray thee, the trespass of thy 28 handmaid: for the Lord will certainly make my lord a sure house, because my lord fighteth the battles of the Lord; and evil shall not be found in thee all thy days. And though man be risen up to pursue 29 thee and to seek thy soul, yet the soul of my lord shall be bound in the bundle of [3]life with the Lord thy God; and the souls of thine enemies, them shall he sling out, as from the hollow of a sling. And it shall 30 come to pass, when the Lord shall have done to my lord according to all the good that he hath spoken concerning thee, and shall have appointed thee prince over Israel, that this shall be no grief unto thee, nor 31 offence of heart unto my lord, either that thou hast

[3] Or *the living*

Let them become equally reckless, and so expose themselves to destruction. Vs. 28, "make my lord a sure house": a prediction of David's future success, because he fights the battles of Jehovah. "Bound in the bundle of life": David's life is too valuable to be lost. Like a precious treasure, tied up in a bundle as a family possession, it shall be safeguarded, in contrast with the life of his foes, which God would cast away like a stone from a sling. Vs. 31, "this shall be no grief unto thee": When David has achieved success, he will be thankful that he did not avenge Nabal's insult shed blood without cause, or that my lord hath avenged himself. And when the Lord shall have dealt well with my lord, then remember thy handmaid.

32 And David said to Abigail, Blessed be the Lord, the God of Israel, who sent thee this day to meet me:
33 and blessed be thy discretion, and blessed be thou, that hast kept me this day from bloodguiltiness, and
34 from avenging myself with mine own hand. For in very deed, as the Lord, the God of Israel, liveth, who hath withholden me from hurting thee, except thou hadst hasted and come to meet me, surely there had not been left unto Nabal by the morning light so
35 much as one man-child. So David received of her hand that which she had brought him: and he said unto her, Go up in peace to thy house; see, I have hearkened to thy voice, and have accepted thy person.
36 And Abigail came to Nabal; and, behold, he held a feast in his house, like the feast of a king; and Nabal's heart was merry within him, for he was very drunken: wherefore she told him nothing, less or

---

with blood. He ought to thank Abigail for holding back his arm from violence. Vs. 32, "who hath sent thee": David saw the providential nature of Abigail's visit to him, and was grateful. Otherwise the whole household of Nabal would have perished. Vs. 35, "I have hearkened": He accepted both her gift and her counsel, and was thankful for them. Vs. 36, "very drunken": Nabal, in his drunken revel, was in no condition to be told the

more, until the morning light.   And it came to pass 37
in the morning, when the wine was gone out of
Nabal, that his wife told him these things, and his
heart died within him, and he became as a stone.
And it came to pass about ten days after, that the 38
Lord smote Nabal, so that he died.

And when David heard that Nabal was dead, he 39
said, Blessed be the Lord, that hath pleaded the
cause of my reproach from the hand of Nabal, and
hath kept back his servant from evil: and the evil-
doing of Nabal hath the Lord returned upon his
own head.   And David sent and spake concerning
Abigail, to take her to him to wife.   And when the 40
servants of David were come to Abigail to Carmel
they spake unto her, saying, David hath sent us unto
thee, to take thee to him to wife.   And she arose, and 41
bowed herself with her face to the earth, and said,
Behold, thy handmaid is a servant to wash the feet

---

events of the day, and his narrow escape from death. Vs. 37,
"his heart died": The overwhelming news of his peril, and the
safety he owed to his wife's discretion, proved too much for him.
He sank in a spasm of terror, or perhaps suffered a stroke of
paralysis. Vs. 38, "the Lord smote Nabal": His death soon
after, perhaps from a second stroke, was understood to be a divine
judgment upon him. Vs. 39, "Blessed be the Lord": David
saw in Nabal's death both the punishment of the reckless farmer's
conduct, and the higher meaning in the events which withheld
him from an act of vengeance, which would have left tribal wounds
not easily healed. Vs. 40, "David hath sent us": It was natural
that David should wish to marry so attractive and discreet a
woman. Vs. 41, "thy handmaid is a servant": A modest way

42 of the servants of my lord. And Abigail hasted and arose, and rode upon an ass, with five damsels of hers that followed her; and she went after the messengers of David, and became his wife.

43 David also took Ahinoam of Jezreel; and they be-
44 came both of them his wives. Now Saul had given Michal his daughter, David's wife, to Palti the son of Laish, who was of Gallim.

---

of disclaiming for herself any right, save that of obeying David's will. She came to him, bringing five maids as her servants. Vs. 43, "Ahinoam of Jezreel": Polygamy was a common practice of the time. Jezreel was a town in Judah near Carmel and Ziph (Josh. 15:56). Vs. 44, "Saul had given Michal": The king construed David's flight as a sundering of all ties that bound them. So he gave his daughter, David's wife, to another man. David later reclaimed her for himself (II Sam. 3:12–16).

QUESTIONS

(1) Read over the text carefully, in close connection with the text of Section LIII, where the story begins. Consult the map for the locality, and the dictionary for any names you do not understand. Study the notes to make sure you have the meaning of the different verses. (2)* What incidents led up to the meeting of David and Abigail? (3) Was there any reason why the woman should take the blame for her husband's foolish conduct? (4) Do you think she really despised Nabal as much as her words imply, or was she trying to secure David's favor? (5) How many good results of Abigail's intercession with David can you name? (6) Was it not a rather difficult and dangerous matter to interfere with David's purpose? Do you think it is ever easy to play the part of a peacemaker? What did Jesus say of the peacemakers (Matt. 5:9)? Is it one's right and duty to interpose in any and

every quarrel where there is a reasonable hope of effecting peace? (7) How did Abigail regard David; as a dangerous man who must be placated? as a celebrated warrior who would come to future success? or as the champion of God, a defender of the right? (8)* How did she describe the value of David's life to his people? (9) How did David receive the intercession of Abigail? Was he glad she came, or would he have preferred to go on and take vengeance on Nabal? (10) How would you describe David's final attitude toward Nabal, that of generous forbearance or of contempt? Which would be the nobler attitude? Do you think any truly good and generous nature can ever feel contempt or scorn of any other person? (11)* What effect did Abigail's news have on Nabal? Do you think his collapse was due to anger, terror, shame, or some physical cause? How was it interpreted by those about him and by David? In what manner do men's habits and dispositions bring physical effects, good or evil, upon them? (12)* What is the climax of the story? What qualities in Abigail made David wish to marry her? (13) According to the ideas of that age, was it wrong for David to marry Abigail when he was already the husband of Michal? Was it right for him to marry Ahinoam? What does the change in such ideas since that age prove regarding the growth of ethical ideals?

SECTION LV

DAVID SPARES SAUL'S LIFE, I SAM. 26:1–25

26 And the Ziphites came unto Saul to Gibeah, saying,
Doth not David hide himself in the hill of Hachilah,
2 which is before ¹the desert? Then Saul arose and   ¹ Or, *Jeshimon*
went down to the wilderness of Ziph, having three

EXPLANATORY NOTES

This section recounts an act of generosity on David's part in
his refusal to harm Saul when the latter was in his power. It is
from the early Judean story of David's life. In many respects it is
so similar to the narrative of Saul's escape from injury at David's
hands in chap. 24 (Section LII) that it may well be regarded as
a variant of the same story. In both accounts Saul's informants
are the Ziphites (cf. 23:19 with 26:1); the locality is the same; in
both David refuses to harm the king because he is the anointed
of God; and the conversations between David and Saul are much
alike. The differences in details are probably due to local color-
ing in the transmission of the stories. The present section probably embodies the older of the two accounts. It apparently follows
chap. 23:1–14 (Section XLIX, the story of David at Keilah), which
is itself the parallel of 23:19–29 (Section LI, David's pursuit
by Saul in the wilderness of Maon). The purpose of the story is
to celebrate David's magnanimity to his enemy, and his reverence
for the person of the king. Vs. 1, "Doth not David hide?":
The verse is almost a repetition of 23:19. The people of Ziph†
visit Saul at his home in Gibeah† to inform him of David's place
of concealment in their vicinity. The desert ("Jeshimon" in the
margin) is the eastern and rocky part of Judah, facing the Dead
Sea. Hachilah was probably some hill in the highlands, overlook-
ing the abrupt descent to the sea. s. 2, "three thousand men":
The same number is mentioned in the other account (24:2). Vs.

thousand chosen men of Israel with him, to seek David in the wilderness of Ziph. And Saul encamped 3 in the hill of Hachilah, which is before ²the desert, by the way. But David abode in the wilderness, and he saw that Saul came after him into the wilderness. David therefore sent out spies, and understood that Saul was come ³of a certainty. And 5 David arose, and came to the place where Saul had encamped; and David beheld the place where Saul lay, and Abner the son of Ner, the captain of his host: and Saul lay within the ⁴place of the wagons, and the people were encamped round about him.

Then answered David and said to Ahimelech the 6 Hittite, and to Abishai the son of Zeruiah, brother to Joab, saying, Who will go down with me to Saul to the camp? And Abishai said, I will go down with thee. So David and Abishai came to the people 7 by night: and, behold, Saul lay sleeping within the ³place of the wagons, with his spear stuck in the

Margin notes (left):

² Or, *Jeshimon*

³ Or, *to a set place*

⁴ Or, *barricade*

4, "sent out spies": to learn the size of Saul's forces, and the route they were taking. Vs. 5, "where Saul had encamped": Saul had brought his general Abner† and had presumably made his camp secure against attack. The camp animals and heavy baggage were placed in a circle, within which the king and his soldiers were fairly safe. The margin, "barricade," is much better than "place of the wagons." In so rough a country no wheeled vehicle could have been used. Vs. 6, "Ahimelech . . . . and Abishai"†: Of the first we know nothing further. He was probably one of David's soldiers of Hittite birth, like Uriah (II Sam. 23:39). Abishai was David's nephew, a fearless warrior. Vs. 7, "Saul

ground at his head; and Abner and the people lay
8 round about him. Then said Abishai to David,
God hath delivered up thine enemy into thy hand
this day: now therefore let me smite him, I pray
thee, with the spear to the earth at one stroke, and I
9 will not smite him the second time. And David
said to Abishai, Destroy him not; for who can put
forth his hand against the Lord's anointed, and be
10 guiltless? And David said, As the Lord liveth,
the Lord will smite him; ⁵or his day shall come to   ⁵ Or, *either*
11 die; or he shall go down into battle, and perish. The
Lord forbid that I should put forth my hand against
the Lord's anointed: but now take, I pray thee, the
spear that is at his head, and the cruse of water, and
12 let us go. So David took the spear and the cruse of
water from Saul's head; and they gat them away:
and no man saw it, nor knew it, neither did any
awake; for they were all asleep, because a deep sleep
from the Lord was fallen upon them.

---

lay sleeping": The two men made their way unhindered to the
side of the sleeping king. Vs. 9, "Destroy him not": Abishai was
impatient to end all their troubles by a single thrust of the king's
own spear. David would not consent. The person of the Lord's
anointed was sacred to him (cf. 24:6). Vs. 10, "the Lord shall
smite him": In some way or other God would deal with Saul,
either by sudden death or by disease or in battle; but David would
not interfere. Vs. 12, "spear and the cruse": David wanted to
take these as proofs that he had actually had Saul in his power.
When they had pulled the spear out of the ground and taken up
the water jar, they hurried away, for they were in great peril.

Then David went over to the other side, and stood 13
on the top of the mountain afar off; a great space
being between them; and David cried to the people, 14
and to Abner the son of Ner, saying, Answerest thou
not, Abner?   Then Abner answered and said, Who
art thou that criest to the king?   And David said to 15
Abner, Art not thou a valiant man? and who is like
to thee in Israel?   wherefore then hast thou not kept
watch over thy lord the king? for there came one
of the people in to destroy the king thy lord.   This 16
thing is not good that thou hast done.   As the Lord
liveth, ye are worthy to die, because ye have not kept
watch over your lord, the Lord's anointed.   And
now see where the king's spear is, and the cruse of
water that was at his head.

And Saul knew David's voice, and said, Is this 17
thy voice, my son David?   And David said, It is
my voice, my lord, O king.   And he said, Wherefore 18
doth my lord pursue after his servant? for what have

Vs. 14. "David cried to the people": From a safe distance he
taunted Saul's general, Abner, and his men with their carelessness
in leaving the king unprotected.   The distances at which men
talk to each other in Palestine, especially from one hill to another,
are remarkable. Vs. 16, "ye are worthy to die": The spear and
water jar were proofs of the truth of what he said.   In lands where
the king has supreme power, the chief officer of the court is often
held responsible with his life for the safety of the monarch.   It is so
in Turkey today. Vs. 17, "my son David": Something of Saul's
former affection for David returned at this proof of the latter's generosity. Vs. 19, "let him accept an offering": If God has moved Saul

19 I done? or what evil is in my hand? Now therefore, I pray thee, let my lord the king hear the words of his servant. If it be the Lord that hath stirred thee up against me, let him accept an offering: but if it be the children of men, cursed be they before the Lord; for they have driven me out this day that I should ⁶not cleave unto the inheritance of the Lord, saying,

20 Go, serve other gods. Now therefore, let not my blood fall to the earth away from the presence of the Lord: for the king of Israel is come out to seek a flea, as when one doth hunt a partridge in the mountains.

21 Then said Saul, I have sinned: return, my son David; for I will no more do thee harm, because my life was precious in thine eyes this day: behold, I have played the fool, and have erred exceedingly.

22 And David answered and said, Behold the spear, O king! let then one of the young men come over and

6 Or, *have no share in*

---

against David, it must be because he is angry with him; in that case David will make an offering to atone for his sin, whatever it is. But if *men* have prejudiced Saul against David, then his curse is upon them. "Go, serve other gods": The common belief of the times, which David seems to share, was that each land had its own god. As David had been driven out of his own land, it was the apparent purpose of his enemies to deprive him of Jehovah's protection. Vs. 20, "let not my blood fall": He implores Saul not to drive him from the land, where Jehovah his God will be unable to avenge him in case of his death. "A flea . . . . a partridge": language similar to that in 24:14. Another and perhaps better reading is, "the king of Israel is come out to seek my life, as the eagle hunts the partridge on the mountains." Vs. 21, "I have played the fool": Saul confesses his fault, and invites

fetch it.   And the Lord will render to every man his 23
righteousness and his faithfulness; forasmuch as
the Lord delivered thee into my hand to-day, and I
would not put forth my hand against the Lord's
anointed.   And, behold, as thy life was much set by 24
this day in mine eyes, so let my life be much set by
in the eyes of the Lord, and let him deliver me out
of all tribulation.   Then Saul said to David, Blessed 25
be thou, my son David: thou shalt both do mightily,
and shalt surely prevail.   So David went his way,
and Saul returned to his place.

David to return, either to the court or to the encampment from
which he just took the spear and cruse. Vs. 25, "David went his
way": He said nothing in answer to Saul's invitation. He
contented himself with pointing out his own conduct toward the
king, and they separated. The object of the narrative is of course
to show David's generous treatment of Saul.

QUESTIONS

(1) Read over the lesson carefully, and also Section LII,
and see if you think they are different accounts of the same
incident. What points of resemblance do they have? In
what do they differ?   (2) What scouting duty did David take
upon himself alone?   (3)* How was the camp of Saul arranged?
(4) What companion did David take on his second visit to the
camp of Saul?   (5) What did Abishai want to do? Would
not such an act have been natural in the circumstances?   (6)
What motives kept David from consenting to Saul's death?
Do you think it was David's kindness or his prudence that
withheld him from killing the king?   (7)* How did David
make certain that the king should know his narrow escape?
(8) What duty did Abner owe to Saul? How had he dis-

charged it? Was David right in saying that Abner ought to be put to death for sleeping when the king was in peril? What is the usual punishment for a sentinel or guard who sleeps at his post? (9)* What instances are there in our own day in which human lives, and public welfare, depend on the sleepless vigilance and care of watchers and workers? Would you say that our daily safety and ability to live and work comfortably depend upon the carefulness and punctuality of many people we never see? Do you think we owe anything to them? (10) How was Saul affected when he knew what David had done? Was this a case of "heaping coals of fire" on the enemy's head (Rom. 12:20)? (11) What did David seem to fear most in being driven from his land? Was he a patriot in the modern sense of the term? What is a patriot? How can patriotism best be shown by the average man? (12) *Would you call this meeting of Saul and David a reconciliation? Why did not David accept Saul's invitation to return to him? What is the purpose of the entire narrative?

SECTION LVI

DAVID AMONG THE PHILISTINES, I SAM.
27:1—28:2

And David said in his heart, I shall now perish **27** one day by the hand of Saul: there is nothing better for me than that I should escape into the land of the Philistines; and Saul will despair of me, to seek me any more in all the borders of Israel: so shall I escape out of his hand. And David arose, and passed over, **2** he and the six hundred men that were with him, unto Achish the son of Maoch, king of Gath. And **3**

EXPLANATORY NOTES

In spite of the apparent change in Saul's attitude toward David recorded in the last section, David seems to have despaired of any safety in the land of Israel. He determines therefore to offer himself and his men to the king of Gath as a vassal, thus securing his protection, and in return giving him his aid in war. The section is from the early Judean narrative of David's life. It will be remembered that in 21:10–15 (Section XLVI) there is given one of the popular stories regarding his flight to the court of King Achish. It is probable that the present section is the original account in its proper place, and that the other is a distorted variant, inserted out of its chronological order. It is hardly likely that David would again visit a court from which he had departed under such humiliating conditions as set forth in 21:15—22:1a. Vs. 1, "Saul will despair": will see that it is useless to pursue further. Vs. 2, "king of Gath"†: the nearest of the Philistine cities. Vs. 3, "every man with his household": David brought his company of outlaws and soldiers with him, and they were quartered with their families in Gath. They would be of great assistance to the king, who had to wage constant warfare with the

David dwelt with Achish at Gath, he and his men,
every man with his household, even David with his
two wives, Ahinoam the Jezreelitess, and Abigail
4 the Carmelitess, Nabal's wife. And it was told
Saul that David was fled to Gath: and he sought no
more again for him.

5 And David said unto Achish, If now I have found
favor in thine eyes, let them give me a place in one
of the cities in the ¹country, that I may dwell there: ¹ Heb. *field*
for why should thy servant dwell in the royal city
6 with thee? Then Achish gave him Ziklag that day:
wherefore Ziklag pertaineth unto the kings of Judah
7 unto this day. And the number of the days that
David dwelt in the ¹country of the Philistines was a
full year and four months.

8 And David and his men went up, and made a raid

Bedouin. Vs 4, "he sought no more": Saul was convinced by
David's departure to the Philistines that nothing more need be
feared from him, since he had apparently given up all thought of
seeking to be king. Vs. 5, "give me a place": David's request for
a town for himself and his men probably grew out of his dislike
of too close relations with the Philistines; his wish for greater
freedom of action; and his desire to keep his men together and in
training for what might be before him. Vs. 6, "gave him Ziklag"†: This town, on the border of Philistia, Judah, and the
desert, would give David the freedom he sought, and at the same
time, his location there would be a protection to Philistia against
the raids of the Bedouin. "Unto this day": in the days of the
writer, or perhaps a later editor. The language implies that the
town, but for this incident, would have belonged to Philistia
(or perhaps to the northern kingdom of Israel, as did Beersheba).
Vs. 8 "made a raid": The Hebrew indicates that this was not a

upon the Geshurites, and the Girzites, and the Amalekites; for those nations were the inhabitants of the land, who were ²of old, as thou goest to Shur, even unto the land of Egypt. And David smote the 9 land, and saved neither man nor woman alive, and took away the sheep, and the oxen, and the asses, and the camels, and the apparel; and he returned, and came to Achish. And Achish said, Against whom 10 have ye made a raid to-day? And David said, Against the South of Judah, and against the South of the Jerahmeelites, and against the South of the Kenites. And David saved neither man nor woman 11 alive, to bring them to Gath, saying, Lest they should

² Or, *from Telem*

---

single action, but customary, habitual. David used to ravage the villages of the Canaanites and Bedouin, and bring the spoil back to Gath. It will be noticed that vss. 8–12 imply that he was still living in Gath. Probably they should come before vs. 5. "Geshurites . . . . Girzites† . . . . Amalekites"†: These were the non-Hebrew and non-Philistine tribes on whose territory the raids were made. As the location of the Geshurites was east of the Jordan (Deut. 3:14; Josh. 13:11) and therefore far away, it is probable that the reading should be simply "Girzites and Amalekites." These were Canaanites and Bedouin in the vicinity. They were the people David used to harass. "Who were of old": This reading gives little meaning. Probably "from Telem"† should be read instead (see margin). This was one of the far southern sites of Judah, on the way to the desert and to Egypt. Vs. 10, "Against the South of Judah": The Negeb or "South" was the entire district lying south of the Hebrew frontier. When David made his reports to Achish he would give him to understand that he had raided the region of Judah, his own tribe This would be sure to sever all bonds between David and the Hebrews, and make him a certain and trusted friend of the Philistines.

tell of us, saying, So did David, and so hath been his
manner all the while he hath dwelt in the ³country   ³ Heb. *field*
12 of the Philistines.   And Achish believed David, saying, He hath made his people Israel utterly to abhor
him; therefore he shall be my servant for ever.

28   And it came to pass in those days, that the Philistines gathered their ⁴hosts together for warfare, to   ⁴ Heb. *camps*
fight with Israel.   And Achish said unto David,
Know thou assuredly, that thou shalt go out with
2 me in the host, thou and thy men.   And David said
to Achish, Therefore thou shalt know what thy servant will do.   And Achish said to David, Therefore
will I make thee keeper of my head for ever.

David wished to give this impression to Achish, that he might not
suspect his loyalty. "Jerahmeelites . . . . Kenites":   Two
tribes in the south, or Negeb, who were friendly to the Hebrews,
and to whom David actually sent presents from the spoil of his
campaign against the Amalekites (30:29).   Vs. 11, "saved neither
man nor woman": His method was to exterminate completely the
population of the raided district, so that no report should reach
Achish but his own.   Vs. 12, "utterly to abhor him": Achish
took David's reports as quite true, and was pleased, because he
thought there could be no return to the Hebrews on David's part
after the injuries he had done them.   In fact, however, David had
been careful to avoid all unfriendly acts toward Judah or any of
its friendly clans.   Vs. 1, "thou shalt go out with me": Achish
felt that now David could be trusted to fight in the Philistine army
against Saul and the Hebrews.   Vs. 2, "thou shalt know": This
reply was meant to assure Achish that David welcomed the occasion to fight against his former countrymen.   In reality, David
had no intention of doing so, and must have been placed in a most
awkward position by this summons.   Had he taken part in the
war against Saul, it would have ruined forever his hopes of being

king of Israel. But he put on a bold front, and pretended to be greatly elated at the opportunity. "Keeper of my head": The king of Gath, pleased at David's ready pledge to do great things in the campaign, promises him that if he fulfils his word, he shall be made his own chief officer, captain of his body-guard. Probably all this time David was perplexed to know how he should extricate himself from his dilemma. It was necessary for him to avoid going on this campaign against his own people, but how he did not know. Fortune favored him beyond his expectations, as we shall see.

QUESTIONS

(1) Read over the lesson with care to get its meaning firmly in mind. Study the notes, in order to understand that which the text does not explain, and look up strange words in the dictionary, and places on the map. (2)* What were David's reasons for leaving Judah and going to Philistia? How do you reconcile this action with Saul's apparent friendliness in 26:17-25 (Section LV)? Do you think he had reason to suspect Saul's sincerity? (3) To what place did David go? Why to that city? Who went with him? (4)* How did Achish receive him? Of what value were David and his men to Achish? (5) What effect did David's departure have upon Saul? Do you think he was pleased or otherwise? Why did Saul fear David? Would his hostility be likely to end if he thought David was no longer aspiring to be king? (6) What reasons did David have for wishing to have Achish give him a town for himself at some distance from Gath? What town was given him? Where was it? (7)* What policy of deception did David practice on Achish all the time he lived in Philistia? Why did he wish to represent himself as hostile to Judah and its allied tribes? (8) Do you think such deception justified by David's condition? Would you call such lying "military strategy," or "diplomatic representation," or simple falsehood? Do you think there are some kinds of lies which are allowable, and others which are wholly

bad, or are all alike evil? (9) What was David's method in his raids? What could excuse the wholesale slaughter of defenseless people? Would such conduct be excused in war today? What has made the difference since David's time? Note that it has been one of the most notable achievements of Christianity that it has modified the horrors of war, and seeks constantly to banish war itself. (10)* What was David's dilemma when Achish summoned him to the campaign against Saul? Why could he not tell him frankly the reasons why he could not fight against the Hebrews? What would have been the result if he had actually taken part against them? Must not David have been in extreme anxiety over his situation? Would you say that his suffering and trouble was brought upon himself by his policy of deception? Is this often the case in human life?

SECTION LVII

SAUL AND THE WOMAN OF EN-DOR, I SAM.
28:3–25

Now Samuel was dead, and all Israel had lamented 3
him, and buried him in Ramah, even in his own city.
And Saul had put away those that had familiar spirits,

EXPLANATORY NOTES

In this section there is given what appears to be one of the
popular prophetic stories of an incident near the close of Saul's
life. In its high esteem for Samuel and its censure passed upon Saul
it resembles chap. 15:1–35 (Sections XXXI, XXXII), one of the
Ephraimite narratives of Samuel's life. But it is somewhat more
sympathetic in its treatment of the unhappy king and is probably an
independent tradition. Saul, who has banished all necromancers
and spiritists from the realm, goes in his despair to a medium at
En-dor. At his request she calls up the spirit of Samuel, who, however, only adds to the king's distress by announcing the fate of himself, his sons, and his kingdom on the morrow. This story may
be regarded either as (1) an actual incident, in which the medium
practiced on the fears of the king whom she probably recognized
from the first, or (2) a popular tradition, without foundation in
fact, but intended to emphasize Saul's superstitious fear, his frantic
resort to witchcraft upon his failure to receive answers from the
God whom he had neglected, and his final appeal to Samuel, the
prophet whose counsel he had too long disregarded. It is probable
that both the writer and the people who handed down the tradition
accepted the story as true, for an unenlightened age is quick to
put faith in witchcraft and other forms of intercourse with the
dead. Viewed thus the account is valuable chiefly as an illustration of the ease with which fortune tellers and other traffickers in
the arts of mystery in every age have made dupes of the victims
of sorrow, anxiety, or misfortune. Vs. 3, "Samuel was dead":

4 and the wizards, out of the land.   And the Philistines
gathered themselves together, and came and encamped in Shunem; and Saul gathered all Israel
5 together, and they encamped in Gilboa. And when
Saul saw the host of the Philistines, he was afraid, and
6 his heart trembled greatly.   And when Saul inquired
of the Lord, the Lord answered him not, neither by
7 dreams, nor by Urim, nor by prophets.   Then said
Saul unto his servants, Seek me a woman that hath a
familiar spirit, that I may go to her, and inquire of
her.   And his servants said to him, Behold, there is a
woman that hath a familiar spirit at En-dor.

This is the statement of 25: 1, which (as explained in Section LIII)
was probably copied back from this account. The death of the
great prophet was an untold loss to Israel. He was buried in
Ramah, his home city. The grave of Samuel is shown today at
Nebi Samwil ("The Prophet Samuel") or Mizpah, three miles
northwest of Jerusalem; but the tradition is late and worthless.
"Saul had put away": Saul's zeal in banishing diviners, fortune
tellers, and spiritists was probably due to Samuel's influence and
advice (cf. 15: 23). The campaign of exclusion probably was
directed against the people who practiced such things and the
images, teraphim†, talismans, instruments, and objects used in
such superstitious rites. Vs. 4, "Encamped in Shunem"†: a
town on the slope of "Little Hermon," facing Mt. Gilboa across
the valley of Jezreel to the south. "Encamped in Gilboa": the range
to the east of Esdraelon. Vs. 5, "he was afraid": Saul was no
coward, but the strength of the enemy, commanding the plain as
they did, was enough to cause him grave anxiety. Vs. 6, "inquired of the Lord": Not so much to secure counsel as to learn the
issue of the battle. Dreams, which were regarded as tokens of the
divine will, Urim†, the oracular instrument of priestly inquiry,
and the revelations of the prophets were regarded as the means of

And Saul disguised himself, and put on other 8
raiment, and went, he and two men with him, and
they came to the woman by night: and he said,
Divine unto me, I pray thee, by the familiar spirit,
and bring me up whomsoever I shall name unto thee.
And the woman said unto him, Behold, thou knowest 9
what Saul hath done, how he hath cut off those that
have familiar spirits, and the wizards, out of the land:
wherefore then layest thou a snare for my life, to
cause me to die? And Saul sware to her by the Lord, 10
saying, as the Lord liveth, there shall no ¹punish-
ment happen to thee for this thing. Then said the 11
woman, Whom shall I bring up unto thee? And
he said, Bring me up Samuel. And when the woman 12
saw Samuel, she cried with a loud voice; and the
woman spake to Saul saying, Why hast thou deceived

¹ Or, *guilt
come upon thee*

---

learning the will of God. In none of these inquiries was Saul successful. Vs. 7, "hath a familiar spirit": a woman who was a
medium, or possessed a charm or talisman that had the power to
summon the dead. "At En-dor"†: a village some ten miles away,
on the other or northern side of "Little Hermon." Vs. 8, "Divine
unto me": It is pathetic to think of the king of Israel resorting to
a person of this sort, whose life-business was the practice of
fraud. Vs. 9, "Thou knowest": The woman, who probably
recognized the king at once in spite of his disguise, sought to increase the value of her services by pretending to be afraid to work
her spells. She alludes to the king's recent suppression of all
diviners† as proof that she can do nothing for him, and that she
believes him to be seeking to entrap her. Vs. 11, "Bring me up
Samuel": Reassured by the king's oath, she is ready to practice
her arts. Vs. 12, "thou art Saul": It will be noticed that Saul

13 me? for thou art Saul. And the king said unto her, Be not afraid: for what seest thou? And the woman said unto Saul, I see ²a god coming up out of the ²Or, *gods*
14 earth. And he said unto her, What form is he of? And she said, An old man cometh up; and he is covered with a robe. And Saul perceived that it was Samuel, and he bowed with his face to the ground, and did obeisance.

15 And Samuel said to Saul, Why hast thou disquieted me, to bring me up? And Saul answered, I am sore distressed; for the Philistines make war against me, and God is departed from me, and answereth me no more, neither by prophets, nor by dreams: therefore I have called thee, that thou
16 mayest make known unto me what I shall do. And Samuel said, Wherefore then dost thou ask of me, seeing the Lord is departed from thee, and is become
17 thine adversary? And the Lord hath done unto thee, as he spake by me: and the Lord hath rent the kingdom out of thy hand, and given it to thy neighbor

---

saw nothing, but was told by the medium that she saw gods, or spirits, rising from the earth. The darkness, the king's anxious and exhausted condition, and his superstitious fear, combined to place him in the power of the woman. Vs. 14, "did obeisance": The description of Samuel by the woman, to whom so noted a prophet would be a familiar figure, convinced Saul that the dead seer was before him, and he fell on his face before the imaginary ghost. Vs. 15, "Samuel said to Saul": The conversation was of course carried on by the woman. The Greek diviners used ventriloquism to dupe their patrons. Vs. 17, "as he spake by me":

even to David.   Because thou obeyedst not the voice 18
of the Lord, and didst not execute his fierce wrath
upon Amalek, therefore hath the Lord done this
thing unto thee this day.   Moreover the Lord will 19
deliver Israel also with thee into the hand of the
Philistines; and to-morrow shalt thou and thy sons
be with me: the Lord will deliver the host of Israel
also into the hand of the Philistines.

Then Saul fell straightway his full length upon 20
the earth, and was sore afraid, because of the words
of Samuel; and there was no strength in him; for
he had eaten no bread all the day, nor all the night.
And the woman came unto Saul, and saw that he 21
was sore troubled, and said unto him, Behold, thy
handmaid hath hearkened unto thy voice, and I have
put my life in my hand, and have hearkened unto
thy words which thou spakest unto me.   Now there- 22
fore, I pray thee, hearken thou also unto the voice
of thy handmaid, and let me set a morsel of bread
before thee; and eat, that thou mayest have strength,
when thou goest on thy way.   But he refused, and 23

The reference is of course to chap. 15.   Saul's failure completely
to destroy the Amalekites is again made the ground of his rejection.   This scene completes the denunciation of the former one.
Vs. 19, "thou and thy sons be with me": in the region of the dead.
Vs. 20, "Saul fell straightway": The message could not be worse.
Faint from fasting and his long journey, he had no strength left.
Vs. 22, "let me set a morsel of bread": The human and sympathetic side of the woman was roused at the sight of the king's
distress.   She had been unable to give him any hope, knowing

said, I will not eat. But his servants, together with the woman, constrained him; and he hearkened unto their voice. So he arose from the earth, and 24 sat upon the bed. And the woman had a fatted calf in the house; and she hasted, and killed it; and she took flour, and kneaded it, and did bake 25 unleavened bread thereof: and she brought it before Saul, and before his servants; and they did eat. Then they rose up, and went away that night.

---

his helplessness in the face of the Philistine hosts. But she could at least strengthen him with food, and after that he and his men went back the long road to the camp, to meet death like the brave men they were.

QUESTIONS

(1) Master as fully as possible the details of the story, consulting the notes, dictionary, and map. (2) What were the locations of the two camps? About how far were they apart? (3)* How was Saul affected by the sight of the Philistine host? What added to his distress? Is one who has neglected prayer and a holy life likely to obtain the comforts of religion in a time of trouble? In what circumstances may answers to prayer be expected? (4) What sort of people had Saul banished from the land? Did he do right in thus suppressing their business? Are there such frauds today? From what class of people do they secure patronage? What would be your estimate of one who consulted a fortune teller or clairvoyant? (5)* What happened when Saul visited the medium? How did the woman make Saul believe that Samuel was really talking with him? Do you think the writer of the account believed that Samuel was actually called up? (6) Suppose the medium had given Saul an encouraging

message, predicting his victory, might it have affected the results of the battle? How far do you think kind, inspiring, and encouraging words may go in affecting the success of other people? Will the reverse be true if discouraging and pessimistic forecasts are made? What bearing has this upon one's responsibility not only for acts but for words? (7) If Saul was convinced that the battle of the following day would be fatal, why did he not escape that night? Does this courageous return into danger help in interpreting the character of Saul? Does it help us to understand why his people loved him and remained faithful to him in spite of his faults? (8)* What do you think is the purpose of this section? Would you regard it as a literal recital of facts or as the account of a clever fraud practiced on King Saul by the woman or as an unfounded tradition?

SECTION LVIII

DAVID AND THE PHILISTINE INVASION
I SAM. 29:1–11

29 Now the Philistines gathered together all their
hosts to Aphek: and the Israelites encamped by the
2 fountain which is in Jezreel. And the lords of the
Philistines passed on by hundreds, and by thousands;
and David and his men passed on in the rearward
3 with Achish. Then said the princes of the Philistines, What do these Hebrews here? And Achish

---

EXPLANATORY NOTES

This section continues the story of 27:1—28:2 (Section LVI)
and like it, is from the early Judean account of David's career.
It explains his fortunate escape from the necessity of fighting
against his own people. The Philistine chiefs, discovering that
he was in the camp as a vassal of King Achish, insisted on his
departure, as one who was too likely to turn against his present
allies in the battle, and by this means secure the favor of his former
lord, Saul. David was apparently much chagrined at the demand,
but in reality must have hailed it as a providential solution of the
serious dilemma in which he found himself (cf. Section LVI).
Vs. 1, "to Aphek"†: Probably some place in the plain of Esdraelon
nearer to Mt. Gilboa than their former camp at Shunem. "The
fountain which is in Jezreel": This may mean the Spring of
Harod at the foot of Gilboa, in the plain of Jezreel, or the spring of
the town of Jezreel itself. Vs. 2, "passed on by hundreds and by
thousands": perhaps in a final military review before the battle.
Vs. 3, "What do these Hebrews here?" The Philistine leaders
thought it unsafe to have David and his men in their army.
Achish tried in vain to convince them that David had completely
broken with Saul and had been a faithful Philistine vassal for two

271

said unto the princes of the Philistines, Is not this
David, the servant of Saul the king of Israel, who
hath been with me these days, or rather these years,
and I have found no fault in him since he fell away
unto me unto this day?   But the princes of the Phil- 4
istines were wroth with him; and the princes of the
Philistines said unto him, Make the man return,
that he may go back to his place where thou hast
appointed him, and let him not go down with us to
battle, lest in the battle he become an adversary to
us: for wherewith should this fellow reconcile himself unto his lord? should it not be with the heads
of these men? Is not this David, of whom they 5
sang one to another in dances saying,

> Saul hath slain his thousands,
> And David his ten thousands?

---

years or more. Vs. 4, "with the heads of these": i.e., with the
lives of Philistine soldiers, against whom David and his men might
turn at a critical moment in the battle. This would be sure to
reinstate him in Saul's favor. Vs. 5, "of whom they sang":
when David returned from his victory over the Philistines, 18:7.
The same song is alluded to in the popular tradition of David's
presence at the court of Achish, 21:11. Vs. 7, "Wherefore now
return": The king of Gath was embarrassed to have to send
David back, but it was the only thing to do, since the other Philistine leaders were so suspicious of him. Vs. 8, "what have I
done?": David pretended to be greatly chagrined at the necessity
of abandoning the campaign. In reality, it was the very event he
wanted, saving him as it did from the danger of having to ruin his
prospects by fighting against his own people. Vs. 9, "as an
angel of God": The references to the God of the Hebrews on

6 Then Achish called David, and said unto him, As
the Lord liveth, thou hast been upright, and thy
going out and thy coming in with me in the host is
good in my sight; for I have not found evil in thee
since the day of thy coming unto me unto this day:
7 nevertheless the lords favor thee not. Wherefore
now return, and go in peace, that thou displease not
8 the lords of the Philistines. And David said unto

THE PLAIN OF JEZREEL

Achish, But what have I done? and what hast thou
found in thy servant so long as I have been before
thee unto this day, that I may not go and fight
9 against the enemies of my lord the king? And
Achish answered and said to David, I know that
thou art good in my sight, as an angel of God: notwithstanding the princes of the Philistines have said,
10 He shall not go up with us to the battle. Wherefore
now rise up early in the morning with the servants of
thy lord that are come with thee; and as soon as ye

are up early in the morning, and have light, depart.
So David rose up early, he and his men, to depart 11
in the morning, to return into the land of the Philistines. And the Philistines went up to Jezreel.

---

the part of Achish, a Philistine, might not be unnatural in speaking to one like David, whose life and religion he knew so well.
Vs. 10, "the servants of thy lord": Achish alludes to David's
men as servants of King Saul, as indeed nominally they were. He
knew how hard a thing he was asking of David to forbid him to
fight, and must have done all he could to remove any sense of
anger or insult that David would be supposed to feel. Vs. 11,
"into the land of the Philistines": back to the city of Ziklag†,
the place where David and his men lived.

QUESTIONS

(1) Study the lesson carefully, using first the text, then the
comments, the dictionary, and the map. (2) What people
invaded the land of Israel? What was their purpose?
Where did they encamp? (3)* How did the Philistines learn
that David was among them? Why were they displeased?
Is it usual for a man of one nation to enter the army of another
people? Can you remember other examples? (4) Do you
think the Philistine chiefs were justified in having David sent
away? When had they heard of him before? What do you
think David really would have done if he had not been ordered
away? (5)* How did Achish feel when the chiefs of the
Philistines made their decision? If David should feel insulted
at his rejection, would it not be dangerous to send him back
into their land? Does it seem certain that Achish trusted
him completely? If Achish had known all the facts of David's
career, would he have put as much confidence in him? (6)
What do you think were David's feelings as he departed from
the camp? Would you say that it was a fortunate escape

from a delicate and embarrassing position? Has one a right to get into such trouble in the hope that he may be lucky enough to escape? Do you think David's conduct in this matter was worthy of imitation? (7)* Where did David and his men go when they left the Philistine camp? Had they left their homes guarded in any way?

SECTION LIX

DAVID AND THE AMALEKITES, I SAM. 30:1–31

And it came to pass, when David and his men were 30
come to Ziklag on the third day, that the Amalekites
had made a raid upon the South, and upon Ziklag,
and had smitten Ziklag, and burned it with fire, and 2
had taken captive the women and all that were there-
in, both small and great: they slew not any, but
carried them off, and went their way. And when 3
David and his men came to the city, behold, it was
burned with fire; and their wives and their sons
and their daughters, were taken captive. Then 4
David and the people that were with him lifted up
their voice and wept, until they had no more power

EXPLANATORY NOTES

The narrative in this section is continued from the earliest
source, the Judean account of David's life. When he returned
from following the Philistines to battle in the plain of Jezreel,
sent back because of their suspicion of him, he found that the
town of Ziklag† where he and his men lived, had been raided by
Amalekites. The place was burned and the women and children
carried off After the first outburst of grief and anger, David
and his men followed the raiders and by a sudden attack recovered the captives and the spoil. Vs. 1, "had made a raid":
The Amalekites†, who lived on the southern border of Philistia
and Judah, had noted David's departure with his followers
They took advantage of his absence to raid Ziklag. Vs. 2, "slew
not any": In this they differed from David's own treatment of the
regions he raided (27:8, 9). But probably their purpose was to
sell their captives to Egyptian slave dealers. Vs. 4, "lifted up

5 to weep. And David's two wives were taken captive, Ahinoam the Jezreelitess, and Abigail the wife
6 of Nabal the Carmelite. And David was greatly
distressed; for the people spake of stoning him,
because the soul of all the people was grieved, every
man for his sons and for his daughters: but David
strengthened himself in the Lord his God.

7   And David said to Abiathar the priest, the son of
Ahimelech, I pray thee, bring me hither the ephod.
And Abiathar brought thither the ephod to David.
8 And David inquired of the Lord, saying, ¹If I pursue
after this troop, shall I overtake them? And he
answered him, Pursue; for thou shalt surely overtake
9 them, and shalt without fail recover all. So David
went, he and the six hundred men that were with
him, and came to the brook Besor, where those that
10 were left behind stayed. But David pursued, he
and four hundred men; for two hundred stayed
behind, who were so faint that they could not go over
the brook Besor.

¹ Or, *Shall I pursue*

---

their voice and wept": It was a sudden and crushing blow.
Oriental people are violent in expressing their emotions. Vs. 6,
"the people spake of stoning him": David was in straits, in great
danger from his own men.   Their grief at their loss quickly turned
to anger against their leader. Vs. 7, "bring me hither the ephod"†:
In this extremity David wished to lose no time, and wanted the
divine direction. Abiathar† was his priestly friend and adviser.
Vs. 8, "Pursue; for thou shalt surely overtake": The oracle was
favorable, and David was bidden to follow the raiders. Vs. 9,
"came to the brook Besor": one of the wadies or valleys whose

And they found an Egyptian in the field, and 11
brought him to David, and gave him bread, and he
did eat; and they gave him water to drink; and they 12
gave him a piece of a cake of figs, and two clusters
of raisins: and when he had eaten, his spirit came
again to him; for he had eaten no bread, nor drunk
any water, three days and three nights. And David 13
said unto him, To whom belongest thou? and whence
art thou? And he said, I am a young man of
Egypt, servant to an Amalekite; and my master
left me because three days ago I fell sick. We made 14
a raid upon the South of the Cherethites, and upon
that which belongeth to Judah, and upon the South
of Caleb; and we burned Ziklag with fire. And 15
David said to him, Wilt thou bring me down to this
troop? And he said, Swear unto me by God, that
thou wilt neither kill me, nor deliver me up into the
hands of my master, and I will bring thee down
to this troop.

---

location is unknown. Here he left the two hundred men who
were too weak to go further. Vs. 11, "found an Egyptian† in the
field": This man, a slave abandoned by his Amalekite master in
the desert, was the means of discovering the route and size of the
Amalekite host. Vs. 12, "his spirit came again": The man had
been left sick, without food or water, and was nearly dead. Vs.
14, "We made a raid": The Cherethites† were a clan of the Philistines. Caleb was the conqueror of Hebron (Josh. 14:6–15).
It is evident that Ziklag was only one of the districts which they
plundered. Vs. 15, "Swear unto me": The slave was willing to
tell all he knew if he could be protected, especially from those he

16 And when he had brought him down, behold, they
were spread abroad over all the ground, eating and
drinking, and dancing, ²because of all the great spoil _* Or, amidst_
that they had taken out of the land of the Philistines,
17 and out of the land of Judah. And David smote
them from the twilight even unto the evening of the
next day: and there escaped not a man of them, save
four hundred young men, who rode upon camels and
18 fled. And David recovered all that the Amalekites
19 had taken; and David rescued his two wives. And
there was nothing lacking to them, neither small nor
great, neither sons nor daughters, neither spoil, nor
anything that they had taken to them: David brought
20 back all. And David took all the flocks and the
herds, which they drove before those other cattle,
and said, This is David's spoil.
21 And David came to the two hundred men, who
were so faint that they could not follow David,
whom also they had made to abide at the brook

---

betrayed. Vs. 16, "spread abroad": The camp was scattered,
and wholly unprotected. They expected no pursuit, for the men
of Ziklag were supposed to be with the Philistines in the campaign
against Saul. They were holding a revel in celebration of their
success. The dancing shows that religious exercises in honor
of their gods were not neglected. Vs. 17, "David smote them":
It is not likely that it took a whole day to disperse the Amalekites.
Rather it seems probable that David and his men remained in
hiding till the twilight of the next day, when the orgy had wearied
the host. Then his attack was sharp, swift, and decisive. Before
darkness had fallen all was done. Only one company of the
enemy escaped, by swift camel riding. Vs. 20, "This is David's

Besor; and they went forth to meet David, and to meet the people that were with him: and when David came near ³to the people, he ⁴saluted them. Then answered all the wicked men and base fellows, 22 of those that went with David, and said, Because they went not with us, we will not give them aught of the spoil that we have recovered, save to every man his wife and his children, that he may lead them away, and depart. Then said David, Ye shall not do so, 23

---

spoil": The Hebrews recovered all their relations and possessions. In addition, they took a large amount of spoil captured from other places than Ziklag. This was assigned to David. Vs. 21, "the two hundred men": The ones who had been left at the brook Besor came out with joy to meet their returning comrades. Vs. 22, "we will not give them aught": Some of David's men wanted to exclude these two hundred from any share in the victory beyond the return of their wives and children. Vs. 24, "as is his share": David would not consent to any such selfish conduct. The men who remained in camp and guarded the possessions left there should share equally with the men who fought. This became a rule in Israel, and was later incorporated in the law of the nation, and attributed to Moses (Num. 31:27). Vs. 26, "a present for you": This shows that the spoil included much more than was taken from Ziklag. It also reveals David's wisdom in securing the friendship of the leading men of Judah. Later on it led to his choice as king. Vss. 27–31, "to them that were in Bethel"†: The towns here mentioned were all in the tribe of Judah or near its borders. Bethel was the well-known place, a few miles north of Jerusalem; or the name may stand for the Bethel or Bethuel of Josh. 19:4 and I Chron. 4:30, a town mentioned as near Hormah and Ziklag; Ramath or Ramah of the South (Josh. 19:8) is not known but was probably some thirty or forty miles south of Hebron; Jattir is mentioned (Josh. 15:48; 21:14) along with Eshtemoa as a town in the hill country of

my brethren, with that which the Lord hath given
unto us, who hath preserved us, and delivered the
24 troop that came against us into our hand.   And who
will hearken unto you in this matter?   for as his
share is that goeth down to the battle, so shall his
share be that tarrieth by the baggage: they shall

HEBRON

25 share alike.   And it was so from that day forward,
that he made it a statute and an ordinance for Israel
unto this day.
26   And when David came to Ziklag, he sent of the
spoil unto the elders of Judah, even to his friends,
saying, Behold, a [5]present for you of the spoil of the   [5] Heb. *blessing*
27 enemies of the Lord: to them that were in Beth-el,

and to them that were in Ramoth of the South, and
to them that were in Jattir, and to them that were in 28
Aroer, and to them that were in Siphmoth, and to
them that were in Eshtemoa, and to them that were 29
in Racal, and to them that were in the cities of the
Jerahmeelites, and to them that were in the cities
of the Kenites, and to them that were in Hormah, 30
and to them that were in Bor-ashan, and to them 31
that were in Hebron, and to all the places where
David himself and his men were wont to haunt.

Judah, not far from Hebron; Aroer, perhaps a site in the Wadi
Arara, twenty miles south of Hebron, and twelve miles southeast
of Beer-sheba; Siphmoth, probably south of Eshtemoa; the latter
is mentioned in Josh. 15:50; 21:14 with Jattir as being in the highlands of southern Judah; Racal should perhaps be Carmel,†
already familiar in the story of David. The Jerahmeelites and
the Kenites† were non-Hebrew but friendly tribes living on the
southern border of Judah. Hormah was a city on the southern
frontier of Canaan where a victory was gained over the Canaanites
during the period of the Exodus (Num. 21:3). For the unknown
Bor-ashan it seems better to read Beer-sheba,† whose omission
from the list is singular. Athach is unknown. Hebron was the
chief city of Judah, the place where David was made king shortly
after. The presents sent seem to have been both a return of kindness for hospitality enjoyed during David's period of wandering,
and a promise of further favors in the future. The entire story
shows David's ability, promptness and success in meeting an
emergency, and the manner in which ill-fortune was changed by
him into brilliant victory.

QUESTIONS

(1) Study the text carefully to learn all the incidents of the
story. Consult the notes and dictionary for explanations of

points not understood, and locate the places on the map, as far as they are known. (2)* Where had David and his men been just previous to this narrative? (3) What did they find on their return to their home in Ziklag? Who were the raiders? Did David know who had burned the town? What means did he have of tracing them? (4) How did David and his men show their emotion? Why did the men blame David for what had occurred? Is it often the case that people seem to find satisfaction in blaming someone, even though he is innocent, for their misfortunes? Was this blame of David just? Who of them all had lost most? (5)* Where did David find strength? Would a person who had been indifferent to the practice of prayer derive much benefit from its sudden use in an emergency? (6) How did David ascertain the will of God? What was the method of consulting God by means of the ephod? What assurance did David receive? (7) Why did he leave part of his army on the way? Who gave David information? What was the Egyptian's explanation of his condition? (8)* In what condition did David find the Amalekites? Why had they not killed the prisoners they took at Ziklag? What was the great slave market of that time? (9) When did David attack the camp? What did they recover? Did they take anything in addition to their own people and possessions? (10) How were they greeted by the two hundred men they had left on the road? What proposal was made by some of those who had been in the fighting line? What did David say in opposition? What rule did David make for his army henceforth? Do you think this rule just and wise? (11)* What did David do with the surplus spoil after their return to Ziklag? Name three motives that led to this conduct. In what way does this entire narrative add to David's glory? How does it differ from Abraham's similar conduct (Gen. 14)?

SECTION LX

THE BATTLE OF MT. GILBOA, I SAM. 31:1-13

Now the Philistines fought against Israel: and 31 the men of Israel fled from before the Philistines, and
¹ Or *wounded* fell down ¹slain in mount Gilboa. And the Philis- 2 tines followed hard upon Saul and upon his sons; and the Philistines slew Jonathan, and Abinadab, and Malchi-shua, the sons of Saul. And the battle went 3 sore against Saul, and the archers overtook him; and he was greatly distressed by reason of the archers.

EXPLANATORY NOTES

The final section is taken from the main narrative, the early Judean story of David's life. It reveals Saul, in spite of all his defects, fighting valiantly for his country, and dying at last when all hope of victory was past. Vs. 1, "Philistines fought": Israel's old enemy had come up from its lowland home to fight in the mountains. This should have given the Hebrews the advantage, but it did not. "Fell down slain": The size of Saul's force is not stated, but his army was entirely routed and either slain or dispersed by the Philistines. "In mount Gilboa"†: The range of mountains that rises on the south side of the plain of Jezreel. It would afford admirable advantage to an army posted on its side or top. Vs. 2, "slew Jonathan": How quietly a great tragedy can be told. Jonathan's death was an irreparable loss to David and to all Israel. He and his brothers staid by their father till the last, and died fighting by his side. "Abinadab": In 14:49 (Section XXX) he is called Ishvi. Vs. 3, "he was greatly distressed": The Hebrew army had doubtless been broken up by Philistine charges, many of them killed and still more put to flight (vs. 7), and now the archers centered their fire on Saul and

4 Then said Saul to his armourbearer, Draw thy sword, and thrust me through therewith, lest these uncircumcised come and thrust me through, and ²abuse me. But his armourbearer would not; for he was sore afraid. Therefore Saul took his sword, and fell 5 upon it. And when his armourbearer saw that Saul was dead, he likewise fell upon his sword, and died 6 with him. So Saul died, and his three sons, and his armourbearer, and all his men, that same day together. 7 And when the men of Israel that were on the other side of the valley, and they that were beyond the

² Or, *make a mock of me*

---

his little surviving company. Vs. 4, "thrust me through": Saul wished to avoid the disgrace of falling by a Philistine sword, as Abimelech wanted to escape the shame of being slain by a woman (Judg. 9:54). Probably, as the marginal rendering hints, he feared that they might insult and torture him before killing him. "Uncircumcised" is a term often applied to the Philistines, as denoting non-Hebrews, and especially men of a wholly unrelated race, who did not practice the rite of circumcision which most Semitic nations seem to have observed. "His armourbearer would not": Perhaps the terror of the circumstances rendered him incapable of any action, or his high respect for Saul made him unwilling to injure his king. "Saul took his sword": He preferred suicide to captivity or torture. Another story of Saul's death was told by the messenger who brought David the news (II Sam. 1: 5–10). Perhaps, however, it was only in hope of obtaining a reward from David. This is one of the rare cases of suicide in the Bible (cf. Ahithophel, II Sam. 17:23, Zimri, I Kings 16:18, and Judas Iscariot, Matt. 27:5). Vs. 5, "died with him": The armorbearer would not survive his master. Vs. 6, "all his men": The tragedy was complete. Saul and his servant were the last of the group to die. Vs. 7, "forsook the cities and fled": This verse points out not only the immediate consequences of the

Jordan, saw that the men of Israel fled, and that Saul
and his sons were dead, they forsook the cities, and
fled; and the Philistines came and dwelt in them.
And it came to pass on the morrow, when the Philis- 8
tines came to strip the slain, that they found Saul
and his three sons fallen in mount Gilboa. And they 9
cut off his head, and stripped off his armour, and sent
into the land of the Philistines round about, to carry
the tidings unto the house of their idols, and to the
people. And they put his armour in the house of the 10
Ashtaroth; and they fastened his body to the wall of
Beth-shan. And when the inhabitants of Jabesh- 11
gilead heard concerning him that which the Philistines had done to Saul, all the valiant men arose, and 12
went all night, and took the body of Saul and the
bodies of his sons from the wall of Beth-shan; and
they came to Jabesh, and burnt them there. And 13
they took their bones, and buried them under the
tamarisk-tree in Jabesh, and fasted seven days.

---

battle, but those more remote as well. A panic seized the Hebrews
dwelling near the scene of the battle, and even those across the
Jordan. They abandoned their towns, and the entire region was
occupied by the Philistines. Vs. 8, "strip the slain": No doubt
the battle had lasted till darkness fell, and there was no chance
to gather the spoil till the next day. Clothing, armor, and weapons
would of course be taken from the bodies of the slain. Vs. 9,
"to carry the tidings": They cut off Saul's head and sent it about
among their cities and shrines to delight their people with the
news of the death of their foe. Vs. 10, "house of the Ashtaroth"†:
"House of Asthoreth" or Astarte, would be a better rendering.
It is not known where it was. Trophies of war were often placed

in temples. The sword of Goliath was hung in the sanctuary at Nob (21:9). So in this case the armor of Saul was kept as a trophy in one of their sanctuaries. "Fastened his body": This exposure of the bodies of foes was common in ancient warfare. It was an act of savage triumph. The bodies of Saul's sons shared the same fate (vs. 12). Vs. 11, "inhabitants of Jabesh-gilead"†: an east Jordan city which Saul rescued from the Ammonites in the beginning of his reign (I Sam. 11:5 f.; Section XXIII). Its people did not forget this service, but bravely rendered such honor to the king as the tragic occasion permitted. Vs. 12, "burnt them there": By a night march they secured the bodies from the wall of Beth-shan, either under cover of darkness, or by a fight with the Philistine garrison, and prevented further disturbance of the corpses by burning them. Burning was an unusual treatment of a corpse among the Hebrews, but these friends of Saul doubtless felt this method safest in that dangerous time. Vs. 13, "buried them": The reverent treatment of the remains was completed by burying the bones and ashes under the sacred tree in Jabesh-gilead. The fast of seven days was a mark of respect and grief.

QUESTIONS

(1) Read carefully the lesson. Consult the map to make sure of the localities. Study the notes till you understand each statement. (2)* Where was Saul's last battle fought? (3) Did the advantage of location lie with the Philistines or the Hebrews? (4) Is it probable that the numbers of the Philistines were considerably superior to those of Israel? (5) Which side gained the victory? (6) Who are mentioned especially among those killed? (7) Do you understand from the text that Saul was wounded before he planned to die? (8)* Why did he wish his armor-bearer to kill him? (9) How did he come to his death? Was it right for him to commit suicide? Has one ever the right to take his own life? (10) What did the armor-bearer do, after Saul's death? (11) Is there another version of Saul's death? (12) What were the

consequences of the battle to the Hebrews? How did they show their terror? (13)* What did the Philistines do with Saul's head? With his body? With his armor? (14) Who rescued the bodies of Saul and his sons? What motive had the men of Jabesh for this act of kindness? (15) Does not this act of brave and generous kindness to the dead king reflect great credit on the men of Jabesh? (16)* How did they finally dispose of the remains?

* REVIEW QUESTIONS

(Answers to be written by the pupil)

(1) Why did David's pretended madness preserve him from harm at the court of the Philistine king?

(2) Of what kind of men was David's band of soldiers composed?

(3) Why did David remove his parents from Bethlehem to Moab?

(4) What was the cause of Saul's anger against the priests of Nob, and what light does his massacre of them throw on his character?

(5) Why did David go to Keilah, and why later on did he leave it?

(6) Describe the last meeting of David and Jonathan.

(7) Why did Saul pursue David through the wilderness of Judah?

(8) How did David twice show his generosity toward Saul?

(9) How did David gain a living for himself and his men in the hills of Judah? What bearing has the story of Nabal upon this question?

(10) What did David do while he lived among the Philistines?

(11) Why did Saul consult the woman of En-dor?

(12) What prevented David's presence at the battle of Mt. Gilboa?

(13) What were the results of that battle?

REVIEW QUESTIONS ON THE FIRST BOOK OF SAMUEL

To the Pupil:

The object of these review questions is to help fix the main features of I Samuel in your mind, so that they will stay with you always. If you can do this, it will make this book more useful to you all your life. Take time enough for the review to do the work thoroughly. On the questions that refer to the names of events and sections, you can find help in the titles given at the head of the successive sections in the body of the book. In the Introductory Remarks you will find some statements about the name of the book, its contents, divisions, sources, and purpose that will help you.

(1) How many chapters are there in I Samuel?

(2) Why is the book called "Samuel"? Did Samuel write it?

(3) Of what larger work is I Samuel a part?

(4) What three men are the chief persons in the book? Which of them is the most conspicuous?

(5) Did the writer or writers of this book write it from personal knowledge of the facts, or from past traditions or from written documents in their possession?

(6) What two series of narratives are most prominent in the book?

(7) Is the leading purpose of the book to give the history of the age of Samuel? If not, what is the purpose?

(8) Do you think the state of society in Samuel's time one to be imitated? If not, what is the value of such a book?

(9) What were the leading characteristics of Samuel's parents?

(10) Was there a close relation between the character of Samuel and that of his mother? Can you think of other great men in whose lives the same thing is seen?

(11) To what collection of poems in the Old Testament does the "Song of Hannah" bear resemblance? To what poem in the New Testament?

(12) What good results came to the nation from the worship at the Shiloh sanctuary? What evil results?

(13) What conditions at this sanctuary made Samuel's presence timely and necessary?

(14) What caused the destruction of the sanctuary, the loss of the ark, and the extinction of the house of Eli?

(15) What was Samuel's method of teaching and preaching to the nation?

(16) What relation did the people's request for a king bear to the work Samuel had been doing for twenty years?

(17) What two views are given of Samuel's feelings regarding the choice of a king? (Compare Section XVII with Section XX.)

(18) Do you think it was best that Israel should have a king?

(19) What qualities did Saul display in his relief of Jabesh-gilead (Section XXIII)?

(20) What was Samuel's plea in his farewell address (Section XXIV)?

(21) In what ways did the Hebrews suffer from the oppression of the Philistines (Section XXVI)?

(22) Draw an outline map of Palestine and on it locate Ramah, Shiloh, Gibeah, Jabesh-gilead and Mizpah.

(23) What qualities did Jonathan display in his exploit against the Philistines (Section XXVII)?

(24) Why did Saul forbid the people to eat (Section XXVIII)?

(25) How was Jonathan saved from death (Section XXIX)?

(26) How many sons did Saul have? What were their names? How many daughters? Name them.

(27) Why did Samuel send Saul against the Amalekites (chap. 15)? How did Saul accomplish this mission?

(28) Why did Samuel rebuke Saul? (Section XXXII. See also Section XXV.)

(29) Where did Samuel go to find another man for king? Whom did he anoint?

(30) What two accounts are given of David's first meeting with Saul? (See Section XXXIV as contrasted with Section XXXVI.)

(31) What were the results of David's victory over Goliath, to David himself? To the nation?

(32) Why was Saul jealous of David (Section XXIX)? Did he have just cause for this feeling? How did he show his jealousy?

(33) How did David come to marry Michal? Was this an advantage or a disadvantage to him? Why?

(34) What was the character of the friendship between David and Jonathan? (Section XVIII. See also sections XXXVIII, XLIV, and L.) What influence do you think it had upon the life of David?

(35) By what means did David secure the help of the priest at Nob (Section XLV)? What did he obtain?

(36) In what places did David take refuge from Saul (Section XLVII)? Why did he go to Moab? Why did he return to Judah?

(37) What vengeance did Saul take upon the priests for their assistance to David? Was he justified in this act? How must it have affected the nation's regard for him?

(38) On the outline map locate Moab, Gilgal, Bethlehem, Gath, Nob.

(39) What did David accomplish by going to Keilah? Why did he leave it so soon? Would you approve the action

of the people of Keilah in their treatment of David, or not?

(40) Why did Saul think it necessary to pursue David? Do you think he attempted to capture him on several occasions, or are the various accounts different stories of one effort? (See Sections LI, LII, LV.)

(41) What was David's conduct toward Saul as shown in these narratives? What were his reasons for treating Saul with such consideration?

(42) What do you think was the writer's purpose in telling the story of David's relations with Nabal and Abigail (Sections LIII, LIV)? How would you describe the kind of life David and his men lived during this period?

(43) With whom did David afterward take refuge (Section LVI)? Where did he live? How did he obtain a living?

(44) Why did Saul consult the woman of En-dor? Was there a law against such practices? What was the result of the interview?

(45) Why was David prevented from accompanying the Philistines on their campaign against Saul? Do you think that David regarded their feeling toward him as fortunate for him, or otherwise?

(46) What happened to David's city of Ziklag in his absence (Section LIX)? What did he do in this distressing emergency?

(47) What rule of military conduct grew out of this event (I Samuel 30:21-25)?

(48) Where did the overthrow of Saul's army take place? What leaders lost their lives?

(49) What was done with the bodies of Saul and his sons? Who finally gave them fitting burial?

(50) What were the results of the battle of Mt. Gilboa to the nation? To the house of Saul? To David?

(51) As you recall the entire narrative of I Samuel, what principles seem to be illustrated by the careers of Samuel, Saul, and David, respectively?

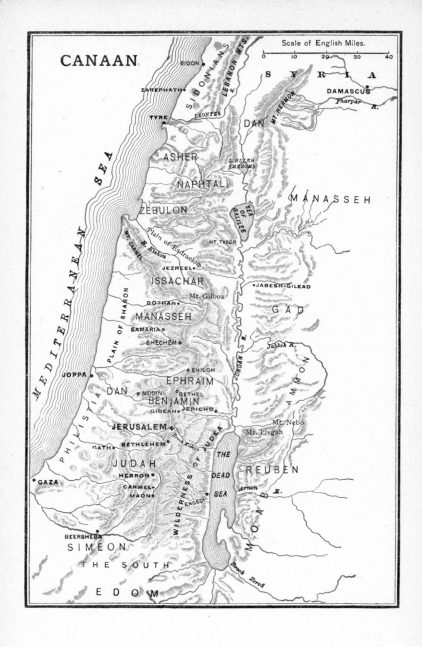

DICTIONARY

Aaron. Brother of Moses, and for this reason appointed to serve as priest. In consequence of this fact the tribe to which they belonged, that of the Levites, was set apart to priestly functions. It was the custom of the compilers of Israel's laws to put all statutes into the setting of a command of God to Moses as to what Aaron should do (cf. the books of Exodus, Leviticus, and Numbers). Aaron died at Mt. Hor near Petra, where his supposed grave is still pointed out by the Arabs.

Abiathar. A priest, son of Ahijah or Ahimelech. He was the sole survivor at the time of Saul's massacre of his family (I Sam. 22:20). He joined David, taking with him the ephod (23:6), and was of signal service to him in his later career. David was strongly drawn to him because of his own connection with the tragic death of Abiathar's family (22:20–23).

Abishai. A son of Zeruiah, David's sister (I Chron. 2:16) and a brother of Joab. These two nephews of David were fearless, relentless, rash, and headstrong warriors. Their brother Asahel was younger, but noted for his swiftness of foot. Abishai accompanied David in his wilderness wanderings, and was his companion in the night visit to Saul's camp (I Sam. 26:6). where he was only prevented from killing the sleeping king by the words of David. He was later one of David s most renowned leaders (I Chron. 11:20, 21).

Abner. The captain of the host, or chief general, in Saul's army. He was Saul's cousin, son of Ner, the brother of Kish (I Sam. 14:51). His place was near Saul in the household and the camp (I Sam. 20:25; 26:5). After Saul's death he secured the kingdom for Ish-bosheth (Ish-baal) Saul's son (II Sam. 2:8–10), but was treacherously murdered by Joab, to the great grief of David (II Sam. 3: 27–29).

Adullam. A city of Judah, in the valley of Elah. It was an old city (Gen. 38:1) and was known in the days of the conquest (Josh. 12:15). In it was the stronghold (rather than "cave," I Sam. 22:1) in which David took refuge from Saul. A "cave of Adullam" is shown six miles southeast of Bethlehem, but the tradition lacks basis. The modern town is Aid el-Ma, twelve miles nearly west of Bethlehem.

Agag. The name of the Amalekite king captured by Saul and put to death by Samuel (I Sam. 15:8, 32, 33). Perhaps (Num. 24:7) the word is a title rather than a proper name (cf. "Pharaoh").

Ahijah. Priest in the days of Saul (I Sam. 14:3). He was with the army when Saul wished to learn the will of God, and ordered him to consult the ephod which was used as an oracle (I Sam. 14:18). But the king would not wait for the answer (vs. 19). Later on the same day the priest advised consultation, but received no answer (vss. 36, 37). The same priest (whose name now appears as Ahimelech) was consulted by David at Nob in his flight from the court (I Sam. 21:1; 22:9, 10). For his kindness to David on this occasion he and his brethren, the seventy priests, lost their lives (II Sam. 22: 11–18).

Ahimelech. See "Ahijah.

Aijalon, or Ajalon. A place on the western slope of the highland of Ephraim. The valley is mentioned in the words of Joshua "thou moon in the valley of Ajalon" (Josh, 10:12), transcribed from the Book of Jashar. To this point Israel pursued the Philistines in the battle of Michmash (I Sam. 14:31).

Amalek, Amalekites. A desert tribe living on the plateau of et-Tih south of Judah, and in the region of Kadesh-barnea (Gen. 14:7). They were met and defeated by the Hebrews on the way from Egypt to Canaan (Exod. 17:8–16), and for their hostility on this and other occasions were held as hated foes by Israel (Deut. 25:17–19). On the attempt to enter Canaan from the south the Amalekites were the chief cause of their defeat and discomfiture (Num. 14:43–45). In the days of the judges they joined with the Midianites in raids upon the crops of Israel (Judg. 6:3). They had settlements in central Canaan as shown by such passages as Judg. 5:14 and 12:15. Against them Saul carried on successful wars (I Sam. 14:48) and nearly exterminated them (I Sam. chap. 15).

Ammonites. A nation living east of the Jordan between the rivers Jabbok and Arnon (see map). South of them beyond the Arnon lay Moab and to their north lay Gilead. They were of Semitic stock, closely related to the Hebrews, but like other neighboring people similarly related were usually either at war with Israel or in subjection to it. Earlier than the period of occupation of Canaan by the latter, the Ammonites had been driven back from the Jordan and the Dead Sea by the Amorites, and upon the conquest of these lands by the Hebrews the tribes of Reuben and Gad settled in them. It was the dispute over these possessions that led to the war in which Jephthah defeated Ammon (Judg. 11:4–33). Early in the days of Saul, the king of the Ammonites, Nahash by name, attempted to take the Israelitish city of Jabesh-gilead, but was defeated by the young king (I Sam., chap. 11). More amicable relations were established between the two nations in the beginning of David's reign, and Nahash, the king of Ammon (either the one mentioned in Saul's time, or his son), "showed kindness to David" (II Sam. 10:2). A friendly message sent by David to his successor however was met with insult, and in the war that ensued, all memory of former friendship was washed away in blood (II Sam. 12:26–31.) The later history of the Ammonites showed similar vibration between victory and defeat. They were cruel in war (Amos 1:13–15) and their worship of the god Moloch was a reflection of their chief characteristics

Amorites. Among the native populations of Palestine the Canaanites are spoken of as dwelling in the lower sections, along the seacoast and in the

Jordan valley, while the Amorites are described as the mountain dwellers of the central highland region. In such a passage as I Sam. 7:14 the name apparently includes all the non-Israelite inhabitants of Palestine. At least it refers to the neighbors of the Israelites in the days of Samuel.

Aphek. A town mentioned in I Sam. 4:1 as the place at which the Philistines encamped before battle with the Hebrews. From the indications there afforded it is probable that the place was in the Plain of Sharon, a few miles north of Lydda, and almost due west of Shiloh, at a distance of somewhat more than twenty miles. In I Sam. 29:1 it is said that the Philistines assembled at Aphek before the battle of Mt. Gilboa. This may mean either that they gathered their forces at the Aphek in Sharon, mentioned above, and then came up to Gilboa through the plain of Dothan, or that there was an Aphek in the Plain of Esdraelon to which the Philistines moved from Shunem. The effort to identify such a place has not been successful.

Ark. The sacred box or chest regarded by the Hebrews as representing Jehovah. Sacred chests, often shaped like boats, were carried by the Egyptians in procession. The ark was carried by means of rods run through staples on its sides. It was covered with gold, and had over it a lid on which there were kneeling figures of cherubim or angels, between which the glory of God rested (I Sam. 4:4). According to Hebrew tradition it contained at one time the tables of the law, Aaron's rod and the pot of manna. It was carried at the head of the hosts of Israel on the march to their new home in Canaan. It was believed to be endowed with magical properties for the defeat of enemies (I Sam. 4:3). Its presence in the new capital founded by David at Jerusalem was secured by events that still further enhanced its sacredness.

Ashtaroth. Astarte was the female divinity of the Phoenicians, the consort of Baal. The usual form in which the name appears in the Old Testament is Ashtoreth. Of this the plural is Ashtaroth, and refers to the various images and shrines of the goddess. Her worship was celebrated on the tops of hills in groves (called Asherah), and was accompanied by impure and degrading practices. For this reason, and because the worship of any false deity lowered the religious life of the people, the prophets of Israel always denounced the practice of offering sacrifices to the Baals (Baalim) and the Astartes (Ashtaroth). (See "Baalim.")

Azekah. A city of Judah a short distance east and upward from the Philistine city of Gath. It was near Socoh, between which and itself lay Ephesdammim, where the Philistines pitched their camp at the time of David's victory over Goliath (see map).

Baalim. Plural of Baal, the sun-god of the Phoenicians. His worship was attended with cruel rites, such as the sacrifice of children. As Phoenicia was not far to the north, along the sea-coast, the idolatrous practices of its people easily spread into the land of Israel in periods when the activity of the prophets ceased. It was the business of these men of God to rid the land of such immoral and unholy practices.

Barak. A leader whom the prophetess Deborah summoned from the northern tribe of Naphtali to deliver Israel from the yoke of Jabin, king of Hazor (Judg., chap. 4). In the battle of Mt. Tabor he won a notable victory, crushing the army of the Canaanites. One of the oldest fragments of Hebrew poetry is the ode in memory of this triumph (Judg., chap. 5).

Bedan. Probably an error for Barak in I Sam. 12:11.

Beer-sheba ("Well of the Oath"), One of the oldest places in Palestine, the home of Abraham (Gen. 21:31), of Isaac (Gen. 26:23), and of Jacob (Gen. 28:10). Its frequent mention as a geographical landmark ("from Dan to Beer-sheba," I Sam. 3:20) was owing to its extreme southern position. It was about forty-five miles southwest of Jerusalem and twenty-five miles from Hebron, in the same direction. It is named as the residence of the two sons of Samuel, whom he appointed as judges (I Sam. 8:2).

Belial. Used in the expressions "Sons of Belial," "Daughters of Belial." The origin of the word "Belial" is obscure. It perhaps signified wickedness, vileness, destruction, or the abyss, i.e., the underworld of the dead. The phrases above quoted apparently refer to vile, worthless persons, destined to ruin. In the New Testament the word appears, in at least one instance (II Cor. 6:15) to be equivalent to Satan.

Beth-aven ("house of vanity"). A town near Bethel and west of Michmash. By the later prophets, like Hosea, the name was used for Bethel itself as a reflection upon its golden calf, set up by king Jeroboam.

Bethel ("House of God"). One of the most ancient sanctuaries in Palestine. It was here that Jacob rested on his journey to Padan-aram, and saw the vision of the ladder set up between heaven and earth (Gen. 28:10-22). It was known in earlier days as Luz. The modern name is Beitin. It is on the highway north from Jerusalem, about ten miles distant, on high ground. It was at one time a fortress (I Sam. 13:2), used by Saul as headquarters for a part of his army.

Beth-horon. There were two places of this name, upper and lower Beth-horon, situated a few miles northwest of Jerusalem, one at the top the other at the bottom of a pass leading from the central highland of Ephraim down to the lower plateau called the Shephelah. Along this pass took place the battle in which Joshua defeated the Canaanites (Josh. 10:9-13). Later, the Philistines on their raids from Michmash sent one of their three bands toward Beth-horon (I Sam. 13:18).

Bethlehem ("house of bread"). A town five miles south of Jerusalem. It was the home of David's family (I Sam. 16:1, 4). A well, said to be the famous well of whose water David longed to drink (II Sam. 23:14, 15) is shown to travelers. In the Book of Micah it is represented as David's city, the place from which his great successor, the Messiah, would come (Mic. 5:2). Here Jesus was born (Matt. 2:1-5). It was also believed to be the same as Ephrath or Ephrathah (Gen. 35:19; Mic. 5:2; I Sam.

17:12), though the identification is far from certain.

Beth-shan. A city in the Jordan valley at the lower end of the Valley of Jezreel. It was an important town, commanding the entrance to Palestine from the East-Jordan side. The Philistines obtained possession of the place, and hung the bodies of Saul and his sons upon the walls. This shows how far eastward the Philistine dominion extended after Saul's downfall. The modern name of the place is Beisan.

Beth-shemesh. A town on the border of the tribe of Judah, situated about half way between Ashdod and Jerusalem. The words mean "House of the Sun," and may point to heathen worship of the sun practiced before the days of Samuel. From Ekron, the last place at which the ark was kept among the Philistines, it was the nearest point, about twelve miles on the way to the hill country on which Jerusalem and Shiloh were situated. Beth-shemesh was just at the mouth of one of the valleys (the Vale of Sorek) at the point where it opened from the Judean hills into the Philistine plain.

Bezek. A town, whose modern name is Ibzik, about thirteen miles northeast from Shechem (see map). It was the mustering point for Saul's army before the relief of Jabesh-gilead (I Sam. 11:8).

Blood. The law of Israel forbade the eating of blood in any form because it was sacred to Jehovah and was to be poured out as a libation to him at the foot of the altar. Therefore all beasts killed for food must be regarded as sacrifices and killed in the proper manner. The sin of I Sam. 14:32 consisted in the disregard of this necessity for the sacrificial killing of the beasts and the offering of their blood to deity. Saul remedied it by consecrating a stone as an altar, and thus making proper the slaughter of such sheep and oxen as were brought to him there.

Bottle. Usually a leather bag made from the skin of a young kid, goat, cow, or buffalo. The larger ones were squared. The smaller sizes usually retained the shape of the animal whose skin was used. The capacity would range from two or three gallons upward.

Carmel. A city of Judah, about ten miles southeast of Hebron. Here Saul set up a monument or trophy on his return from his expedition against the Amalekites (I Sam. 15:12), and here Nabal lived in the days when David was an outlaw (I Sam. 25:2 f.).

Cherethites. A tribe mentioned as living in the southern portion of Canaan (I Sam. 30:14; Zeph. 2:5). In II Sam. 15:18 they are mentioned along with the Pelethites and Gittites as among David's hired guards, and are often referred to in a similar manner. That they were Philistines seems obvious. It has been thought that the name is derived from the belief that the Philistines originally came from Caphtor or Crete, and thus the name Cherethites = Cretans took form.

Cubit. A Hebrew measure of distance, whose exact value is not known. By some it is given as low as sixteen inches; by others as high as twenty-five. The height of Goliath at an average estimate would have been not far from ten feet.

Diviners. Men who practiced magic, or the art of finding out the future. They had various methods of operating, the use of the bowl or cup (Gen. 44:5), or the shooting of arrows (Ezek. 21:21), in order to determine whether the plans of those who consulted them were likely to succeed. They were the same sort of people as the modern fortune-teller, who practices on the credulity of the ignorant. All these kinds of divining or fortune-telling were forbidden to the Israelites, but they persisted in spite of the law.

Eben-ezer. A place at which Samuel set up a stone of memorial after the victory over the Philistines, as recorded in I Sam. 7:12. It was between Mizpah (Nebi Samwil) and Shen ("the tooth") or Jashana, which latter place has not been satisfactorily located. This makes the site of Eben-ezer only conjectural. It was somewhere in the highland region of Judah, and not far from Mizpah.

Edom, Edomites. The region to the south of the Dead Sea was called Edom (Idumea in the days of Jesus). Its people, the Edomites, were usually hostile to the Israelites, although individuals sometimes took service with them. Doeg, an Edomite, was the chief muleherd of Saul (I Sam. 21:7; 22:9).

Egypt. A country in Africa lying along the River Nile, and in the delta formed by its various mouths. The Hebrews lived there for several generations during the earliest portion of their history, and were held as slaves by the Egyptians and their king, the Pharaoh (I Sam. 2:27). Their deliverance was accomplished by Moses, and their departure was called the exodus. The marvelous events which resulted in this deliverance were often recalled in the later history (I Sam. 4:8).

Ekron. One of the five cities of the Philistines, situated about ten miles almost directly north of Gath (Tell-es-Safi). The modern name is Akir. It was one of the places to which the ark was taken according to the story in I Sam. 5:10, and was the refuge of the flying Philistines after the death of Goliath (I Sam. 17:52).

Elah, Valley of ("valley of the terebinth"). Probably the modern Wadi-es-Sunt, a valley that leads up from the Philistine plain near Gath (Tell-es-Safi), and after an hour divides in the directions of Hebron and Jerusalem. At this junction point the battle between David and Goliath probably took place (I Sam. 17:2).

Elders. As their name implies, the men of age and wisdom, the heads of households or clans, the sheiks as they would be called today in the Orient, were the ruling class in the cities and towns of Israel. They acted as judges (Deut. 22:15) and gave advice to the king or ruler of the state (I Sam. 8:4). Their good opinion was regarded as indispensable to a king (I Sam. 15:30).

Eli. The head of the priestly order in the closing days of the judges. He combined the duties of priest with those of judge. He is already an old man when he first appears. In all regards save the control of his sons he bears an upright character. His faults were due to weakness and leniency. He presided over civic and religious affairs at Shiloh, and there he came to his death on hearing of the death of his two sons and the capture of the ark by the Philistines (I Sam., chaps. 1–4).

En-dor ("spring of Dor"). A village on the northern slope of "Little Hermon," opposite Mt. Tabor. It was the home of the medium consulted by Saul on the night before his death. It still bears the ancient name. It would require a journey of ten to twelve miles to reach it from Saul's camp.

En-gedi ("fountain of the kid"). A spring on the western shore of the Dead Sea at about its middle point from north to south. The ancient name of the town was Hazazon-tamar (Gen. 14:7; II Chron. 20:2). The spring bursts out from the rock at an elevation of 612 ft. above the sea. The place is rich in vegetation, though the surrounding region is a desolate, rocky wilderness. Among the caves in the mountains near by David found a refuge from Saul, and in one of them occurred the incident of I Sam., chap. 24 in which David showed his generosity by sparing the life of the king.

Ephah. A Hebrew measure of capacity, used for measuring grain, flour, etc. It was equivalent to about seventy pints, and roughly corresponds to our bushel.

Ephod. A garment worn by priests and those of priestly class (I Sam. 2:18). It was usually of linen. The word is also used to describe an image worshiped as an idol (Judg. 8:27). It is not always easy to tell in which of the two senses the word is employed (cf. I Sam. 14:3 where the meaning may be either "wearing an ephod" i.e., serving as priest, or "bearing an ephod" for the purpose of inquiring the will of God).

Ephraim. One of the twelve tribes, named after a son of Jacob. Its territory lay in the lofty central portion of Palestine, between Benjamin on the south and Manasseh on the north. It was the strongest of the northern tribes. The sanctuary or tabernacle was located at Shiloh, within its borders.

Ephrath, Ephrathah, Ephrathite. See "Bethlehem."

Feasts. The Hebrews, like other nations, held sacred feasts at special seasons of the year. Among these were the feasts of sheep-shearing and grape-gathering, the new moon festival, the family feasts. It seems to have been the custom also in Samuel's day to make an annual pilgrimage to the nearest shrine for the purpose of celebrating a feast. There annual feasts gradually took precedence over others (Exod. 23:14, 17; 34:23); these were: (1) the Feast of Unleavened Bread (Exod. 23:15) which began with the Passover, commemorating the departure from Egypt, on the fourteenth day of the first month, Abib (= March–April), and continued for seven days (Deut. 16: 1–8); (2) the Feast of Weeks (Exod. 34:22), called also the "feast of harvest" (Exod. 23:16), in Sivan (= May–June) which came some weeks (fifty days, hence called "Pentecost") after the Passover (Deut. 16:9–12); and (3) the Feast of Tabernacles or "feast of ingathering" (Exod. 23:16; 34:22), at the close of the year, in the seventh month, Tisri (= September), when the crops were gathered (Deut. 16:13–17). At these feasts it was the expectation that all the men of the nation should appear with suitable offerings. This was probably not obligatory, however, and the man who faithfully observed the custom of keeping even one of the feasts from year to year was esteemed as a pious Israelite (I Sam. 1:3).

Gad. A tribe of the Hebrews which remained east of the Jordan in the settlement of Canaan. Their territory lay on the eastern border of the Dead Sea, near its northern end.

Gad. A prophet or seer who was with David in his outlaw life in Moab (I Sam. 22:5) and who reproved him in later life for the royal census (II Sam. 24:11). In I Chron. 29:29 he is named as a biographer of David.

Gath ("wine press"). One of the five chief cities of the Philistines. In David's time it had a king (I Sam. 21:10), with whom the young Hebrew took refuge. Its site is not known with certainty, but Tell-es-Safi, eighteen miles east and somewhat south of Askelon, has been thought to occupy the place where Gath stood.

Geba ("hill"). A town now called Jeba, about seven miles north of Jerusalem on the south side of the gorge Wadi Suweinit, opposite Michmash. Here Jonathan had a division of the Hebrew army at the time of Saul's first campaign against the Philistines, and from this place he started on the adventure which brought on the battle narrated in I Sam., chap. 14.

Gibeah ("high place"). A town situated some four miles north of Jerusalem on the road to Ramah and Bethel. It was the home of Saul, and from this fact was also called Gibeah of Saul (I Sam. 11:4); and because it had a local sanctuary, it was sometimes called Gibeah (or the hill) of God (I Sam. 10:5), while in I Sam. 13:2 it is called Gibeah of Benjamin. Here Saul held his simple court.

Gilboa. See "Mt. Gilboa."

Gilead. A region east of the Jordan and north of the territories of the tribes of Gad and Reuben. It was mountainous. Jabesh-gilead was one of its cities.

Gilgal ("a circle"). The name of several places in Palestine. It appears to have been the custom in antiquity to mark a sacred place with cairns or monuments. Such a place would naturally be known in later years as a "gilgal." The town mentioned in I Sam. 7:16 seems to have been in the same general district as Bethel and Mizpah. It has been identified with the modern Jiljiliyah, seven miles north of Bethel and about four miles southwest of Shiloh. It may be that it gathered to itself some of the renown and religious significance of Shiloh after the loss of the ark. That it was not the Gilgal in the Jordan valley seems clear. That would have been far down from the highlands, outside of the main part of the land, and difficult to reach.

Girzites. See "Gizrites."

Gizrites. Probably the correct reading for the word "Girzites" in I Sam. 27:8. It undoubtedly refers to the inhabitants of Gezer the modern Tell Jezer, a site recently excavated, on the way from Jaffa to Jerusalem. Gezer was a strong city, not included among the Canaanite conquests of the Hebrews, but later on given by the king of Egypt to his daughter as a dower at the time of her marriage to Solomon (I Kings 9:16). Its population was therefore still Canaanite in the days of David.

Goliath. A Philistine giant, whose home was in Gath. He challenged the army of King Saul and was slain by David (I Sam. 17:1–54). In II Sam. 21:19 a man of the same name is mentioned as having been slain by Elhanan of Bethlehem. This has led some to suppose that Elhanan was another name of David. Goliath belonged to a family of giants (II Sam. 21:22).

Guilt offering. A gift or sacrifice made in those cases where the sinner has robbed or defrauded either man or God of that which is their due. It is usually called " trespass-offering " in the English Bible. It was intended as a reparation or compensation for the injury done. Thus the Philistines sent back with the ark certain golden images representing the form in which they had suffered for carrying away the ark.

Harp. A lyre or stringed instrument much loved by the Hebrews. It was used by the bands of prophets in their wild minstrelsy (I Sam. 10:5) and was the instrument which the youthful David played (I Sam. 16:16). It was small enough to be carried easily in processions, and was used to accompany odes, chants, or war hymns.

Hazor. The capital of King Jabin near Lake Merom (Huleh) on the highlands of Western Palestine (see map).

Ichabod. The son of Phinehas, and grandson of Eli. His mother died at his birth on learning of the death of her husband and the loss of the ark (I Sam. 4:21). He is mentioned (I Sam. 14:3) as the uncle of Ahitub, priest in the reign of Saul.

Idolatry. The worship of idols or images, representing both Jehovah and other gods (see "strange gods"). Such worship was usually carried on at some shrine where an image of wood or stone, representing the god in the form of a man or beast, was adored. The law of Israel sternly forbade all such practices, and the prophets spent their lives in leading the people away from idolatry to the worship of the living God.

Ishvi. A son of Saul mentioned in I Sam. 14:49. The name seems to be a contraction of Ishijah, "man of

Jehovah." In I Chron. 8:33 he is called Eshbaal, "man of Baal" (i.e., of the Lord). But in the days when the prophets saw the danger of using "Baal" ("Lord") at all, lest it should lead to the worship of the god of that name, the name was changed to Ishbosheth, "man of shame" (II Sam. 2:8, where the change for religious purposes is apparent). No parent would ever have named his son Ishbosheth. In the days of Saul, however, Ish-baal, "man of the Lord," was quite proper.

Jabesh-gilead. A city whose name seems to survive in the Wadi Yabis, a river which flows into the Jordan from the east some ten miles below Beisan (Bethshan). The city was probably a short distance north of the river, and about seven miles from Pella (see map). According to Judg. 21:8–12, it was destroyed in the pre-kingly period. In the times of Saul it had risen again, and was delivered by him from a siege by the Ammonites (I Sam. 11:1–11). In remembrance of this rescue its people at the death of Saul heroically recovered the bodies of the dead king and his sons and gave them honorable burial in their city (I Sam. 31:8–13).

Jacob. The patriarch from whom the twelve tribes were traced (Gen. 25:19–49). His name "Israel" was also borne by the nation. After living the life of a herdsman in Canaan, famine at home and the presence of his son Joseph in high favor at the court of Egypt led to his removal to that land, where his death occurred. The change of royal attitude toward their descendants brought on their experiences as serfs, and led at last to their departure from Eygpt under Moses and Aaron.

Jephthah. Hebrew warrior and judge. His home was in Gilead, east of the Jordan and when the region was raided by the Ammonites, he was called to lead his people in the war. He gained a complete victory, but was compelled to offer up his daughter in fulfilment of a rash vow that if successful he would sacrifice the first person who came out from his tent on his return (Judg. chap. 11).

Jerubbaal. A judge of Israel usually called Gideon (Judg., chaps.

6–8), a native of Manasseh, who in a time when the desert tribe of Midian invaded the land in great force raised an army, and after reducing it by various tests to the small but effective number of three hundred, won a great victory, freed the district from its enemies and was importuned to accept the title of king, which he declined.

Jerusalem. The capital of the united kingdom under David and Solomon, and after the division the capital of the kingdom of Judah. It was captured by David from the Jebusites (II Sam. 5:5–10). It is mentioned as the place to which David took the head of Goliath, but this is of course an error, for it was not in Israel's possession till several years after that event.

Joab. Son of David's sister Zeruiah, and brother of Abishai and Asahel. He does not appear in the earlier portion of David's career, being merely mentioned as the brother of Abishai in I Sam. 26:6. He was David's chief captain, a man of fiery, implacable nature, yet devoted to the king. He was put to death by Solomon (I Kings 2:28–35).

Jonathan. Son of Saul, a young man of exceptionally high character, chiefly known because of his strong friendship for David. His first appearance is at Geba of Benjamin as commander of a thousand men (I Sam. 13:2). Soon after, his exploit in stampeding the Philistine garrison at Michmash led to Saul's great victory.

Keilah. A town, four miles south of Adullam on the western slope of Judah, on the road from Philistia to Hebron. It was a fortified city with walls and gates (I Sam. 23:7). David delivered its people from the Philistines but was unable to remain in it at the time Saul pursued him, owing to the unwillingness of its people to face Saul's wrath.

Kenites. A desert tribe of Midian which accompanied Israel from the wilderness to the borders of Palestine. Hobab, the father-in-law of Moses, was of this tribe (Judg. 1:16), and Heber the Kenite lived in north Palestine at the time of the battle of Mt. Tabor (Judg. 4:11, 17). They seem to have been friendly to Israel, and for that reason Saul warned those

of the tribe who lived among the Amalekites to save themselves at the time of his southern campaign (I Sam. 15:6).

Kiriath-jearim (" town of the woods"). A town of Judah situated some nine or ten miles west and slightly north from Jerusalem, and about the same distance northwest from Beth-shemesh. The modern name is Kuriet el Enab, and it is locally known as Abu Gosh, after a famous robber of the last century. Attempts to locate it elsewhere do not seem so satisfactory. It was on the highland of central Palestine, so that the journey of the ark from Beth-shemesh was *upward* all the way (I Sam. 6:20, 21).

Michal. Younger daughter of Saul and wife of David. Saul offered her to David for the proofs of a hundred slain Philistines, hoping by this means to bring about his death (I Sam. 18:20–28). When David left the court she was given to Palti, or Paltiel the son of Laish of Gallim (I Sam 25:44), but she was restored to David by Abner after Saul's death (II Sam. 3:12–16). In II Sam. 21:8 Michal is called the wife of Adriel the Meholethite, but it is probable that Merab is meant (I Sam. 18:19).

Michmash. A town situated on a high hill east of Bethel and about eight miles north of Jerusalem, near Ramah. It was held by Saul and two thousand of his forces soon after the opening of his reign (I Sam., chap. 13), but when the exploit of Jonathan in smiting the Philistine garrison in Geba became known the Philistines gathered in numbers, took Michmash, and posted a camp there (I Sam. 13:5). From this they were dislodged by the Hebrews after Jonathan's heroic adventure (I Sam. 14:31).

Mizpah ("watchtower"). There were several places of this name in Palestine, as would be natural from the meaning of the word. The town mentioned in I Sam. 7:5, 10:17, etc., was situated on a high hill, five miles northwest from Jerusalem. Its modern name is Nebi Samwil (" the prophet Samuel") from the tradition which connect his name with the place, It is a conspicuous landmark on the horizon, just such a spot as might well be chosen for a rendezvous of the Israelites.

Moab. The high region east of the Dead Sea, extending from its southern end to a movable frontier on the north that was at times some distance up the Jordan from its mouth, at others near the northern end of the sea, and at times still further south. The people were Semites, related to the Ammonites, their neighbors on the northeast, the Edomites, joining them on the southwest, and the Hebrews across the sea. In the days of the judges Eglon, king of Moab, in company with the Ammonites and Amalekites, subdued a considerable part of Canaan and oppressed the people. Deliverance was gained by Ehud, who put Eglon to death (Judg. 3:12-30).

Moses. The great leader of the Hebrews in the period of their departure from Egypt (Exod., chaps. 2 f.). Under his direction they made their escape from oppression at the hands of the Egyptians, crossed an arm of the Red Sea when the waters were driven back by a strong wind, traversed the desert to the region of Sinai, and there received the primitive institutes or constitution of the nation. With varying fortunes they continued to Kadesh-barnea south of Judah, and then after abortive efforts to enter Canaan, passed to the country east of the Jordan. Here Moses after a long life spent in the service of his people died, without the privilege of setting foot on the soil to the margin of which he had led the nation. The legal material from Exod., chap. 20 to the close of Deuteronomy is set in the framework of Moses' life. He continued throughout the later history the most conspicuous figure of the past.

Mt. Gilboa. A range of hills, rising to the height of 1,700 ft. on the east of the Plain of Esdraelon, and south of the Valley of Jezreel. It was the site of the camp of Saul in his final campaign against the Philistines (I Sam. 28:4) and the scene of his defeat and death in the battle that followed (I Sam. 31:8). In his lament over the issue of the battle, David mentioned the "mountains of Gilboa" reproachfully as the field of the tragedy.

Naioth. A part of the town of Ramah, the home of Samuel (I Sam. 19:18; 20:1). The meaning of the word is unknown. Some have supposed it to be a house in which the prophets dwelt, such as is mentioned in II Kings 6:1-7.

Nazirite. One who became "consecrated," as the word implies. Nazirites were under vows, either for life, or for a given period. The vow, made either by the Nazirite himself, or by his parents, forbade his use of wine or other strong drink, forbade the cutting of his hair, and did not permit any contact with a dead body. Samson is an example of this order of men (Judg. 13:5). Samuel had at least some of the characteristics of a Nazirite. (I Sam. 1:11).

Nob. A city of Benjamin, just north of Jerusalem on the edge of the elevation called Scopus in New Testament days. In the ideal picture of the Assyrian approach from the north to Jerusalem (Isa. 10:28-32) it is named as nearest to the holy city on a road that passed through Michmash, Geba, Ramah, Gibeah of Saul, Gallim, Anathoth, and Nob. It was the site of an ancient sanctuary in the days of Saul, and here David found assistance from the priest Ahimelech (Ahijah) in his flight from Saul (I Sam. 21:1).

Paran. A region lying far south of Judah, identified with Kadesh (barnea) in Num. 13:26, and mentioned often in connection with Seir, Edom, Teman, and Sinai (Deut. 33:2; Hab. 3:3). The wilderness of Paran was the place to which Hagar and Ishmael fled, which is said to be on the way from Beersheba to Egypt (Gen. 21:21). In Num. 12:16 and 13:3, 26, Paran was one of the stations in the wilderness journey of the Hebrews. It lay some fifty miles south of Beersheba. The attempt to identify Paran with the Oasis of Firan near Mt. Serbal in the peninsula of Sinai is unsatisfactory. In I Sam. 25:1 David is s id to have gone down to the wilderness of Paran. The improbability of such a long journey has perhaps led the Septuagint to substitute Maon for Paran in agreement with vs. 2.

Pharaoh. The designation of the kings of Egypt. It was a title rather than proper name. In I Sam. 2:27 reference is made to Israel's stay in Egypt as bondservant under the government of the Pharaoh.

Philistines. A race living along the borders of the Mediterranean Sea, south of Joppa in a strip of territory which included the five cities of Gaza, Ekron, Ashkelon, Gath, and Ashdod. They were not natives of Canaan, but came probably from the island of Crete. Later on their name was given to the entire land of Canaan by the Greeks ("Palestine," from "Philistine"). They were a warlike people, among whom there were men of gigantic stature, like Goliath. They worshiped a god called Dagon. They continued to be enemies of the Hebrews till they were subdued by David. In the days of Saul and Samuel they held possession of large portions of Hebrew territory, keeping garrisons in the various parts of the land, such as Gibeah (I Sam. 10:5).

Priests. These men were the regular ministers of religion among the Hebrews. They belonged to the tribe of Levi, and were intrusted with the work of teaching the people, of offering sacrifices. and, in certain cases, of deciding disputes. At first they lived in the various towns and cities. Later they preferred to remain at the central sanctuary. They were not always men of unblemished lives, as the cases of Hophni and Phinehas show (I Sam. 2:12).

Prophesy. The meanings of this verb are various. Sometimes it implies the simple exercise of religious instruction, as in the preaching of Samuel. Elsewhere, and more frequently in I Samuel, it signifies the ecstatic rites of the prophetic guilds, consisting of songs, religious dances, and such violent performances, accompanied by music, as left the participants breathless and exhausted, and even drew the observers into the circle as with a spell (I Sam. 10:5-13; 19:20-24). (See "prophet.")

Prophet. There were two sorts of religious teachers in Israel, the priests and the prophets. The former attended to the services at the sanctuary, and belonged normally to the tribe of Levi. The latter were more concerned with preaching and teaching, and were of no one tribe. The prophets were the reformers who reproved the people for their sins and exhorted them to righteousness. In the earlier part of the history there

appeared groups of men who often went about in bands, and their "prophesying" consisted to some extent of singing and incoherent ecstatic utterances, stimulated by the use of musical instruments, accompanied by violent gestures, and resulting at last in a swoon (I Sam. 10:5-11; 19:23-24; 18:10, where the marginal reading for "prophesied" is "raved"). Very different was the character of the great prophets in Israel, like Samuel and Elijah, under whose direction the prophets, or "sons of the prophets" as they were called, the untrained and roving preachers, settled in groups, at towns like Ramah, Bethel, and Jericho, led a more ordered life and thus created centers of instruction and reform throughout the land. They were the preachers of righteousness. Their number must have been considerable. Samuel was their recognized leader as long as he lived. They received their messages through dreams, visions, or intelligent appreciation of the needs of the times, as they reflected on God's nature and his disclosure of his will to the people. They therefore spoke for God, and their utterances were usually begun with the words, "Thus saith the Lord" (I Sam. 2:27). But the great prophets, from Samuel onward, were vastly superior to the many prophets around them, and often had occasion to reprove and denounce them.

Rachel's sepulcher. Rachel was the wife of Jacob and the mother of Joseph and Benjamin. She died on the journey from Bethel to Ephrath, and was buried by the road (Gen. 35:19, 20). It is probable that the words "the same is Bethlehem" in vs. 19 are an incorrect note added by a later writer. The exact place of Rachel's sepulcher is therefore unknown. A tomb with this name is shown today on the highroad from Jerusalem to Bethlehem and near the entrance to the latter. But as Saul passed the sepulcher on his way from Ramah to Gibeah, it cannot have been so far south as Bethlehem. Jeremiah (Jer. 31:15) speaks of the dead Rachel as weeping for her children at the time the exiles went northward into Babylon. This would strengthen the probability that the tomb lay somewhere on the northern border of Benjamin, and that the traditional site near Bethlehem is erroneous.

Sacrifice. This was the offering of animals, brought by Israelites to the altar of God. The animal, an ox, a ram, a lamb, or a goat, was taken to the priest, and by him put to death. Its blood was poured out at the foot of the altar as a libation to God, and the fat was burned upon the altar as God's portion. A part of the meat was given to the priest as his pay for the service he rendered, and the remainder was eaten by the worshiper and his family as a holy meal. Other offerings, such as meal, wine, and salt were also made. A "whole burnt offering" was made by consuming the entire body of the victim upon the altar, in cases of exceptional peril or sin (I Sam. 7:9).

Saul ("asked"). The first king of Israel (for the attempt of Abimelech, son of Gideon, to secure the kingship a generation earlier see Judg. chap. 9). Saul was the son of Kish, a prosperous farmer of the tribe of Benjamin, residing at Gibeah, usually known in the records as "Gibeah of Saul." Two records of his first appearance are given. According to the early Judean document of Saul's life (I Sam. 9:1—10:16; chap. 11) he went forth from his home accompanied by a servant to search for some strayed asses. Failing in the search they turned to the town of Ramah to seek the assistance of the seer Samuel. The latter recognized in Saul the subject of his prophetic vision of a king, and after entertaining him over night, anointed him privately and gave him certain signs to assure him of his selection by God. Soon after Saul, who had returned to his agricultural tasks, learned of the distress of Jabesh-gilead, and summoning his countrymen, delivered the city, gaining thus the public recognition of the nation as its king.

The late Ephraimite narrative of Samuel's career as a prophet tells a very different story (I Sam., chap. 8; 10:17–27; chap. 12). In his old age Samuel is requested by the people to give them a king, his sons not being suitable rulers. He is disappointed and grieved at this request, but, directed by God, accedes to it. At a public assembly at Ramah Saul is chosen by lot, and Samuel soon after delivers his farewell address, charging the nation with sin in asking for a king,

and warning them against further errors.

Septuagint. A Greek translation of the Hebrew Old Testament made by Jewish scholars in Egypt between the years 250 and 150 B.C. It is a valuable help in determining the correct Hebrew text of the Old Testament. At many points its readings are given in the margin of the Revised Version.

Sheol. This word is used in the Old Testament to describe the world of shades, where the dead abide. It is translated variously, as grave, pit, hell. It does not denote a place of torment or of blessedness, but one to which the dead go to remain in silence and weakness. This is of course very different from the Christian belief in a future life. It was Christ who "brought life and immortality to light through the gospel" (II Tim. 1:10).

Shiloh. A town in the highlands of the tribe of Ephraim, about nineteen miles north of Jerusalem. Here a sanctuary was established after the Hebrews settled in Palestine. The ark of God was kept in the sacred tent or building. To this place pilgrims came at the times of the great feasts. The town was probably destroyed by the Philistines after the battle of Aphek when the ark was captured (I Sam., chap. 4). To this destruction Jeremiah seems to refer (Jer. 7:12, 14; 26:6). The modern town is called Seilun. There is still visible a leveled quadrangle, on the hillside above the town, where it is thought the sanctuary may have stood.

Shunem. A town mentioned in connection with Jezreel in Josh. 19:18. It was the camping place of the Philistine army before the battle of Mt. Gilboa (I Sam. 28:4). The modern town of Sulem is supposed to occupy its site. It lies on the slopes of Jebel Dahi ("Little Hermon"), which rises north of Jezreel. The Hebrew camp was across the valley of Jezreel at the foot of Mt. Gilboa. Whether this is the Shunem mentioned in II Kings 4:8 as the town in which Elisha stopped on his journeys, and the home of the heroine of the Song of Songs, is not certainly known.

Shur. A district on the northeast border of Egypt, mentioned as the place of Hagar's wandering (Gen. 16:7), and the region into which the Israelites went after passing the Red Sea (Exod. 15:22). In this direction Saul pursued the defeated Amalekites (I Sam. 15:7).

Sisera. The general of King Jabin of Hazor, in the region near Lake Merom (Huleh), who was defeated in the battle of Mt. Tabor by Barak and Deborah (Judg., chaps. 4, 5). In his flight from the field he made his way to the encampment of Heber, the Kenite, whose wife Jael lured him to trust to her hospitality, and then put him to death, thereby winning the praise of the Israelites.

Socoh. A town on the west border of Judah, almost directly west of Bethlehem, on the edge of the shephelah or plateau which looks down upon the plain of Philistia. At this point the roads from Jerusalem and Hebron unite on the way to Philistia through the valley of Elah (Wadi es-Sunt).

Spirit of God. This term is used in the Old Testament not only to describe the divine activity in the creation of the world (Gen. 1:2) and of man (Job 33:4), in revelation to the prophets (Ezek. 11:24), and in the endowment of certain men with special gifts (Exod. 31:3), but also such arousal of soul to meet an emergency as renders a man capable of a great deed. In this sense it is said that the Spirit of God came upon Samson (Judg. 14:6) and he killed a lion, or upon Saul and he joined the band of "prophets" in their uncouth performances (I Sam. 10:10). The term represents the unusual intensity of emotion which is displayed in man's behavior. In this sense the expression "of God" is really equivalent to "great," as "the trees of Jehovah," i. e., great trees (Ps. 104:16), "mountains of God," i.e., great mountains (Ps. 36:6), "the dread of Jehovah," i.e., a strong terror (I Sam. 11:7). Yet it is probable that in all instances where the term "Spirit of God" is used, the writer intended to indicate direct divine activity.

Strange gods. The nations around Israel worshiped the various gods of their lands and religions. It was the general belief of that age that each country was under the protection of its own deity. Thus the Phoenicians worshiped Baal, the Philistines, Dagon, and the Ammonites, Molech, etc. In several instances there was a female divinity or goddess who was honored beside the god. Thus the consort or companion of Baal was Astarte or Ashtoreth. These deities were represented by idols or images, and their worship was carried on at sacred places or shrines. It was the early belief of the Hebrews that these gods were actual beings who ruled in their own lands. It was the work of the prophets to prove that there is but one God, and that he is worthy of the worship and love of all men.

Telaim. A town in the south of Judah where Saul assembled his army for the campaign against Amalek. It is probably the same as Telem (Josh. 15:24) near the border of Edom in the far south of Judah.

Telem. See "Telaim."

Temple. The structure which Solomon erected in Jerusalem as the center of worship in Israel. In earlier periods, from the days of the Exodus, there was a portable structure, called the Tent of Meeting, at which religious exercises were conducted. Such a tent was, perhaps, set up at Shiloh after the occupation of Palestine. If so, it was doubtless inclosed with wood for protection (its door-post is mentioned), and is called "the temple" in I Sam. 1:7. This expression probably reflects also the usage of the times of the author, when the Temple had long been standing.

Teraphim. Images, in human form, probably representing the ancestor of the family, kept in many households in Israel, and even worshiped. It was a form of superstition denounced by the prophets as degrading and useless. Yet it was practiced even in leading families (I Sam. 19:13) and persisted in many parts of the land until a late period.

Threshing-floors. Grain was threshed by placing it on a high, flat rock, where the wind had full sweep. There it was "trodden out" by cattle dragging a sledge, which separated the grain from the straw. Then the whole was tossed aloft in the wind with a winnowing shovel, called sometimes a "fan" (Matt. 3:12), and the wind blew away the straw and chaff, leaving the grain to be gathered into the granary.

Thummim. See " Urim."

Urim and Thummim ("lights and perfections"). The names applied to a method of securing knowledge of the divine will in Israel. In I Sam. 28:6 it is said that Saul could not gain response either by dreams or Urim or by prophets. In "the blessing of Moses" (Deut., chap. 33) the use of Thummim and Urim is assigned to the priestly tribe of Levi (vs. 8). Neither of these passages describes the method of augury. But the Septuagint renders I Sam. 14:41, "And Saul said, Jehovah, God of Israel, why hast thou not answered thy servant this day? If the guilt be in me or in Jonathan my son, Jehovah, God of Israel, give Urim; but if thus thou say: It is in my people Israel, give Thummim." This indicates that Urim and Thummim were two objects used by the priests, perhaps two stones, one of which signified the answer "yes," the other the opposite.

Witch, Witchcraft. It was a common superstition in Israel that there were people, usually women, gifted with the power to control demons, to hold converse with the dead, to foretell the future and to curse or benefit their fellow-beings. The practice of witchcraft or sorcery was strictly forbidden in the law (Exod. 22:18). Saul used harsh measures against these practices, but at the last resorted to a witch at En-dor to learn his approaching fate (I Sam. 28:6–12).

Ziklag. A town in the territory of Judah (Josh 15:31) or Simeon (Josh. 19:5), which was in Saul's days assigned to David by Achish, the king of Gath (I Sam. 27:6). Its site is uncertain. It probably was about twenty-five miles southwest from Gath, and half as far southeast from Gaza, on the way to Beersheba. It was plundered by the Amalekites in David's absence, but the raiders were overtaken and the spoil recovered (I Sam. 30:1–26). It is mentioned as one of the cities occupied by the post-exilic Jews (Neh. 11:28).

Ziph, Wilderness of. The town of Ziph was a few miles (six or seven) southeast of Hebron. The wilderness of the same name was of course the surrounding region, rocky and convenient for concealment. Here David took refuge from Saul (I Sam. 23:14, 19).

Zobah. An Aramaean kingdom on the northeast frontier of Palestine, probably in the Hauran south of Damascus. It is mentioned in I Sam. 14:47 as one of the enemies against which Saul fought successfully. At a later time the Ammonites hired the Syrians of Zobah and other allies to assist them in repelling Israel under David (II Sam. 8:3 f.; 10:6 f.). It is probable therefore that Zobah lay not far beyond the northern frontier of Ammon east of the Jordan.